BRINGING TALK TO LIFE

Do you want to encourage purposeful talk between students in your classroom but feel you do not have the time or the permission? Do you wish you had more opportunity to listen to your students and include discussion of pressing and controversial issues in their lives and society today in your curriculum? Amidst rising recognition of how being articulate improves life chances, this book takes a look at these questions, outlining an alternative approach to curriculum and pedagogy.

Bringing Talk to Life is firmly grounded in classroom experience and research evidence, and explores how a dialogic approach to teaching can improve students' confidence and agency and restore teachers' professional judgement. It outlines the social and linguistic barriers some students find in accessing knowledge through the school curriculum and identifies ways that teachers can help them become more confident and articulate by modelling different behavioural norms and introducing concept vocabulary in an accessible way.

Using transcripts of classroom dialogues, teachers' plans, and examples of students' work, chapters show by contrast that a talk-focussed, enquiry curriculum can free up teachers and pupils to explore ideas together, reigniting curiosity. Examples of this dialogic approach come from primary classrooms where Philosophy for Children (P4C) is adapted to suit a school's aims and curriculum. In addition, there are chapters on how talk is used in further and higher education to develop students' critical thinking skills.

Designed to stimulate thinking and debate, and restore teachers' confidence in their own professional judgement, this book is intended for those training to be teachers. It will also be of interest to schools that are keen to learn how to include more talk in their curriculum, and to experienced practitioners who feel that there is another way to plan and teach.

Paul Gurton was a primary school teacher, head teacher, and a senior lecturer in primary initial teacher education at the University of Wolverhampton, UK.

Meghan Tipping is an experienced primary school teacher currently working in the education and heritage sectors.

BRINGING TALK TO LIFE

Thinking Through Dialogue in the Classroom

Paul Gurton and Meghan Tipping

Routledge
Taylor & Francis Group

LONDON AND NEW YORK

Designed cover image: © Getty Images

First edition published 2025
by Routledge
4 Park Square, Milton Park, Abingdon, Oxon, OX14 4RN

and by Routledge
605 Third Avenue, New York, NY 10158

Routledge is an imprint of the Taylor & Francis Group, an informa business

British Library Cataloguing-in-Publication Data
A catalogue record for this book is available from the British Library

ISBN: 978-1-032-58680-9 (hbk)
ISBN: 978-1-032-58679-3 (pbk)
ISBN: 978-1-003-45104-4 (ebk)

DOI: 10.4324/9781003451044

Typeset in Interstate
by Apex CoVantage, LLC

CONTENTS

ACKNOWLEDGEMENTS

This book would not have been possible without the participation of pupils and staff past and present of St. Catherine's Catholic Primary School, Sheffield. Our thanks go to them and to Warwickshire College Group (WCG).

Paul would like to thank the many colleagues he has had conversations with over the years but particularly the late Jean Jeffreys, who was an early advocate of children's talk. Above all, thanks go to Sue for her unstinting support and insightful thinking. Talking with her always helps clarify his ideas.

Meghan would like to thank her husband Luke for his constant support and belief. She would also like to acknowledge all of the wonderful people she has met on her journey so far that through meaningful connection have given her the opportunity to learn, unlearn, and grow. And finally, a special mention for her brother Adam, who has always been there to talk to and listen from the very beginning.

FOREWORD

In a way, this book reminded me of Edward Thomas' fine poem, *Words:*

> *I know you:*
> *You are light as dreams,*
> *Tough as oak,*
> *Precious as gold,*
> *As poppies and corn,*
> *Or an old cloak . . .*

Bringing Talk to Life is both light to read and tough as oak. It is often intriguing and occasionally surprising, but always thought-provoking.

I urge the reader to immerse themselves in the story, enjoying the clarity and its well-developed argument. It is a book about talk and how we learn it and teach it. But it is more than this.

I learned afresh that children's language and thought are linked inextricably, that language and concept development go hand in hand, and that critical reflection and dialogic learning should not be seen as an 'optional extra' in our education system but need to be fundamental to it.

We have known for a long time that our 'national curriculum' needs an overhaul, not just in relation to content but in the methods we use to 'deliver' it as teachers wherever we work. Books like this one will form essential reading for anyone interested in where our education system needs to go. The careful use of much published research work that lies behind it provides an opportunity for the reader to think again about the nature of language development, how children learn effective dialogue, and how adults come to be critical and thoughtful beings. In later chapters, we learn that staff in further and higher education are encouraged and even expected to teach critical thinking, often without the tools to do it. This book opens a door to experiences in all phases of education, which we can identify with and explore.

Paul Gurton, Meghan Tipping, and their contributors will help educators in all phases of education to explain to themselves and to policymakers why dialogic learning may be crucial for active citizenship. Skills in debate and critical thinking around major concepts are of immense value at any age. The authors suggest with great skill how we can enhance our teacher education to ensure greater critical thinking and challenge. We can also help all our pupils and students to be contributors and leaders, no matter what the topic, through the teaching methods we use.

And now is the time when more than ever we need citizens who are critical thinkers and who are active in constructive debate.

'Culture is ordinary,' said Raymond Williams. He argued over thirty years ago that he could not accept that education is only useful as 'a training for jobs, or making useful citizens. It is a society's confirmation of its common meanings, and of the human skills for their amendment.' And aren't we in dire need for such amendments?

Williams goes on to say,

> I ask for a common education that will give our society its cohesion and prevent its disintegration. . . . We must emphasise not the ladder but the common highway, for every man's ignorance diminishes me, and every man's skill is a common gain of breadth.
>
> (1989, p. 14-15)

It is this voice I hear when I think about the purpose of education, and the purpose cannot only be 'training for jobs' or for 'usefulness' among citizens.

Although *Bringing Talk to Life* is about how children learn to talk and why it matters, how we learn to converse, and why the curriculum needs changing to reflect this, it is also about the value of teaching and learning in a dialogic way. Further, it is about teaching new teachers to work to a broader and more exciting purpose in all phases of education. Without this, what is the chance of helping individuals to create their own 'amendments' to the world?

Dr. Peter Lavender
Emeritus Professor of Education,
University of Wolverhampton

Reference

Williams, R. (1989) *Resources of Hope: Culture, Democracy, Socialism*. Edited by Robin Gable. New York: Verso.

AUTHORS & CONTRIBUTORS

Dr. Paul Gurton spent twenty years as a primary school teacher and headteacher before becoming senior lecturer in primary teacher education at the University of Wolverhampton where he led the BA route. He has an abiding interest in languages and language acquisition and has published on talk, dialogic teaching, language learning and reflective teaching.

Meghan Tipping is a Freelance Consultant working across the education and heritage sectors. She previously worked as a primary teacher leading the development of a History curriculum and embedding a whole school approach to Philosophy for Children before becoming a Design Lead for a centralised curriculum provider. Her organisation, Rooted in Talk, offers innovative learning experiences that foster a love for dialogue and ignite a passion for self-expression and critical thinking. Meghan has published several articles on the power of dialogue in tackling sensitive subjects and in engaging young people in heritage.

Dr. Hilary Wason is Associate Professor and Head of Curriculum Enhancement at Kingston University, London. Originally a business educator, she has authored a series of critical thinking toolkits which are used nationally and internationally.

Sue Lay is Tutorial Manager at Warwickshire College Group. She has 24 years working in FE as a teacher and later as a pastoral tutor. In her current role, she develops materials on themes of social, political, and personal development and supports the pastoral staff in their work with students.

INTRODUCTION

As humans, one thing we do all the time is talk. And when we talk, we endlessly go back over our experience. Whether it's in person - on a walk, in a restaurant, or in the car - or at a distance - on a Zoom call or on the phone - we talk to others, sometimes individually and sometimes in a group. We recount our experiences and impressions, exchange views and opinions, and compare theories. Talking together allows us to make sense of the world. No one person has exactly the same understanding as another, even when they share an experience. My understanding will be influenced by all my prior experiences, my background and culture, and even my mood at the time. Yours will differ. I will impute reasons to events or people's behaviours. You may see others, although there will be commonalities. Talking together allows us to share our experiences and bridge the gulf between minds. It allows us to discuss issues and solve problems. When we talk, we sometimes change our views based on what someone else has said. Or we may even represent what we think differently or selectively, depending on who we are talking to. Language helps us build an understanding of how things are but also to interrogate why they are the way they are. In this way, we build our representation of the world. We use our past experiences to anticipate or predict future events and actions, and we also greatly influence each other's representation.

Language is not the only tool we have at our disposal to represent our world. But it is probably the most significant. It is the way we think together. The German philosopher Jürgen Habermas, in his *Theory of Communicative Action* (1984), sees the inherent aim or *telos* of language as reaching a consensus. In fact, he argues that the primary function of speech is to coordinate the actions of individuals and provide invisible tracks along which their interactions can unfold in an orderly and conflict-free manner (Finlayson, 2005, p. 34). Others, whose ideas will be explored in this book, have also attributed a preeminence to language in human construction of meaning - the Russian psychologist Lev Vygotsky and the Australian linguist Michael Halliday are two of these. But words can also be used to mislead and misrepresent. They can inflame passions and prey upon prejudice to incite hatred and violence. Those who use language to deceive often rely on people's naïveté, vulnerability, or lack of education. That is why it is so important to become a confident user of the spoken language - to speak up for what you believe in and speak out when you see injustice. The ability to use language to ask questions of what seems at first glance to be 'just the ways things are' allows us to enter into dialogue to scrutinise and evaluate reality, as the Brazilian educator Paulo Freire taught. This developing sense of criticality makes of us citizens who can

DOI: 10.4324/9781003451044-1

enjoy the gift of free speech, one of Roosevelt's four essential human freedoms, fundamental to the functioning of democracy.

Children learn to speak in the microcosm of the home and within their local environment. Parents and carers, siblings, grandparents and other members of the wider family, and friends all play a role in their developing ability to express themselves. And so do teachers. A large part of a child's life is spent in the classroom, and a teacher's role in facilitating their pupils' language development is significant. Classroom opportunities for talk can greatly enhance a child's ability to understand the world and build a picture of their place in it. If they are encouraged to use talk to develop their thinking as they come across new and different ideas, they learn to reason. And whilst it might be a daunting experience at first to express yourself in front of the teacher and your peers, it should be a safe space where you can try out ideas and build upon your knowledge. Classrooms that operate like this help children build confidence and a sense of their own worth and agency. They can provide meaning and enable them to have aspirations for their own life. Equally, classrooms can be places of fear for children where talk is discouraged and what is modelled is a sort of unthinking conformity inherited from the Victorian notion of children being seen and not heard, and the saying 'only speak when you are spoken to.' The dual demands upon the teacher of keeping order within the classroom and 'delivering' the curriculum – a very misleading notion – can lead to a situation where, as Douglas Barnes put it, 'the overcontrol of knowledge by teachers must in the long run hinder learning, whatever social functions it performs then and there in the classroom' (1987, p. 128).

Teachers bear a heavy responsibility for children's all-round achievement socially and academically. The classroom is a unique social environment where talk is concerned because unlike many other situations in life where communication is necessary for a transaction, like buying something in a shop, a school's central focus is on talk. Education is about communication. But how that occurs can have a profound effect on how much is learned and how confident children become, and it depends largely upon how teachers understand the nature of the knowledge they are teaching. If teachers see their role as simply transmitting authoritative knowledge, they are less likely to listen to their pupils. But if they understand that knowledge is socially constructed and meaning is built in a community and draws on previous experience, they will be more disposed to listen to children's contributions, validate them, and interact more closely with them.

As learning is emphatically not a one-way street with the teacher transmitting and the learner receiving – hence the inappropriacy of the metaphor of 'delivery' for teaching – the classroom environment is critical for a child's ability to make progress. The way pupils participate in class depends on their individual characteristics – their intelligence, confidence, and ability to articulate their understanding. But these, in turn, are influenced by other factors. Children enter school with very different language experiences, depending on their language heritage, socio-economic background, race, religion, and culture, as well as simply how much adult attention they receive and how talkative their parents are. These aspects of preschool experience differentially affect children's access to learning in school, creating barriers for some and advantages for others. But how a child participates also depends on how confident they feel within the classroom. A teacher should try to reduce barriers and make adaptations to meet the needs of their pupils. A school sets the expectations for the teachers, but the teachers set the expectations in the classroom. These are created over time and reinforced on a daily basis by what a teacher says, their tone of voice, physical stance, and gestures. How approachable are they? Do they listen? Is it okay to have a go, to get it wrong, or do answers have to be correct? To what extent do they allow children to articulate their understanding using their own way of speaking? Or do they insist upon a correct 'school language' – and if so, how is this modelled?

Figure 0.1 is an extract from a lesson in a primary classroom of ten and eleven year olds (Year 6). They are discussing the question 'Is life always in our control?' It has come about through a class project on what life was like in Edwardian Britain with a focus on the sinking of the *Titanic*. Through researching the passenger lists and other historical data, they have found out about the class system and how rigidly society was structured at the time. This has piqued their curiosity and led them to think about their own life experiences (as described in more detail in Chapter 10). The class has had a number of discussions and enquiries on themes such as *power*, *class*, and *equality*. The teacher has helped them use these concept words to articulate their understanding, but the themes have been largely chosen by the children. This latest discussion on the theme of *control* leads them to consider how much autonomy people have over significant aspects of their lives, like the food they eat or the friends they make.

It is 10.50 on a dark, drizzly, December day. Children have been outside to play at a primary school on a housing estate just outside the centre of a northern English city. As they enter the classroom, they calm their voices and sit on a carpeted floor space in front of an interactive whiteboard. Until now, there has been no sign of a teacher present, but as one boy tries to push in between another two, a voice comes from a space slightly to the side of the children. A woman in her late twenties, with curly, brown shoulder-length hair is sitting cross-legged in front of a laptop at eye level with the children. She only speaks one word, quietly, but clearly, with an upward intonation,

'Aiden!'

Hearing his name, the boy looks up to where the voice comes from, spots the teacher, and moves swiftly, seating himself at the edge of the semicircle of children without any further ado.

Shortly after Aiden has settled himself, the teacher announces the theme of the enquiry, 'Is life always in our control?' The question is also displayed on the whiteboard in front of them. The extract that follows is taken from near the beginning of the lesson. Mostly, children choose each other to speak by placing their hand out, palm upwards. The teacher does not choose who speaks, unless otherwise indicated, but she occasionally makes statements herself as a facilitator of the discussion or to regulate behaviour or interactions.

Teacher:	**The next theme is 'The food we eat.'**
Jerome:	I think we have some control, but sometimes we might get forced.
Niall:	I agree with Jerome, but I also wanted to say that poor people don't have much control.
Mary:	If you are in prison, you cannot decide.
Teacher:	**Nice loud voice!**
Hajra:	I agree with Niall. If you are poor, you do not have as much control, but I also agree with Mary, too, because the food is just cooked in the prison. You cannot go and buy it.
Mohammed:	If you are a child, you might eat what you are given, because your parents have decided . . .
Teacher:	**So do we see a theme coming through here?**
Aiden:	Yes, CHOICE! (*loud voice*)
Teacher:	**The next theme is 'Death.'**
	The teacher chooses the first child to express an opinion.
Aneesa:	You have some control if you are sick and don't take your medicine because then you might die. Or you might be in a car accident and be really badly hurt and die.
Teacher:	**So, what control would you have then?**
Aneesa:	None.
Tyler:	You can make choices – like whether you wear a seatbelt.
Teacher:	**Are there always things that are preventable?**
Niall:	It might not be preventable if you decide to kill yourself.
Joelle:	I agree. You could decide to kill yourself.
Kiran:	If you just got a disease and died it would not be your fault.
Teacher:	**If you chose to take your own life, would it be wholly your choice if you had heard something about it?**

There is a brief discussion which revolves around the very recent case of 14-year-old Molly Russell, who took her own life after allegedly reading how to do so on her Instagram account. The teacher does not ignore it. In fact, after Kiran moves carefully away, suggesting you might die from a disease, she moves it back to the theme of suicide briefly, acknowledging that you could be influenced to take your own life if, as was suggested with the case in question, you read about how to do it.

Teacher:	**The next theme is 'Dreams.'**
Hazaneen:	I do not think we have any control because God makes dreams.
Jack:	What type of dreams are we talking about . . . nightmares?
Ben:	You could choose to watch some scary stuff.
Nafeesa:	Miss, I'd like to question you. By dreams, do you mean nightmares or wishes?
Teacher:	**I think I meant dreams, not life goals.**

Figure 0.1 Beginning of class enquiry 'Is life always within our control?'

There are several things going on in this extract. You might notice the way the children respectfully agree with each other or the ease with which they discuss their chosen themes with each other and the teacher. You might notice that the traffic is not all one way – it is not only the teacher asking the questions. At the end of the exchanges, Nafeesa asks the teacher to clarify what she means by the word 'dreams.' You might be surprised or feel uneasy at the mention of suicide by the children and the way the teacher returns to it, albeit briefly. If you are unfamiliar with primary education, you might think that these sorts of discussions are commonplace – to be seen every day in schools. But although they do take place, they do not feature regularly in many schools and certainly do not occur on a day-to-day basis. In this school, however, they are a regular feature of lessons. As we describe in more detail in Chapters 9 and 10, the approach is based on the school's aims for their children. They want them to develop independence and agency, to be able to take on some responsibility for their own learning, and to be able to develop an understanding of what we may call social concepts, such as *justice, equality* and *freedom*. Above all, they want them to be confident speakers. To this end, they have devised what they call a concept-curriculum, which integrates National Curriculum requirements with an enquiry approach underpinned by Philosophy for Children (P4C), a thinking skills programme.

At the heart of the classroom discussion in Figure 0.1, and fundamental to the argument of this book, is that learning is significantly enhanced when children are trusted to develop their understanding of the world by talking about it with each other and the teacher. How teachers can go about this, how trusting relationships are formed and a classroom becomes a genuine community, as well as the curriculum and pedagogy this entails, will be discussed in subsequent chapters. But our recurrent message is we become better teachers when we cease to pretend to pupils that we know everything and when we learn to listen to what they are saying. Listening means listening with our whole soul. It means asking students questions that do not require simple one-word answers but show that we, too, are trying to understand them. The approach this book advocates is based on the view of good teaching as an essentially human endeavour in which we are open to our pupils. We do this by showing our fallibility. The teacher who regularly shows they can be wrong, who shows they are interested in and concerned about their pupils, and who can share a bit of themselves, too, will develop trusting and respectful relationships that no amount of rewards or sanctions can replace. A teacher who can listen to their pupils in this way will find it easier to enter into genuine dialogue, as we saw in Figure 0.1. Like a parent, it is only when the teacher notices how a pupil is seeking to make sense of their learning by listening to them, and following their gestures, that real progress is made. Teaching is above all about relationships. It does not mean being a friend to the pupils, but it does mean showing your humanity.

The significance of classroom relationships cannot be overstated. But in order for children to be able to share thoughts, ideas, and experiences with each other and the teacher, they need to be able to understand the language of the school and express themselves so that others can understand them. School language differs considerably from what many children experience in the home, whether or not they are native speakers. So, teachers need to take time to introduce, explain, and give children opportunities to explore the language of the school. The words they need to become confident with are often abstract concepts such as *multiplication* and *division* in Maths or *evaporation* in Science. Sentences might be longer and grammatical constructions more formal. Children should also be able to explore concepts which we might see as religious, ethical or philosophical, words such as *freedom, justice* or *equality*, words which help them understand their place in the world. Yet this is very rare, especially in primary schools. Current classroom practice, focussed as it is on the individual, on meeting targets, and passing exams, leaves little time for pupils to talk together. A paradigm of measurability has led to a dogma that suggests that knowledge is immutable – something to be parcelled up and delivered and that there is a simple input-output algorithm at the heart of learning. Of course, in reality, this is not how we learn or build concepts, whether they are scientific, historical, artistic, literary, or religious. The most powerful learning comes from the sharing of ideas through exploratory talk, comparing our understanding, and making tentative attempts to build upon and articulate what we already know, trying out new ideas and using new words to encapsulate those ideas.

In Figure 0.1, we saw children participating in just such exploratory talk, sharing their ideas and drawing on their existing knowledge and experiences. We also saw a teacher who was confident to let them discuss together and who was listening to what they said, not asking questions to test their factual knowledge. It was this close listening that led her to ask the questions she did to test and extend their understanding. But she also did something else which led directly from her active listening. She encouraged the children to use a word to identify a concept. She asked, 'do we see a theme coming through here?' to which Aiden answered immediately in a loud voice, 'Yes, CHOICE!' Here, she was guiding the children to draw out concepts, to help with their thinking. Figure 0.2 is a further, much shorter extract from the same lesson. It comes at the end, when children are deciding, after their discussions, how much control they have over different aspects of their lives. There is a 'concept line' (a long, narrow strip of card about a metre long) on the carpet stretching out before them. It is marked out with the statements 'No control' at the top, 'Some control' in the middle, and 'Full control' at the bottom. As they feed back in their groups, children place pieces of paper with the titles of the themes such as 'Food,' 'Friends,' or 'Weather' at various points on this line. They have placed 'Weather,' for example, midway between 'Some control' and 'No control' and 'Friends' just above 'Some control.'

Farzana:	We put ours ('Health') in the middle because we thought that you do get some choice. We considered the situation of a child who is a baby as different from kids of our age. We can choose if we eat chips or crisps or unhealthy things, especially if we get pocket money, and even if we cannot choose what our parents cook at home, we can refuse to eat it.
Shobna:	I agree with that position.
Miriam:	We put ours ('Thoughts') in between 'Full' and 'No control' because someone else might introduce an idea into your head. . . . So, someone else makes you think something . . .
Teacher:	**So, are you talking about the concept of 'influence'?**
Catherine:	Ours was 'Behaviour.' We said some people might have problems like mental health – they don't get to choose! But, like you said, you could be influenced by your friend to do something wrong which you might not choose to do yourself, like if you were scared of them or something.

Figure 0.2 End of class enquiry 'Is life always within our control?'

In Figure 0.2, we again see the teacher drawing out a concept word. On this occasion, she supplies it for them. But notice how carefully she does so. She does not say, 'I think you are talking about the concept of influence.' Nor does she say, 'You mean the concept of influence.' She enters into the dialogue with them as an equal by introducing the word as a suggestion framed as a question – 'Are you talking about the concept of influence?' We can see too how the word is immediately taken up by the next child, Catherine, this time as a verb to explain their group's consideration of the theme of 'Behaviour.' Classroom learning which encourages dialogue of this sort is empowering for child and teacher alike. It makes lessons come alive, and although it cannot be a model for all learning, as there are skills that need direct teaching, it needs to be practised much more widely than is currently the case. A balance of individual and communal learning, in which students raise questions and witness each other talking about their own past learning and experiences, can be achieved. This book sets out to show how this is possible, from the first words a child utters to showing how teachers can create talk-friendly classrooms.

The book is divided into two parts. The first looks at how children learn to talk, the role of talk in learning and its current status in schools. It shows how talk pedagogies can considerably enhance the development of children's cognitive, social, and emotional skills. This is followed by a critique of the 'behavioural objectives' model of curriculum design which has almost total dominance in schools and colleges at present. Is it appropriate for developing subject knowledge? Does it give too much power to the teacher? We explore the alternative, an enquiry-based or process model of curriculum through the writings of Lawrence Stenhouse. This approach has significant advantages to learning amongst which are the proper testing and exploration of ideas with students and room for more teacher autonomy and professional decision making. The second part of the book shows what is possible by an extended consideration of the actions of one primary school which has adopted a talk pedagogy and uses this to underpin a concept-led curriculum. We learn how this approach evolved from their aspirations for their pupils, and we are taken term by term through a year in a Year 6 class at the school. We see how subject areas like History, Geography, Art, and Design and Technology are integrated within ethical, social, and religious themes which can sometimes be controversial in nature. A chapter is devoted to this aspect of using talk to develop children's criticality showing what it means for the teacher but also underscoring its importance in a world where young people are constantly exposed to the pressures of social media and the potential dangers of AI and fake news. Later chapters focus on how talk is used to develop critical thinking in Further and Higher Education. In Chapter 13, Sue Lay explains how to manage discussions with sixteen to eighteen year olds on a wide range of political and social themes, as well as sensitive issues such as Consent and Sexual Harassment. In Chapter 14, Hilary Wason lets us hear the voices of three university lecturers as they set out to develop the skills of critical thinking through talk in their classes. Throughout the book, points are illustrated and discussion is focussed on examples from the classroom. There is a range of lesson extracts, examples of students' work from different subject areas, and we hear teachers' voices as they reflect on their changing classroom practice.

A note on terminology

The word *talk* is used throughout this book, despite the increasing popularity of the term *oracy*. Oracy was coined by Andrew Wilkinson (1965) and used by the National Oracy Project in the 1980s and 1990s to represent an all-embracing philosophy of learning through talk. But it has more recently often been associated with a narrower set of measurable skills, or communicative competences, which do not fully reflect its origins. Although anything which focusses on improving students' ability to express themselves verbally should be welcomed, the approach we advocate entails significant changes to teachers' classroom practice. We believe that talk must arise from meaningful learning contexts and be embedded within the curriculum, promoting students' authentic voices and involvement in their own learning (Knight, 2023). Those who, like us, are seriously concerned with the value of talk for sustained learning opportunities need to be wary of the potential for useful tools such as the Oracy Skills Framework to be co-opted to serve the ends of current classroom practice with its focus on measurement and target setting. Talk must not become yet another 'bolt on' to curriculum, without serious thought given to learning context, purpose, and audience.

We use children, pupils, and students as almost interchangeable terms throughout the book, with a heavier emphasis on the word students for the older age groups included.

References

Barnes, D. (1987) *From Communication to Curriculum*. London: Penguin Books.

Finlayson, J.G. (2005) *Habermas: A Very Short Introduction*. Oxford: Oxford University Press.

Habermas, J. (1984) *The Theory of Communicative Action*, Vol 1. London: Heinemann.

Knight, R. (2023) Really saying something? Speaking up for authentic classroom talk. *Forum*, 65(1), pp. 98–107.

Wilkinson, A. (1965) The concept of oracy. *Educational Review*, 17(4), pp. 11–15.

PART I
Learning through talk

1 Learning to talk

Children's language development is phenomenal. By the age of six, most of us have a vocabulary of between ten and fourteen thousand words (Bloom and Markson, 1998; Clark, 1993). Estimates vary, and arriving at an estimate is not straightforward. But it is nevertheless a remarkable achievement. By the time we leave school, this has risen to an estimated fifty thousand words (Nagy and Anderson, 1984). But it does not stop there. Millions of typically developing children produce and understand an infinite number of sentences of increasing complexity and precision over time. We start to say individual words around the age of a year, although development can vary considerably and is no indication of later achievement. Moreover, we have been understanding words and phrases, along with other sounds and gestures, for a lot longer. Research even tells us that the newborn infant brain responds differently when it hears a foreign language to that of its mother (May et al., 2011) and that newborns can differentiate between a story which has been read to them many times when they were still in the womb (DeCasper and Spence, 1986). This does not mean, of course, that they understand it, but these prelinguistic behaviours demonstrate a developing readiness for language use. Simple two- or three-word phrases such as 'Rosie milk' typically come after a child uses words individually. They are context-dependent and require you to be with the child to understand her meaning. Does Rosie want some milk, is she stating that the milk is hers, or is she saying something else? Initially, children use some words generically, like *dad* for any man. Perhaps milk means any drink, and Rosie actually wants juice? The stage at which children use phrases or sentences to report an action, 'Rosie and Mummy see ducks in the park' – in this case narrated to her Granny after they return from the park – is a further step forward as language is being used to refer back to an experience in the past. It is not just being used in the here and now. This stage can happen roughly at any time between two years of age and older. It is an example of what Halliday called the *Grammatical Generalisation Phase* (1993).

Semantics: how children learn the meaning of words

Over fifteen hundred years ago, the philosopher and theologian St. Augustine of Hippo in his *Confessions* attempted to explain how he learned to speak, describing his elders pointing at objects in order to teach him their names. This direct correspondence between the object and the word has been repeated by other philosophers, such as Locke. It holds similarities too with a more recent account of word learning known as the 'computational model.' But is

DOI: 10.4324/9781003451044-3

it really as simple as that? As Wittgenstein pointed out, this view assumes every word has a meaning which is fixed and unalterable (1968). It seems to disregard the social context. Think of how the phrase 'I like that' could be used with very different emotions and different tones of voice to convey completely different meanings. It is not the words themselves that convey humour or aggression. It is where they come in the sequence or flow of social interaction, the tone of voice used, and often the accompanying gestures. Any utterance can have multiple possible meanings. Wittgenstein termed the phrase 'Language Games' to refer to the concrete and social activities which involve specific forms of language. The meaning of a word, then, is not the object to which it corresponds but rather the use made of it in what he termed 'the stream of life.' There was a larger philosophical problem associated with the view of language learning that suggested a direct relationship between meaning and each individual word which bothered him too and which has been at the centre of philosophical arguments around meaning and thinking in the Western European tradition. The assumption that the contents of an individual's mind are foundational, as most famously articulated by Descartes in his statement *Cogito ergo sum*, suggested to Wittgenstein a conundrum as far as language was concerned. We can only talk about the contents of our own mind once we have learned a language, and we can only learn a language by taking part in the practices of a community. By this token, he went on to argue, the starting point for philosophical reflection is not our own consciousness but our participation in communal activities. This means that the public is logically prior to the private, not the other way round, as Descartes' famous statement implies. This view of language development and meaning making is essentially social. It is a central theme of this book. It forms the basis for the argument that we return to again and again of the primacy of sharing thinking and building ideas together through talk. Chapter 2, for example, explores Vygotsky and Halliday's ideas of the primacy of language in concept formation and the restructuring of experience. But for now, we will return to a consideration of how children become able, apparently effortlessly, to manipulate the nuts and bolts of language – vocabulary and grammar.

If we were for a moment to accept Augustine's apparently 'common sense' explanation of how children learn words – by an adult pointing to an object or animal and saying a word – would it be that easy? Surely it could lead to multiple possible interpretations? I could say 'apple' as I point to it, and a child may think I am referring to its colour (as with an orange) or its shape or its ability to roll! Or I might point to a cat running across the road and say 'cat.' The child could well infer the movement, the colour, tail, or even the behaviour. Perhaps I was suggesting that this was a bad thing to do? There are countless possible meanings to narrow down, and yet the child does so, seemingly effortlessly. This situation, known as the problem of translation, was illustrated well by the philosopher Quine (1960) when he invented the *gavagai* problem. Quine imagines a linguist visiting a culture which is new to him. As a rabbit hops by, a native says, *gavagai*, and the linguist promptly writes down the word 'rabbit' as a tentative translation. But how sure can he be that the native was naming the animal? Of course, the answer is he can't. The term might refer to anything from the whole class of rodents, any part of the rabbit's anatomy, or the movement it was making and so on and so forth, as with the earlier example with the word 'apple.'

So, how do children make sense of individual words within the flow of speech? There has been much research in this area over the last fifty years or so, but there is still no consensus, although there is some agreement over the fact that the human brain seems to have a built-in bias or 'constraint,' which rules out certain possibilities being considered when we are trying to make sense of new words (Markman, 1990). The pioneer of children's language development, Roger Brown, for example, noticed the human tendency to generalise across items with very different uses but which share some qualities – like the kitchen utensil called a fork and the garden fork used for digging (1957). This tendency was later named the 'shape bias' (Landau et al., 1988). Other constraints, such as the function bias, mutual exclusivity, and the whole object assumption, have also been posited. Others have suggested that there may be certain dedicated modules or a fast-mapping system within the brain to aid language learning (Carey and Bartlett, 1978). A different view of how children learn word meanings is proposed by those who, similar to Wittgenstein, see meaning as context dependent, within a sequence of interactions (see, for example, Tomasello, 2001). This view, known as the social pragmatic approach, sees young children drawing on social pragmatic cues to learn the adult's referential intent in a given situation. Carpendale, Lewis, and Muller put it thus: 'Yes, some words are learned by simple association, but the complexity of language is such that children need a rich communicative environment in order to learn the meaning of words' (2018, p. 187). But is early language development only about naming things? Canfield (2007) notes eight patterns which form the basis of language interactions. Amongst these, making requests and refusing appear early, whereas naming appears later and may not even be universal across cultures.

Syntax: stringing it together

When we move from individual words and their meanings to how words are put together in phrases and sentences to make grammatical sense, otherwise known as syntax, a very influential but highly controversial account was given by the American linguist Noam Chomsky. Chomsky posited what he termed a 'Universal Grammar.' Chomsky's ideas were not based on empirical research. They were nevertheless so radical as to turn the study of language acquisition on its head. Although his ideas have been paraphrased as regarding language as innate, his phrasing is somewhat more careful, stating that 'language is largely determined by internal factors' (1966, p. 64). Nevertheless, the idea that all of us are born with the facility to learn the grammar of a language (bearing in mind that there are estimated to be more than 7,000 languages currently spoken in the world) sounds, at first glance, far-fetched. His theory was that we are all born with the genetic blueprint for language to develop, almost like an organ, much as other parts of your body develop. Those who adopt this approach are often termed 'nativists' in the literature, and it has been very influential in linguistics and developmental psychology. His principal aim was to come up with what he called the 'Transformative Generative Grammar,' a set of rules determining all the possible grammatical sentences in a language. One of the problems with this theory is that it rests upon the assumption, made before empirical research was conducted, that the sentences children hear are often incomplete and ungrammatical. A second argument, known as 'Poverty of the Stimulus,' stated that even if all the language children heard were error free, it still would not enable them to learn the abstract principles upon which language is based, as it is just too complicated.

There is not space here to devote to a discussion of Chomsky's arguments, nor is it of specific significance to the focus of this book. However, the following section, which is devoted to a more careful look at how parents and adults in general talk to young children, serves in part as evidence that adults do enable children to understand how to use correct grammar, even if it is not by explicit instruction, contrary to Chomsky's assertions. Teachers also engage children in talk activities, using the discourse norms of conversation and dialogue, often subconsciously using the same approach. The way parents and teachers interact with children has also been shown to influence children's development of memory and organisation of experience (Goswami, 2015). For while young children have remarkably good semantic and episodic memories (Bauer, 2010), they do not structure experience in memorable ways unless they have a temporal framework for doing so. Reese, Haden, and Fivush (1993) found that what they termed an 'elaborative' conversational style involving amplifying information recalled by the child then elaborating it seemed to result in children developing more organised and detailed memories. Longitudinal studies have also shown that it is the experience of verbalising events as they occur that is critical for long-term retention (Fivush and Schwarzmueller, 1998).

So, it would seem that the way we talk to and with children, as they grapple with the task of explaining and representing what they are experiencing, not only helps them in getting to terms with articulating experience using correct grammar and vocabulary but is also helping them develop and organise memories to be drawn upon in future knowledge building.

Child-Directed Speech

Have you ever noticed how we talk to very young children? The extra stress we put on certain words, the repetition and recasting of sentences, the higher pitch and exaggerated lilt in phrasing? Maybe you have noticed yourself doing it with your own children or siblings or observed it in other family members or friends. The way adults speak to children has been variously termed 'baby talk,' 'motherese,' 'caregiver talk,' 'parentese,' and a whole host of other names. For ease of discussion here, we will adopt the term 'Child-Directed Speech' (CDS). There is good research evidence to support all of the features of this particular 'register' of speech listed earlier and others, too. Register is a term that is very useful when we are referring to how we adapt our speech for a different audience, and it can overlap style and dialect (Saxton, 2008). Imagine the difference in how you might tell your friends you are going to the toilet in a restaurant or café to how you might ask the waiter. You might say 'I'm just going for a wee' or 'I'm off to the loo' to friends. But the register you use for the waiter would be entirely different. You would probably say something like 'Could you please tell me where the toilets are?,' both adapting your vocabulary and using the more polite addition of the modal verb 'could.' And, of course, this phrasing may alter depending on the age of the waiter and how formally or informally they are dressed. We make these snap decisions subconsciously, but they also form part of a complex set of social expectations.

The way we talk to very young children has been the subject of research since the 1970s. And researchers have looked at how this different register is manifested at the different levels of linguistic analysis - phonology, vocabulary, morphology, and syntax. For example, at the level of phonology, it has been found that overall pitch is higher (e.g., Garnica, 1977; Werker and McLeod, 1989), that adults enunciate more clearly, and that speech tends to be slower with some syllable lengthening (Fernald and Simon, 1984; Albin and Echols, 1996). As Saxton points out (2008), although this exaggerated intonation has been ridiculed as the minority pursuit of Western middle-class mothers, there is good evidence from across the globe in languages and cultures as diverse as German, Italian, Japanese, Hebrew, Luo, and Spanish (Söderstrom, 2007). Brown (1973) found that although children hear a number of incomplete sentences, phrases are nearly always syntactically correct. We use shorter sentences and utterances of shorter duration with young children, and there are fewer complex sentences containing subordinate clauses (Sachs, Brown and Salerno, 1976). Research has also found that the subject of sentences in child-directed speech is nearly always the agent. So, we rarely use the passive with young children. This has the effect of making the relationship between meaning and grammar clear (Rondal and Cession, 1990).

The use of CDS also changes over time. In their first three months of life, babies tend to respond to a comforting tone of voice, whereas from three to six months, they respond to a more approving tone. Kitamura and Lam (2009) suggest that by nine months, children respond to a more directive tone of voice. So, it would seem that adults respond intuitively to the developing needs of the child in the way they speak to them.

Recast and correction

Adults are continually recasting young children's speech, and, just as they may speak more slowly or with exaggerated intonation, they do it more or less unconsciously. An adult follows the child's lead, using the same structures that the child uses, changing or adding to them to model more 'correct' grammar. For example, when young Henry said, 'Brum-brum up' as his mum pushed his pushchair past a car transporter parked at the roadside, and he noticed cars parked on the ramps high above ground level, his mother said, 'Yes, the brum-brums are up, aren't they, Henry? The cars are high up.' By using the same linguistic structure as the child, it seems there is less of a cognitive demand placed on the child's processing and memory. This helps ensure that the child will more easily assimilate new vocabulary – in this case, the word 'car' and maybe even 'high.' Many studies have established the value of such recasts with typically and atypically developing children (for example, Forrest and Elbert, 2001; Seitz and Stewart, 1975; Swensen, Naigles and Fein, 2007).

Contrary to Chomsky's initial assertions and indeed repeated subsequently by some child language researchers (e.g., Weissenborn, Goodluck and Roeper, 1992), adults do also 'correct' children's errors regularly. Brown and Hanlon (1970, p. 197) were the first to recognize these adult corrections, which they felt 'could be instructive.' In the earlier example and ones evidenced by Brown and Hanlon, the repetitions of the child's speech contain corrections. Henry's mum includes a grammatical element, missing from his utterance, by adding the verb 'are.' Examples cited by Brown (1973) include 'Oh, you want lunch?' by Eve's mother when she states, 'Want lunch' and 'Mummy's gone' for 'Mummy gone.' Children, like all language users, make mistakes early on. We are all familiar with some of the most common, such as the 'ed' ending wrongly added to irregular verbs by young children and even occasionally by adults when they are not thinking. Saxton, in his 'Direct Contrast Hypothesis' (1997) explores how the correct adult form is especially evident when the adult sentence directly follows the child's.

Socio-economic and cultural background

So far in this chapter, we have looked at how children pick up language and adults interact with them in general terms. But there is, of course, a great degree of variation. Individual children will have very different experiences, depending on how much attention, interaction, and child-directed speech they experience. A study by Hart and Risley (1995) in the US revealed stark differences in the amount of language children heard, both in terms of quality and quantity. They divided parents into three bands according to their socio-economic status (SES) and investigated the length and complexity of sentences and types of utterances, such as prohibitions or commands or language designed to control behaviour. The findings revealed that those children with parents in the high-SES band were estimated to hear 215,000 words per week, those in the mid-SES band 125,000, and those in the low-SES band 62,000. The high-SES band parents tended to use longer, more complex sentences with their children and a greater range of vocabulary. Those in the lower bands were in receipt of more prohibitions and directive utterances, two features which are more commonly associated with poor language growth (Taylor et al., 2009). But if it seems that there is a simple correlation between high socio-economic status and children's language growth, it is not quite so simple. Other studies reveal a more direct link between talkative parents and children's language development. More talkative parents use a wider vocabulary and express more complex ideas (Rowe, 2012), and children show a corresponding ability to use more complex structures (Vasilyeva, Waterfall and Huttenlocher, 2008). It has also been observed that culture and language spoken can make a significant difference with low SES Spanish-speaking mothers in San Francisco in one study producing a higher number of utterances per minute (17.5) than those of both mid- and high-SES band English-speaking mothers in another study (Hoff and Naigles, 2002).

So, although SES does have a significant impact, the amount your parents talk is of greater importance in predicting your own rate of language development than what SES band you belong to. Children of talkative mothers develop larger vocabularies (Fernald and Weisleder, 2015; Hart and Risley, 1995; Hurtado, Marchman and Fernald, 2008). Of course, if your parents just talk and you don't get a look-in, that may not be advantageous, and a recent US study of the talk between parents and preschool children suggests that adult-child turn taking may be a greater predictor of future academic success than mere exposure to a wider range of vocabulary (Gilkerson et al., 2018). There is also good evidence that children who are engaged in regular and good quality literacy activities like book reading develop larger and more varied vocabularies (Farrant and Zubrick, 2013; Sylva et al., 2010). This can also provide an advantage when they first start school. Wolf puts it clearly in her book, *Proust and the Squid: the story and science of the reading brain,*

> Children who begin kindergarten having heard and used thousands of words, whose meanings are already understood, classified and stored away in their young brains, have the advantage on the playing field of education. Children who never have a story read to them, who never hear words that rhyme, who never imagine fighting with dragons or marrying a prince, have the odds overwhelmingly against them. (2008, p. 20)

Yet how well do we address the need for a significant group of children to develop to become confident and articulate speakers? Is there space in the curriculum to develop this area of learning? And to what extent are teachers and other education professionals confident and competent to support these children?

References

Albin, D.D. and Echols, C.H. (1996) Stressed and word-final syllables in infant-directed speech. *Infant Behavior and Development*, 19(4), pp. 401–418.

Bauer, P.J. (2010) Early memory development. In Goswami, U. (ed.) *Wiley Blackwell Handbook of Childhood Cognitive Development*, 2nd edn. Oxford: Wiley-Blackwell, pp. 153–179.

Bloom, P. and Markson, L. (1998) Capacities underlying word learning. *Trends in Cognitive Sciences*, 2, pp. 67–73.

Brown, R. (1957) Linguistic determination and the part of speech. *Journal of Abnormal and Social Psychology*, 55, pp. 1–5.

Brown, R. (1973) *A First Language*. London: George Allen and Unwin.

Brown, R. and Hanlon, C. (1970) Derivational complexity and order of acquisition in child speech. In Brown, R. (ed). *Psycholinguistics*. New York: Free Press.

Canfield, J.V. (2007) *Becoming Human: The Development of Language, Self and Self- Consciousness*. New York: Palgrave Macmillan.

Carey, S. and Bartlett, E. (1978) Acquiring a single new word. *Papers and Reports on Child Language Development*, 15, pp. 17–29.

Carpendale, J.I.M., Lewis, C. and Muller, U. (2018) *The Development of Children's Thinking: Its Social and Communicative Foundations*. London: Sage.

Chomsky, N. (1966) *Cartesian Linguistics: A Chapter in the History of Rationalist Thought*. New York: Harper and Row.

Clark, E.V. (1993) *The Lexicon in Acquisition*. Cambridge: Cambridge University Press.

DeCasper, A.J. and Spence, M.J. (1986) Prenatal maternal speech influences newborns' perception of speech sounds. *Infant Behavior and Development*, 9(2), pp. 133–150.

Farrant, B.M. and Zubrick, S.R. (2013) Parent-child book reading across early childhood and child vocabulary in the early school years: Findings from the longitudinal study of Australian Children. *First Language*, 33(3), pp. 280–293.

Fernald, A. and Simon, T. (1984) Expanded intonation contours in mothers' speech to newborns. *Developmental Psychology*, 20(1), pp. 104–113.

Fernald, A. and Weisleder, A. (2015) Twenty years after 'meaningful differences' it's time to reframe the 'deficit' debate about the importance of children's early language experience. *Human Development*, 58(1), pp. 1–4.

Fivush, R. and Schwarzmueller, A. (1998) Children remember childhood: Implications for childhood amnesia. *Applied Cognitive Psychology*, 12, pp. 455–473.

Forrest, K. and Elbert, M. (2001) Treatment for phonologically disordered children with variable substitution patterns. *Clinical Linguistics and Phonetics*, 15(1), pp. 41–45.

Garnica, O.K. (1977) Some prosodic and paralinguistic features of speech to young children. In Snow, C.E. and Ferguson, **C.A.** (eds.) *Talking to Children*. Cambridge: Cambridge University Press, pp. 63–88.

Gilkerson, J., Richards, J., Warren, S., Kimbrough Oller, D., Russo, R. and Vohr, B. (2018) Language experience in the second year of life and language outcomes in late childhood. *Paediatrics*, 142(4), pp. 1–11.

Goswami, U. (2015) *Children's Cognitive Development and Learning*. York: Cambridge Primary Review Trust.

Halliday, M.A.K. (1993) Towards a language-based theory of learning. *Linguistics and Education*, 5, pp. 93–116.

Hart, B. and Risley, T. (1995) *Meaningful Differences in the Everyday Experiences of Young American Children*. Baltimore, MD: Paul H. Brookes Publishing.

Hoff, E. and Naigles, L. (2002) How children use input to acquire a lexicon. *Child Development*, 73(2), pp. 418–433.

Hurtado, N., Marchman, V.A. and Fernald, A. (2008) Does input influence uptake? Links between maternal talk, processing speed and vocabulary size in Spanish-learning children. *Developmental Science*, 11(6), pp. 31–39.

Kitamura, C. and Lam, C. (2009) Age-specific preferences for infant-directed affective intent. *Infancy*, 14(1), pp. 77–100.

Landau, B., Smith, L.B. and Jones, S.S. (1988) The importance of shape in early lexical learning. *Cognitive Development*, 3(3), pp. 299–321.

Markman, E.M. (1990) Constraints children place on word meanings. *Cognitive Science*, 14(1), pp. 57–77.

May, L., Byers-Heinlein, K., Gervain, J. and Werker, J.F. (2011) Language and the newborn brain: Does pre-natal language experience shape the neonate neural response to speech? *Frontiers in Psychology*, 2. Published online: 21 September 2011.

Nagy, W.E. and Anderson, R.C. (1984) How many words are there in printed school English? *Reading Research Quarterly*, 19(3), pp. 304–330.

Quine, W.V.O. (1960) *Word and Object*. Cambridge, MA: MIT Press.

Reese, E., Haden, C.A. and Fivush, R. (1993) Mother-child conversations about the past: Relationships of style and memory over time. *Cognitive Development*, 8, pp. 403–430.

Rondal, J. and Cession, A. (1990) Input evidence regarding the sematic bootstrapping hypothesis. *Journal of Child Language*, 17, pp. 711–717.

Rowe, M.L. (2012) A longitudinal investigation of the role of quantity and quality of child-directed speech in vocabulary development. *Child Development*, 83(5), pp. 1762–1774.

Sachs, J., Brown, R. and Salerno, R. (1976) Adults' speech to children. In von Raffler Engel, W. and Lebrun, Y. (eds.) *Baby Talk and Infant Speech*. Lisse: Peter de Ridder Press, pp. 240–245.

Saxton, M. (1997) The Contrast theory of negative input. *Journal of Child Language*, 24, pp. 139–161.

Saxton, M. (2008) What's in a name? Coming to terms with the child's linguistic environment. *Journal of Child Language*, 35(3), pp. 677–686.

Seitz, S. and Stewart, C. (1975) Imitations and expansions: Some developmental aspects of mother-child communication. *Developmental Psychology*, 11(6), pp. 763–768.

Söderstrom, M. (2007) Beyond babytalk: Re-evaluating the nature and content of speech input to pre-verbal infants. *Developmental Review*, 27(4), pp. 501–532.

Swensen, L.D., Naigles, L.R. and Fein, D. (2007) Does maternal input affect the language of children with autism? In Caunt-Nolan, H., Kulatilake, S. and Woo, I. (eds.) *Proceedings of the 30th Annual Boston University Conference on Language Development*. Somerville, MA: Cascadilla Press.

Sylva, K., Melhuish, E., Sammons, P., Siraj-Blatchford, I. and Taggart, B. (eds.) (2010) *Early Childhood Matters: Evidence from the Effective Pre-school and Primary Project*. London: Routledge.

Taylor, N., Donovan, W., Miles, S. and Leavitt, L. (2009) Maternal control strategies, maternal language usage and children's language usage at two years. *Journal of Child Language*, 36(2), pp. 381–404.

Tomasello, M. (2001) Perceiving intentions and learning words in the second year of life. In Tomasello, M. and Bates, E. (eds.) *Language Development: The Essential Readings*. Oxford: Blackwell, pp. 111–128.

Vasilyeva, M., Waterfall, H. and Huttenlocher, J. (2008) Emergence of syntax: Commonalities and differences across children. *Developmental Science*, 11(1), pp. 84–97.

Weissenborn, J., Goodluck, H. and Roeper, T. (1992) Introduction: Old and new problems in the study of language acquisition. In Weissenborn, J., Goodluck, H. and Roeper, T. (eds.) *Theoretical Issues in Language Acquisition: Continuity and Change in Development*. Hillsdale, NJ: Lawrence Erlbaum, pp. 1–23.

Werker, J.F. and McLeod, P.J. (1989) Infant-preference for both male and female infant-directed talk: A developmental study of attentional and affective responsiveness. *Canadian Journal of Psychology-Revue Canadienne De Psychologie*, 43(2), pp. 230–246.

Wittgenstein, L. (1968) *Philosophical Investigations*. Oxford: Blackwell.

Wolf, M. (2008) *Proust and the Squid: The Story and Science of the Reading Brain*. Cambridge: Icon Books.

2 Talking to learn

Talking to yourself

The two most influential educational psychologists of the twentieth century had much to say about children's speech and how they use it. Jean Piaget, who is often identified as the champion of the view of the child as solitary scientist, was the first to write about the fact that young children often talk to themselves. In an early book entitled *The Language and Thought of the Child* (1955), he coined the term 'egocentric speech' to describe this phenomenon, noting that this sort of speech is not expressed to be understood by others, because it is rooted in the child's point of view. He saw it as social but not socially adapted as a means of communication between the child and any other person. It was evidence of the child's egocentrism – their inability to take another's perspective – and therefore a sign of immaturity. Lev Vygotsky, by contrast, thought that egocentric speech had a very significant function as a stage in the development of thought. According to his theory, children learn to talk and then use this tool as a means to develop their thinking. Gradually, 'egocentric' or what some of his followers have termed 'private' speech disappears as it is internalised. It is then abbreviated and becomes 'thought without words' (1986, p. 244).

There is no doubt that children do talk in this way to themselves when playing alone or alongside others (parallel play). Research has shown that this 'private' speech follows a pattern described as an inverted 'U-shaped' trajectory (on the horizontal axis of a graph, where age is what is being measured). That is to say, there is little to no private speech in the very early years, followed by a growth in preschool years, and then it trails off when children start school. Studies have also shown, interestingly, that children use more private speech when there is a task set which is just above their level of competence (Behrend, Rosengren and Perlmutter, 1989) and that they are more likely to use private speech when they have a friend or an adult nearby. But whether the internalisation that Vygotsky suggested occurs is more open to question, as it suggests that thought is contingent on language. And we can all think of examples of thinking that are not language dependent – visualisations, maps, and musical notation are just some examples of other symbol systems. To be fair to him, Vygotsky himself stated that 'there is a vast area of thought that has no direct relation to speech' (1986, p. 88). Indeed, his first objective in *Thought and Language* (1986) was to show that thought and speech have different roots and only merge together at a certain time. But he did argue that thereafter they develop together with reciprocal influence.

DOI: 10.4324/9781003451044-4

Vygotsky saw language as a psychological tool. He claimed that thinking originated in social activity, implying that forms of thought are first external and then become internalised as they are gradually mastered by the child – so thinking is social in its primary manifestation. He summed this up in a much-cited sentence,

> Every function in the cultural development of the child appears on the stage twice, in two planes, first, the social, then the psychological, first between people as an intermental category, then within the child as an intramental category.

> (Vygotsky, 1997)

It is worth comparing this view with Wittgenstein's writing about language and 'Language Games,' as mentioned in the previous chapter. Both described thinking as primarily a social function, in contrast to what was and still is a widely held view of thinking as a private and individual matter (Descartes' *Cogito, ergo sum*).

Vygotsky made two other major contributions, derived from his own work in educational settings. The first is usually termed 'The Zone of Proximal (sometimes Potential) Development' and has been very influential in the field of education. It was an early articulation of the idea that learning is dialogical.

The Zone of Proximal Development

One of Vygotsky's main areas of interest was the study of concept formation. In his limited experimental work – cut short by his death from tuberculosis at the early age of 38 in 1934 – he identified a long process from relatively unorganised categorisation based on physical properties to more mature conceptual thinking. His follower Alexander Luria was able, with much more data, to develop a neuropsychological theory. Vygotsky was particularly critical of methods of mental testing (still used today) of a child left on its own. He argued that a much better assessment of a child's intellectual ability could be made by observing the cooperation of a child with an adult. Here, the unorganised concepts of the child, derived from their everyday experience, meet the more systematic organised concepts used in adult reasoning. This meeting point he described as 'The Zone of Proximal Development' (ZPD). The child's ability to begin to appropriate the adult mental structures (over time) varies with their ability. But once this form of reasoning becomes internalised, it forms part of the child's own reasoning. He defined the ZPD as 'the distance between the actual developmental level as determined by independent problem solving and the level of potential development as determined through problem solving under adult guidance or in collaboration with more capable peers' (1978, p. 86). It is worth noting here that Vygotsky's actual words do draw out that it could be a peer whom the child is working with. It does not have to be an adult.

Vygotsky's view that thinking originates in interaction with others has been a major influence on what are termed socio-cultural or socio-historical approaches to cognitive development. Many in teaching espouse the use of the ZPD through what is known as 'scaffolding' (Ninio and Bruner, 1978). The metaphor refers, of course, to providing a child with a structure to enable them to develop their understanding. As their understanding develops, the structure is gradually removed or becomes no longer necessary. This could apply to all types of learning. We can imagine a parent helping a young child counting a number of objects by placing their finger on an object each time they say the number, for example, or a teacher using a series of cue questions to enable a child to structure a piece of writing. And, indeed, research has been done which reveals scaffolding in action, demonstrating in the best cases, mothers adjusting the level of help needed to the child's abilities. Scaffolding like this has shown positive links to children's cognitive development (Bibok, Muller and Carpendale, 2009; Hammond et al., 2012). But equally, scaffolding can be misused or simply misunderstood. Sometimes parents, teachers, or teaching assistants simply do not show the necessary sensitivity, often doing the work for the child to ensure they get the right answer, demonstrating an insufficient grasp of the child's abilities, or merely not giving the child a chance to have a go. This misunderstanding of scaffolding actually has a negative effect on a child's cognitive development, as does the message it carries. Children who are 'supported' in this way in the 'lower ability' group - another very misleading term - routinely develop low self-esteem and the approach stunts their development in all sorts of ways. In fact, it is very hard to establish children's learning potential, and the best way to help them develop their skills and understanding is through a classroom climate where it is all right to get it wrong, and, indeed, that is the first step to getting it right.

From home language to school language

In Chapter 6 of *Thought and Language* (1986), Vygotsky addresses the issue of what happens when children start to encounter the language used in school. He characterises a transition in which the instruction in school awakens a series of functions lying in the ZPD. He uses words that have been translated as 'everyday' and 'scientific' to distinguish between the way a child learns to talk about their experience in everyday life compared with how they encounter concepts in school. It is the interaction that occurs in school that enables children to appropriate these 'scientific' concepts and thereby develop their thinking. And using the correct words is a significant step on this journey. It is important to understand what he means at this point by these terms. By 'scientific,' he does not mean just concepts we encounter in science. In fact, in his research, he used material from a school Social Sciences programme. Among the small number of terms in the materials he selected for his research with his pupil Shif are the nouns *exploitation* and *revolution* (Wells, 1999, p. 34). He is referring, therefore, to what we might call 'concept vocabulary' such as *tolerance* (in RE or PSHE), *erosion* (in Geography), or *metaphor* (in English or Language), *condensation* (in Science), or *integer* (in Maths). Such terms are usually nouns - what we would call abstract nouns. In contrast to 'everyday' concepts which are learned unsystematically and arise from a child's spontaneous interest and experience, these 'scientific' concepts, encountered in school (but not only in school, it is worth saying) are presented and learned as part of an interaction with an adult, usually a teacher (although remember that Vygotsky does talk about a more able peer). The explanations of the concepts require dialogue which entails a sort of bringing to conscious awareness. As an example of this, let us have a further look at an extract from the introduction to the book as shown in Figure 2.1.

Farzana:	We put ours (Health) in the middle because we thought that you do get some choice. We considered the situation of a child who is a baby as different from kids of our age. We can choose if we eat chips or crisps or unhealthy things, especially if we get pocket money, and even if we cannot choose what our parents cook at home, we can refuse to eat it.
Shobna:	I agree with that position.
Miriam:	We put ours (Thoughts) in between 'Full' and 'No control' because someone else might introduce an idea into your head. . . . So, someone else makes you think something . . .
Teacher:	**So, are you talking about the concept of 'influence'?**
Catherine:	Ours was 'Behaviour.' We said some people might have problems like mental health – they don't get to choose! But, like you said, you could be influenced by your friend to do something wrong which you might not choose to do yourself, like if you were scared of them or something.

Figure 2.1 A section of dialogue on the theme of *control*

In this extract from a classroom enquiry, the teacher introduces the word 'influence' after Miriam states someone else might introduce an idea into your head. It is very quickly picked up by Catherine, the next child to respond, who puts it to use straight away as a verb to help explain her group's consideration of the theme of *behaviour*. It is unlikely that this is the first time the children have encountered the concept expressed by this particular word, although for some, the word may be new. The teacher, in dialogue with her class, is reinforcing the children's understanding and encouraging them to use this 'concept' word to help them articulate their thoughts.

Vygotsky suggested that two processes were at work in concept formation – 'generalisation' and 'systematisation.' At the earlier stage of generalisation, we classify objects into groups. There is no hierarchical relationship between the concepts, but at the later stage, systematisation, there is a hierarchy. What is interesting is that he suggests that as children's thinking develops, as a result of instruction in 'scientific' or what we have called here 'concept' vocabulary, it leads to a restructuring of their spontaneous concepts. He may even be suggesting this restructures their experience. One thing is clear: he ascribes a critical role to teaching in this process, whether in the home, preschool, or school itself.

How language restructures experience

A writer who did suggest that our developing command of language leads to a restructuring of experience was the linguist Michael Halliday. Halliday summarised much of his lifetime's work in a paper entitled *Towards a Language-Based Theory of Learning* (1993). Like Vygotsky, Halliday proposed that a growing vocabulary of abstract nouns had an effect on children's concept development by encoding and thereby objectifying experience. But for Halliday, it was the reconstruction of grammar that occurs at different stages of our development that actually reconstitutes the way we think. He identified four stages of language development: 'protolanguage,' 'grammatical generalisation,' 'grammatical abstractness,' and 'grammatical metaphor.' Particularly important are the changes that come about as children enter formal education. His concepts of grammatical abstractness and grammatical metaphor (see what follows) throw light on how the experience of learning to read and write influences the way a child can organise their experience and articulate their understanding of the world. The neuroscientist Wolf (2008) maybe puts it more succinctly when she suggests that humanity's development of writing, and as a result of it, of reading, rewired the brain.

> We were never born to read. Human beings invented reading only a few thousand years ago. And with this invention, we rearranged the very organisation of our brain, which in turn expanded the ways we were able to think, which altered the intellectual evolution of our species.
>
> (2008, p. 3)

When children learn to read and write, Halliday argued, they enter a phase he calls 'grammatical abstractness,' and it is at this point that they become aware of the medium of language itself. The marks on the page that they are called upon to render into words, through a process called 'reading,' are part of a second-order symbolic system in which symbols stand for other symbols, '[h]ence the learner has to recognise two sets of abstract entities, and also the abstract relation between them – e.g. *word, letter, stand for, spell*, or analogous terms in other languages and writing systems' (1993, p. 109). As he points out, it is not just a matter of mastering a new medium but a new form of knowledge: educational as opposed to 'everyday.' When children present their knowledge in written form, even when it is something they are familiar with and can talk about at length, they consistently show regression, but this is because they are struggling with a new form of representation. Their ability in writing cannot nearly keep up with their fluency in speaking, and besides, it mainly requires a different means of expression. At this stage children come to reinterpret their experiences according to the semantic structures which are characteristic of written texts. It is the grammar and syntax of sentences encountered through reading, and being read to, that are different and influence children's ability to articulate their thoughts. In Halliday's own words, 'In the process of becoming literate, they learn to reconstitute language itself into a new, more abstract mode' (1993, p. 105).

The final stage – what Halliday terms 'grammatical metaphor' – is clearly compatible with what Vygotsky means when he discusses a child's growing awareness of, and ability to explain, 'scientific concepts' through access to the semantic structure of written language and under instruction from a teacher (1986). At this stage, experiences that children are familiar with, and would express using verbs and adjectives in their day-to-day talk, are recast in the written form as nouns. So, for example, when we might say, 'When an engine breaks down, trains are cancelled' in everyday speech, we might come across it recast as 'In times of engine failure, there are cancellations' in a written text. Where we might say, 'Cheetahs are excellent predators because they can move very fast,' it may be recast in a written text as 'because they rely on their great speed.' This is a means of expression children become familiar with through their own reading and begin to use in their own writing. It will also, up to a point, seep into their own speech, depending on the audience they are talking to – because it is a register (see Chapter 1). It will also likely depend upon whether they are exposed to this register of language in the home.

The work of Vygotsky and Halliday sheds light on the cognitive and linguistic processes at work as we go through the first years of schooling. But there are several boundaries to cross when children first start school, including the physical act of entering the building itself! There are new expectations for their behaviour, new relationships to form, and new experiences to assimilate. Good teachers use verbal strategies to support them by building on their own phrases, recasting them, and using elaboration or a series of conversational prompts, as do parents. In their work on dialogic teaching, discussed in Chapter 5, Mercer (2000) and Alexander (2020) identify a range of verbal strategies in common use by teachers which, like elaboration, are an effective means of children building on prior learning and working together to build understanding. Some examples of these strategies are 'recaps' and 'reformulations' (Mercer) or using talk that is 'reciprocal' and 'cumulative' (Alexander). But good teaching isn't just about language. To support children to 'bridge the gap,' teachers make extensive use of nonverbal strategies such as tone of voice, expression, body language, and gestures, alongside other approaches like using visual and physical resources. Indeed, most language derives its meaning from the tone of voice in which it is delivered, or accompanying gestures, in all human communication.

References

Alexander, R.J. (2020) *A Dialogic Teaching Companion*. Abingdon: Routledge.

Behrend, D.A., Rosengren, K.S. and Perlmutter, M. (1989) A new look at children's private speech: The effects of age, task difficulty and parent presence. *International Journal of Behavioral Development*, 12, pp. 305–320.

Bibok, M.B., Muller, U. and Carpendale, J.I.M. (2009) Childhood. In Muller, U., Carpendale, J.I.M. and Smith, L. (eds.) *The Cambridge Companion to Piaget*. Cambridge: Cambridge University Press, pp. 229–254.

Halliday, M.A.K. (1993) Towards a language-based theory of learning. *Linguistics and Education*, 5, pp. 93–116.

Hammond, S.I., Muller, U., Carpendale, J.I.M., Bibok, M.B. and Liebermann-Finestone, D.P. (2012) The effects of parental scaffolding on preschoolers' executive function. *Developmental Psychology*, 48, pp. 271–281.

Mercer, N. (2000) *Words and Minds: How We Use Language to Think Together*. London: Routledge.

Ninio, A. and Bruner, J. (1978) The achievement and antecedents of labelling. *Journal of Child Language*, 5, pp. 1–15.

Piaget, J. (1955) *The Language and Thought of the Child*. Cleveland, OH: Meridian (Original work published in 1923).

Vygotsky, L.S. (1978) *Mind in Society: The Development of Higher Psychological Processes*. Cambridge, MA: Harvard University Press.

Vygotsky, L.S. (1986) *Thought and Language*. Cambridge, MA: MIT Press (Original work published in 1934).

Vygotsky, L.S. (1997) Genesis of higher mental functions. In Rieber, R. and Carton, A. (eds.) *The Collected Works of L.S. Vygotsky*, Vol. 4. New York: Plenum Press.

Wells, G. (1999). *Dialogic Inquiry: Toward a Socio-Cultural Practice and Theory of Education*. Cambridge: Cambridge University Press.

Wolf, M. (2008) *Proust and the Squid: The Story and Science of the Reading Brain*. Cambridge: Icon Books.

3 Talk and social mobility

A class ceiling?

Talk is political. It is no accident that those educationalists who have promoted the value of talk, drawing on learners' life experiences, have also believed strongly in emancipation of the marginalised, economically disadvantaged and oppressed members of society. Whilst the American philosopher and educationalist John Dewey's ideas were vilified in a democratic country, Paulo Freire, the adult educator, was imprisoned and narrowly escaped with his life from his native Brazil when it was in the hands of a right-wing dictatorship. There have been a number of government-commissioned and independent research reports and short-lived initiatives which have promoted good practice in talk in England over the last fifty years, but the advice has not been acted upon - for example, the *Bullock report* (1975) or the *Cambridge Primary Review* (Alexander, 2010). Other initiatives have been short lived and closed down with insufficient explanation - for example, the National Oracy Project which lasted from 1987-1993 (Norman, 1992). As we write this, the current leader of the Labour Party in England, Sir Keir Starmer, has given a recent speech in which he has committed his party to introduce what has been termed 'speaking lessons' by some in the media, citing the National Literacy Trust data suggesting that the poorest students start school 19 months behind the richer ones in language and vocabulary. The speech suggests that a lack of ability to speak well, or be articulate, imposes a 'class ceiling' on children. This is welcome, though not news to many who have been arguing this case for a long time. Very recently, the Oracy All-Party Parliamentary Group launched the final report of their inquiry *Speak for Change* (April 2021), highlighting the effects of the pandemic on an already marked spoken 'language gap' between disadvantaged students and their peers. The report called for a shift in educational culture and values, for shared expectations for oracy across schools, and for teachers and schools to be equipped and empowered to provide the tools and resources to effect this change. There is no doubt that equipping people with the means to discuss and argue, including for better life circumstances, can be seen as a threat by those in power who are keen to keep power for themselves. The phrase 'History is written by the victors,' often attributed to Winston Churchill, has an uncanny echo in Vygotsky's own belief in his early writing that 'Pedagogics was never politically indifferent . . . it has always adopted a particular social pattern, political line in accordance with the dominant social class that has guided its interests' (1997, p. 348). Language use in education, as in other aspects of life, has the potential to reinforce, or loosen, structural inequalities in society. Bourdieu and Passeron's (1977) theory of reproduction

DOI: 10.4324/9781003451044-5

demonstrates how the culture, practice, and consciousness of the dominated group in society are misrepresented, distorted, and given less value. Empowering children who do not belong to the elite to talk eloquently and persuasively might disrupt the social order.

The facts

In 2014, the Centre for Social Justice stated that as many as 10 percent of the UK population may have Speech, Language, and Communication Needs (SLCN). SLCN was defined in the 2008 Bercow Report as including difficulties 'with fluency, forming sounds and words, formulating sentences, understanding what others say and using language socially' (2008, p. 14). Although some schools may have the luxury of a Speech and Language unit, these are few and far between, and children with expressive and/or receptive language needs are not always picked up early. Children with SLCN are significantly likely to come from more disadvantaged areas with some suggesting the prevalence of these needs being as high as 50 percent from this sector of the population (Centre for Social Justice, 2014). There are also clear links with poorer education outcomes (Snowling et al., 2011), mental health needs, and involvement with the criminal justice system (Early Intervention Foundation, 2017).

Another group of children who have different needs are those for whom English is an Additional Language (EAL). In 2019, 21.2 percent of children in British primary schools and 16.9 percent of pupils in secondary schools were recorded as having a first language known or believed to be other than English (DfE, 2019). These figures show a significant rise from a decade earlier when the figures were 14.4 percent and 10.8 percent, respectively (DCSF, 2008). Data from national test results show that children who have English as a first language experience higher rates of educational attainment than those with EAL at each stage of education (NALDIC, 2021). Many children with EAL have significantly lower levels of English vocabulary knowledge than their monolingual English-speaking peers (Cameron, 2003), and their weaker language skills are likely to have a significant impact on their ability to understand what they are being taught (Stuart, 2004).

Narrowing the gap?

But there is another reason why talk is not nearly well-enough used in schools. In addition to its low status in the curriculum, which we shall explore further in Chapter 4, using talk collaboratively requires a completely different mindset, one that challenges many teachers' ideas of what it means to be a teacher. Classrooms are places where there is a marked power differential. The teacher has much greater power than the pupils, and it is through the teacher that the child gets to talk – in answering questions, making presentations, participating in a group – or indeed gets told, politely or otherwise, to stop talking! Teachers are the mediators and interpreters of children's talk, and they are also gatekeepers. They may, and often do, misunderstand a child's utterance or attempt to articulate a concept. But above all, teachers are the ones who talk the most. The famous 'two-thirds rule' first outlined by Flanders in 1961 after examining patterns of talk in US classrooms over a six-year period states: two-thirds of classroom time involves talk; two-thirds of that talk is teacher talk; and two-thirds of teacher talk is devoted to explaining or directing. Subsequent research over decades in UK in both primary and secondary schools has largely corroborated these findings, demonstrating how talk patterns, dominated by 'telling,' reflect the teacher's authority (Edwards and Furlong, 1978; Galton, Simon and Croll, 1980; Galton et al., 1999). Because of the power differential, the child will seldom answer back or question the teacher. This situation is described by the German philosopher Jürgen Habermas as a 'speech-role imbalance' in his *Theory of Communicative Action* (1984). There are other examples of this imbalance – for instance, in the customer-client relationship or when being served in a restaurant. But schools present probably the most extreme example and possibly the one most open to abuse. Where talk has the sole purpose of transmitting knowledge, often characterised by recitation or short question and answers – what Cazden (2001) calls 'traditional' – this conventional power imbalance applies.

But talk can be used as a means of exploration and to develop understanding. In this case, a different kind of communication develops between pupil and teacher. The teacher does away with the trappings of authority and power, making themselves more approachable by lessening the power differential. In this situation, where students are asked to think, not merely remember, and collaborative meaning making is encouraged, the classroom becomes a community of enquiry. Children and teacher are collectively seeking to deepen their understanding. Later in this chapter, for example, we see 'Miss W' exchange a formal and traditional stance for an approachable, accessible persona, encouraging contributions and debate from her pupils. The students bring their life experiences and prior learning to bear in a way which makes the lesson meaningful and the subject matter accessible. This is not to say that every lesson can or indeed should be taught in this way. There is a need for direct teaching of some skills and teacher modelling at times also. Neither is it to deny the authority of the teacher. Some teachers are able to switch between these different modes. But some find the move from more overtly authoritarian and controlling to more human and approachable difficult. It threatens their authority as a teacher. For others, the closer relationship that forms between them and their pupils increases the respect. It is all a matter of confidence. One teacher who was interviewed in research conducted by one of the authors has adapted her pedagogy to accommodate this mode in the context of Philosophy for Children. She states, 'the bit that I really like is that you feel like quite, almost like, connected to your class and I think they do trust you a lot with what they are saying' (Gurton, 2022, p. 89).

Pedagogic communication

In a work entitled *The Structuring of Pedagogic Discourse* (2003), the English sociologist Basil Bernstein demonstrated how pedagogy communicated ideas about social status, the nature and importance of knowledge, and access to it. How a school or the education system selects, organises, and controls the pacing, sequencing, and assessment of knowledge – what we call curriculum, pedagogy, and testing – has a profound effect on student self-concept, he argued. Bernstein devised a way of analysing teaching in which he focussed in on what was taught, how it was taught, and the nature of the relationships in the classroom. Different pedagogies would result in pupils with different degrees of agency and self-worth. Bernstein posed the question, 'How does power and control translate into principles of communication and how do these principles of communication differentially regulate forms of consciousness with respect to their reproduction and the possibilities for change?' (1996, p. 18) In other words, how do we, maybe without realising it, communicate expectations differently to different children? And to what extent can these differential expectations affect the way children see themselves and their agency and potential for achievement? Are we (and for 'we' here, read schools and academy chains, as well as individual teachers and teacher educators) in fact merely replicating social structures of advantage or disadvantage? Bernstein was not what has been termed a 'progressive' in his theorisation. In fact, he believed what he saw as progressive or 'child-centred' discourses in education as harmful, as they did not allow access to academic language and placed success or failure on the head of the child. But he did believe strongly in the potential of education to bring about social change through inclusion and participation (1996, pp. 6-7).

Bernstein believed things were not quite as fixed as they often seem. There was space to negotiate change within your classroom to the set curriculum or alter the ways in which you teach and relate to your pupils. That, of course, is the message of this book, and we believe that action taken to alter these aspects of schooling – at whole school and/or classroom levels – enables teachers to grow a sense of professional empowerment and encourage pupils to develop their own agency. Bernstein's ideas suggested that subject boundaries could be made more flexible, leading to links between teaching themes, as we will show later in the book. Relationships in school could also become closer, given intelligent pacing and sequencing of teaching and use of space and time. He believed that education had the potential for pupils to feel valued within the social order. But one of the major problems in his time – which is still an issue today and exacerbated by the COVID-19 pandemic – was the significant educational inequalities experienced by marginalised communities, socio-economic, race-based, and disability-based. Indeed, recent research from secondary schools in America has demonstrated how the high-stakes standardised testing regime helps to reinforce the social and economic barriers experienced by pupils from these backgrounds and, far from encouraging social mobility, has the opposite effect (Au, 2008). Bernstein also drew attention to the fact that the individualising tendency so prevalent in Western curricula was not the only legitimate approach to teaching and that learning could be constructed as a collective experience. There could be collective social knowledge-building as a community, and individuals could even be representatives for the class, talking their way into the knowledge of the community (Daniels, 2001). Examples from Alexander's cross-cultural study (2001) provide evidence of this approach being routine within Russian classrooms in primary school in which there is a formal structure where, after a brief introduction, one child stands up and represents the class with a series of dialogic questions on a given subject. Despite the apparent formality of the exchange – the child stands up and comes out before the class, acting as the class representative – there is a warmth and closeness in teacher-pupil relationships which is evidenced by gesture, facial expression, proximity, and touch.

Horizontal and vertical discourse

Bernstein uses an idea we are now familiar with but expresses it using different terms. In this way, he allows us to move to a different level of understanding of how the teacher can be the bridge between Vygotsky's 'everyday' and 'scientific' concepts. Bernstein describes what Vygotsky called 'everyday' language as 'horizontal' discourse and 'scientific' language as 'vertical' discourse. School language (vertical) has a strict hierarchy of concepts, built one upon each other, whereas 'everyday' (horizontal) communication does not operate in this way.

For Bernstein, everyday communication operates in a narrative or storytelling way, whereas school language is analytical. He believed that the preponderance of vertical discourse in school differentially disadvantages and regulates the consciousness of children from poor social backgrounds, as it focusses on the transmission of curriculum content without drawing links with pupils' own life experiences and vocabulary. The commonplace of teachers' questions and pupil one-word answers – what Sinclair and Coulthard (1975) described as 'Initiation, Response, and Feedback' (IRF) – he called a 'lexical' pedagogic code (Bernstein 2003, p. 207), setting the pupil as object in the pedagogic discourse. The combination of difficult school vocabulary and lack of time for or no discussion proved a barrier to children accessing the curriculum. The difficulty some children might experience in learning because of these barriers caused by new vocabulary and syntactic structures could be exacerbated by the formal nature of the relationships and power structure in the classroom. Although we might take issue with his analysis being limited to class (and Bernstein experienced considerable opposition to his earlier ideas of restricted and elaborated codes being class dependent), the fact that some children experience barriers with school language is beyond question. It could result from linguistic, cultural, or socio-economic background or, as we have seen, merely because of their parents' taciturnity or lack of sufficient linguistic stimulus (which is not class dependent). The solution, if we can call it that, that he proposed takes us back to Vygotsky and Halliday and, by implication, to the elaboration used by parents to help support and develop young children's partial accounts of their experience. He termed it the 'syntactic' pedagogic code (2003). It is for a teacher to support their pupils in the development of 'concept' knowledge, the disembodied vocabulary of vertical discourse (Vygotsky's 'scientific' language). The skilful teacher does this by relating school language to the more familiar 'horizontal' discourse. The exchange between pupils and teacher is dialogic. But crucially, the means is by relating it to pupils' own life experience. And it manifests itself not just in the language used but in the relationship between teacher and pupils.

Bourne (2003) gives a good example of this technique in an excerpt from an observed English lesson. The teacher, 'Miss W,' is teaching a class of fourteen and fifteen year olds in a multi-ethnic English urban state school. The class are reading a short story by William Trevor, 'Teresa's Wedding.' They are preparing to write an essay discussing characters' feelings and motivations in this story of a Catholic Irish family. The teacher's style is formal and traditional. She sits upright in her chair, holding her hands tightly clasped together, only once getting up and walking briskly around the room to check the pupils' notes and to stop briefly to talk to a few individuals. On one occasion a boy apologises for his language – 'Yeah . . . whatever!' Her questions at the start of the excerpt are formal, checking student understanding of the facts of the text. Bernstein would have described this style of teaching as conservative and overtly regulated, given her formal expectations for pupil behaviour. But, at a certain point, things change. She moves out from behind the desk and sits on a pupil table, 'hand[ing] over the interpretation to the class, using their knowledge to illuminate the text, the text to illuminate their lives' (2003, pp. 513–514). Figure 3.1 provides two extracts from this classroom observation after it changes to this new pattern of interaction.

Extract 5 (sic)

Lucy:	It's like a game.
Teacher:	**Mm, it's like women and men. Men feel free to talk about your - their conquests.**
Lucy:	Men disrespect . . .
Teacher:	**Disrespect** (*handing arm out, conducting debate, encouraging pace, bringing in rapid responses from students*)
Amy:	Disloyal
Teacher:	**Disloyal** (*nods*)
Darcus:	But the women have . . .
Lucy:	But the men have all these expectations of women, but the women never have any expectations of the men.
Teacher:	**Ah! All right! Hold on to that** (*nominates a girl with her hand up*) **Marissa?**

Extract 6 (sic)

The students are all talking at once animatedly, then,

Peter:	(*urgently, leaning forward and jabbing his arm at the teacher from across the classroom, pointing at her*) It is different between men and women. But also, a friend - yeah, he's been his friend for years. Her, he didn't even love her too much.
Students:	*All talking at once. Teacher waits, listening.*
Teacher:	(*Leans back, softly*) **So, men can behave in a certain way. That is acceptable. But a woman can't?**

(*In a performative voice, referring to the text*) **He was cross with Teresa. Didn't even want to sit next to her on the bus. Do you remember?**

Boy:	No - where does it say that?
Teacher:	**Look at your story. Didn't affect his relationship, friendship with Screw Doyle. That's a men thing.**

(*Then, leaning forward, looking at a boys' table, speaking emphatically*)

> **And you boys will need to examine sometimes how you behave towards girls, even in school as well, yes?**
> *The lesson from this point reverts to the earlier, formal, and text-focussed style of discourse. The teacher first stands then returns to her desk. The easy range of physical movement becomes once again more tightly restricted and formalised, gesture and expression are backgrounded, the text is foregrounded.*

Teacher:	**All right, so what happens when he learns the truth? Gemma, find the bit where he is enlightened further as to when this relationship actually took place!**

Figure 3.1 English lesson on 'Teresa's Wedding' by William Trevor (Bourne, 2003, pp. 514–515)

Bourne guides us through the exchange, demonstrating how markedly it differs from the rest of the lesson in a number of ways. The teacher adopts a different stance and position, encouraging debate by the use of hand gestures and greater pace. At one point, it seems like she is conducting an orchestra as she encourages the pupils to share their views with each other and her, and several times a number of students talk together and over each other which does not happen during the rest of the lesson. A significant moment is when a pupil, Peter, challenges her, also using hand gestures with urgency, as he appeals to friendship between men. This is something that could not have happened during the other phases of the lesson both before and after the critical incident described. She steps aside from her teacher persona and for several minutes becomes herself a grown adult woman, defined by her cultural and social circumstances and education, before reverting to her role and using her moral authority when she states 'and you boys will need to examine sometimes how you behave towards girls, even in school . . .'

The teacher's art lies in her ability to step out of her role, 'tightening and relaxing the classification between discourses' (Bourne 2003, p. 515), to use Bernstein's language. We see the pupils use abstract vocabulary and language that will help them in their written work when they come to discuss the characters in the story – *disrespect, disloyal, expectations* – becoming energised in this mini-debate on gender roles and restructuring their experience, to use Halliday's description. She creates an environment where pupils can draw on their own life experiences, using 'horizontal discourse,' by appealing for personal responses. They are 'allowed' to be themselves, active teenage subjects keen to argue and engage, rather than passive objects in the educational process. The markers for this are given when she uses different body language which gives permission for the pupils to do the same. Gestures, movements, and facial expressions all change markedly during the episode. In fact, Bourne herself compares the atmosphere to the emotional charge in an Oprah Winfrey or Jerry Springer televised debate! But the experience is also collective. Students are reflecting together, allowing them to make personal meaning, which will help them in their exams. The increase of pace in this exchange is also productive. In a shorter period of time, a great deal of progress has been made which would have been much harder to achieve in a series of individualised questions and answers in the customary formal context. The benefit of the experience being collective means some students can draw upon the way in which their peers have articulated things, and they are engaged and switched on in a way they would not be in an individualised class question-and-answer session. We almost know also, from the power of the exchange, that this will go beyond the classroom. The permission to engage and debate in this manner has genuinely brought the text to life.

'Miss W's approach to her teaching (what is sometimes rather grandly called epistemology) is drawn from her belief in bringing the learning to life by making it relevant to the students' own experience. It contains a strong commitment to her role 'creating the citizen for the future' and 'striving for a more humane understanding of the world, creating a different world where people don't judge you so much by your differences and see those are things that can enrich society.' The words are hers – as recorded in an interview with the researcher (Bourne 2003, p. 516). Her commitment to bringing the learning to life for her pupils through dialogue derives from her own experience as a Black, African-Caribbean woman who has previously been a youth worker. Her students, who variously describe themselves as 'Half-Black, quarter-English, quarter-Indian, Afro-English, Black and Mixed race,' appreciate this. A group of students interviewed say things like, 'In English we feel like we have got respect . . . it prepares you for the future . . . you look at deeper meaning . . . we voice our opinions.' Interestingly, they also comment on the necessity for the use of formal language (vertical discourse). She will say, 'No, look. What do you mean by that? Don't talk like that, say that again.' Another states, 'I don't think she minds us talking how we talk because that is us, but she wants us to know when to stop' (Bourne, 2003, p. 217).

Opening up a lesson to discussion like this is not without risk for the teacher. But the improved levels of engagement in students' learning are significant. They are gaining access to language that will help them in their coursework and exams. But it will also, very importantly, make a genuine difference to address the inequality they may face in their future lives. They are becoming empowered through this access to what is often termed cultural capital. They are developing their own voice and agency rather than adopting and perpetuating the norms of the powerful.

References

Alexander, R.J. (2001) *Culture and Pedagogy: International Comparisons in Primary Education*. Oxford: Blackwell Publishing.

Alexander, R.J. (ed.) (2010) *Children, Their World, Their Education: Final Report and Recommendations of the Cambridge Primary Review*. London: Routledge.

Au, W.W. (2008) Devising inequality: A Bernsteinian analysis of high-stakes testing and social reproduction in education. *British Journal of Sociology of Education*, 29(6), pp. 639–651.

Bercow, J. (2008) *The Bercow Report: A Review of the Services for Children and Young People (0-19) with Speech, Language and Communication Needs*. London: Department for Children, Schools and Families (DCSF).

Bernstein, B. (1996) *Pedagogy, Symbolic Control and Identity*. London: Taylor and Francis.

Bernstein, B. (2003) *The Structuring of Pedagogic Discourse: Class, Codes and Control*, Vol. 4. London: Routledge.

Bourdieu, P. and Passeron, J. (1977) *Reproduction in Education, Society and Culture*. London: Sage.

Bourne, J. (2003) Vertical Discourse: The role of the teacher in the transmission and acquisition of decontextualised language. *European Educational Research Journal*, 2(4), pp. 496–521.

Bullock, A. (1975) *A Language for Life: Report of the Committee of Enquiry Appointed by the Secretary of State for Education and Science Under the Chairmanship of Sir Alan Bullock, F.B.A.* London: HMSO.

Cameron, D. (2003) Schooling spoken language: Beyond communication. In Qualifications and Curriculum Authority (ed.) *New Perspectives on English in the Classroom*. London: QCA, pp. 5–13.

Cazden, C.B. (2001) *Classroom Discourse: The Language of Teaching and Learning*, 2nd edn. Portsmouth, NH: Heinemann.

Centre for Social Justice (2014) *Closing the Divide: Tackling Educational Inequality in England* [online]. Available at: https://www.centreforsocialjustice.org.uk/wp-content/uploads/2018/03/Closing-the-Divide.pdf (Accessed: 12 April 2024).

Daniels, H. (2001) *Vygotsky and Pedagogy*. London: Routledge.

Department for Children, Schools and Families (DCSF) (2008) *Pupil Characteristics and Class Sizes in Maintained Schools in England*. London: DCSF.

Department for Education (DfE) (2019) *School Pupils and Their Characteristics* [onine]. Available at: https://assets.publishing.service.gov.uk/government/uploads/system/uploads/attachment_data/file/812539/Schools_Pupils_and_their_Characteristics_2019_Main_Text.pdf (Accessed: 12 April 2024).

Early Intervention Foundation (2017) *Language as a Child Wellbeing Indicator* [online]. Available at: https://www.eif.org.uk/report/language-as-a-child-wellbeing-indicator (Accessed: 12 April 2024).

Edwards, A. and Furlong, V. (1978) *The Language of Teaching*. London: Heinemann.

Galton, M., Hargreaves, L., Comber, C., Wall, D. and Pell, T. (1999) Changes in patterns of teacher interaction in primary classrooms 1976-1996. *British Educational Research Journal*, 25(1), pp. 23–37.

Galton, M., Simon, B. and Croll, P. (1980) *Inside the Primary Classroom*. London: Routledge.

Gurton, P. (2022) *Teacher Talk and Pupil Talk: A Case Study of a Thinking Skills Approach to Learning in an English Primary Academy*. University of Wolverhampton. http://hdl.handle.net/2436/625068.

Habermas, J. (1984) *The Theory of Communicative Action*, Vol. 1. London: Heinemann.

National Association for Language Development in the Curriculum (NALDIC) (2021) *EAL Achievement: The Latest Information on How Well EAL Learners Do in Standardised Assessments Compared to All Students* [online]. Available at: http://www.naldic.org.uk/research-and-information/eal-statistics/ealachievement/ (Accessed 12 April 2024).

Norman, K. (ed.) (1992) *Thinking Voices: The Work of the National Oracy Project*. London and Sydney, Aukland: Hodder and Stoughton.

Oracy All Party Parliamentary Group (APPG) (2021) *Speak for Change: Final Report and Recommendations from the Oracy All-Party Parliamentary Group Inquiry*. Available at: https://oracy.inparliament.uk/speak-for-change-inquiry/ (Accessed 12 April 2024).

Sinclair, J.M. and Coulthard, R.M. (1975) *Towards an Analysis of Discourse: The English Used by Teachers and Pupils*. London: Oxford University Press.

Snowling, M., Hulme, C., Bailey, A., Stothard, S. and Lindsay, G. (2011) *Better Communication Research Programme: Language and Literacy Attainment of Pupils During Early Years and Through KS2: Does Teacher Assessment at 5 Provide a Valid Measure of Children's Current and Future Educational Attainments?* DFE Research Brief 172a.

Stuart, M. (2004) Getting ready for reading: A follow-up study of inner city second language learners at the end of Key Stage 1. *British Journal of Educational Psychology*, 74, pp. 15–36.

Vygotsky, L.S. (1997) *Educational Psychology*. Boca Raton, FL: St. Lucie Press (Originally work written 1921-23).

4 Teaching talk

The status of talk in school

Talk in the classroom has both a social and academic function. The teacher sets the expectations for behaviour through what they say and communicates the learning through the spoken word too. It sounds simple, doesn't it? And yet, as teachers, we all recognise the layers of complexity that lie beneath. Managing children's behaviour has multiple challenges, not always best solved through talk, even though it features significantly. And giving explanations requires careful planning and communication. But teaching, as we have seen already, is not just a simple matter of delivery. For us to learn, we need to think, as humans. And much of our thinking is social. It is done out loud and involves talking about our understanding. As teachers, we need to think about how we communicate the subject matter we are teaching. What language are we using? And what vocabulary and grammatical constructions are we expecting the children to be using? Are we providing opportunities for them to articulate what they have learned out loud? Are they able to reformulate what has been explained to them in their own terms to themselves and each other? Or are they working individually most of the time, planning, solving problems, or writing? What is the balance of whole class to small-group activities? Do children get a chance to talk together in smaller groups to solve problems, plan, and talk through their learning? Are there opportunities to argue a point, or build upon their own and others' ideas, and to agree and disagree with each other respectfully? Above all, throughout the whole process, are we listening to them? Not just hearing what they say and moving on to the next child until we have the answer we are looking for, but actively listening, probing, and helping them by using an elaborative conversational style, amplifying information recalled by the child, then elaborating it (Reese, Haden and Fivush, 1993), as we saw parents do in Chapter 1.

These and other questions relate to how teachers use talk to support, develop, and enable children's learning and thinking. So, how is talk seen in schools and to what extent is this facilitated by the curriculum?

Talk has never enjoyed a status in the curriculum in England and Wales anywhere near comparable to that of reading and writing. Even a cursory glance at the English National Curriculum for Key Stages 1 and 2 (DfE, 2013) confirms this. There are eighty-six pages devoted to English, of which a measly page and half is given over to spoken English. The statutory requirements - at twelve bullet points or half a page - are the shortest of any curriculum area. Compare this with seventy-nine pages devoted to reading and writing, and you get the feeling

DOI: 10.4324/9781003451044-6

that speaking and listening are virtually transparent. The truth is a bit more complicated. But evidence shows that the prevalence of 'recitation,' or a question-and-answer pedagogy based on a teacher checking pupil understanding, often requiring single-word answers, has persisted in teaching practices the world over, despite significant developments in our understanding of how we learn (e.g. Alexander, 2020; Smith et al., 2004). Although it is tempting to attribute this condition to the 'standards agenda' with pressure on teachers to 'cover the curriculum' and the requirement for both children and teachers to meet targets, it is maybe not all down to these factors. Schools do seem to see students as containers or receptacles to be filled with knowledge by the teacher, where the better teachers more completely fill the receptacles with knowledge and the better students are those who meekly allow themselves to be filled (Freire, 1970, p. 53). But this is nothing new. Tyack and Tobin (1994), who coined the phrase 'the grammar of schooling,' suggest that modern reforms merely perpetuate an organisation of time and space, pupil groupings, and subject-focussed instruction which has held sway since the introduction of compulsory schooling in 1870. It is what Robinson describes as an industrial model (2015). These cultural expectations prioritise conforming to social norms over the broader aims of education in terms of developing thinking skills, individual agency, and self-realisation – an irony, surely, given the focus on individual attainment in many Western education systems?

A public perception of talk in classrooms as unproductive and time wasting may also have an impact on teachers' practice. In a culture where production holds sway, it is much easier to measure outcomes in written form. And this has had a powerful influence. Talk does not form a part of the assessment programme in English schools, apart from in the early years. There is no assessment of talk or verbal reasoning at Key Stage 1 or 2, and, although there is a spoken element in some English GCSEs, the outcome does not have any weighting in the final exam grade. So, there is no incentive for teachers to focus on developing children's talk as, unlike proficiency in other areas, it is not subject to assessment or examination. Neither they nor their school will get judged on it. Couple that with an inspection regime that is always requiring evidence, it has meant that for decades, schools have been using written evidence of children's performance in English, Maths, and other subject areas to prove attainment to Ofsted, management, governors, and parents. But none for talk. Talk in the classroom can also be misinterpreted. Teachers new to the profession are often sensitive to the level of talk in the classroom, viewing too much 'noise' as an indication of poor classroom management skills. The temptation to view a quiet classroom as a productive one is strong. And of course, the talk in a classroom may be unproductive if children have wandered 'off-task' into social talk. But that may also reflect the nature of the learning task set and whether or not there are opportunities for discussion built into learning. When children are talking about their learning, sharing, and extending their understanding, it is always important. It is how we learn.

Talk as curriculum

At the beginning of the chapter, we explained that talk gets a raw deal in the curriculum. In its current incarnation, the National Curriculum in England for children aged five to eleven lists twelve bullet points as the statutory requirements:

Spoken language - Years 1 to 6

Pupils should be taught to:

- Listen and respond appropriately to adults and their peers
- Ask relevant questions to extend their understanding and knowledge
- Use relevant strategies to build their vocabulary
- Articulate and justify answers, arguments, and opinions
- Give well-structured descriptions, explanations, and narratives for different purposes, including expressing feelings
- Maintain attention and participate actively in collaborative conversations, staying on topic and initiating and responding to comments
- Use spoken language to develop understanding through speculating, hypothesising, imagining, and exploring ideas
- Speak audibly and fluently with an increasing command of Standard English
- Participate in discussions, presentations, performances, roleplay, improvisations, and debates
- Gain, maintain, and monitor the interests of listener(s)
- Consider and evaluate different viewpoints, attending to and building on the contributions of others
- Select and use appropriate registers for effective communication

(DfE, 2013, pp. 17-18)

In addition to these statements, the non-statutory guidance states also that pupils should 'have opportunities to work in groups of different sizes' and 'understand how to take turns and when and how to participate constructively in conversations and debates.' The introduction to the English programme of study also contains a short section on spoken language with the following interesting statement, 'They [sic] must be assisted in making their thinking clear to themselves as well as to others, and teachers should ensure that pupils build secure foundations by using discussion to probe and remedy their misconceptions. Pupils should also be taught to understand and use the conventions for discussion and debate' (DfE, 2013).

There is nothing here to disagree with. Indeed, using talk 'to make their thinking clear to themselves as well as to others' corresponds to the Vygotskian principle that we build our conceptual understanding through articulating it to and with others. In a moment of apparent abandon, the authors of the curriculum also permit themselves to use the word 'thinking' – a word remarkable for its rarity in curriculum documentation. Yet regardless of these statements in the curriculum and despite notable exceptions in some schools, opportunities for debate, discussion, and exploratory talk in groups of varying sizes are not generally evident across the curriculum, and evidence consistently shows talk exchanges are usually limited to a variation of the recitation sequence of 'Initiation, Response, Feedback,' or 'Evaluation' (Edwards and Furlong, 1978; Galton, Simon and Croll, 1980; Galton et al., 1999; Sinclair and Coulthard, 1975).

The previous National Curriculum (DfEE, 1999) had more detail in the English curriculum, but the statements were very similar, and the programme of study for what was then called 'Speaking and Listening' was still placed firmly within the English subject curriculum. In stark contrast, the detailed breakdown of, for example, what spelling patterns must be taught or what grammatical terminology is to be used and understood is exhaustive, and there are statutory requirements for each year group. There is no programme of study for separate year groups in spoken English, only the few statements we have repeated earlier which are meant to be applicable across Years 1 to 6. It might be argued that teachers should use their discretion and professional judgement as to when to focus on statements drawn from the bullet points and non-statutory guidance in this area. However, the reality is, when faced with a large amount of very prescriptive advice for other areas of English and tests in Years 1, 2, and 6 in reading, spelling, punctuation, and grammar and writing, teachers struggle, and opportunities for structured talk lose out. It is easier to 'model the learning' at the board and set individualised tasks for children to perform. It is much harder orchestrating opportunities for class and group discussions or teaching children how to cooperate constructively in group situations.

Talk across the curriculum

The decision to place the requirements for spoken English, what we have chosen to call talk in this book, in the English subject curriculum has applied for the last thirty-five years; that is to say, for as long as there has been a National Curriculum. But is this appropriate? At first glance, it might seem so. And yet, as the medium through which every subject is taught, would it not be more appropriate to consider talk as a strand to be threaded through all curriculum areas? This suggestion is not as radical as it may sound. Successive evidence-based studies, from *The Bullock Report, A Language for Life* (1975), to the *Cambridge Primary Review* (Alexander, 2010) have called for an element of language across the curriculum. *The Kingman Report* (DES, 1988), for example, called for 'Knowledge about Language' (KAL for short) to form a major part of the training of teachers of all subjects to enable students to have a deep understanding of the language, and for teachers to open up, 'the concepts and discourses of any subject' (Alexander, 2020, p. 23). Yet the resultant *Language in the National Curriculum* (LINC) project (Carter, 1990) was closed down almost as soon as it had begun by the same government that had commissioned it, 'on the grounds of its imputed appeal to cultural and linguistic relativism' (Alexander, 2020, p. 23). Politics again!

A strand of talk across different curriculum areas would need, of course, to take into account the disciplinary vocabularies of the different subjects. Wells (1999) was an advocate of a curriculum in which the teacher has agency and is responsible for monitoring the outcomes in terms of students' increasing mastery. But he also believed that students, under supervision, can have some choice in the direction the learning takes. Through research in classrooms in Toronto, he observed teachers who provided opportunities for children to develop their spoken language, predominantly in Science lessons. Drawing on Halliday's ideas of language as a tool which enables us to reflect on our actions (1993) to build meaning into our understanding of the world, he identified two different kinds of use that language is put to in classroom learning: the language of 'acting' and the language of 'understanding,' the empirical and the theoretical. They are never wholly separate, but put simply, the language of acting is used to mediate action and the interpersonal relationships around this – like doing an experiment in Science – and the language of understanding has an emphasis on reflection and has a closer relationship at the level of both vocabulary and grammar with written text.

In this book, we have already come across several terms which different authors use for 'school' language: Vygotsky's scientific, Bernstein's vertical, and now we have the word and phrase Wells uses – theoretical, the language of understanding. As Wells explains, to be able to 'do' History or Science, the student needs to be able to master the 'discourse genres that constitute ways of making meaning in different disciplines' (1999, p. 244). For what children learn with respect to language depends on what they use it to do.

Table 4.1 The language of acting and the language of understanding

Discipline	Empirical (the language of acting)	Theoretical (the language of understanding)
Science	Planning and carrying out experiments	Considering predictions and interpreting results in relation to theory
History	Obtaining and handling artefacts and documentary evidence	Debating and considering the value of the evidence and drawing conclusions
Literature	Reading and responding to a novel, play, poem, etc.	Attempting to explain overall effect of text by referring to key features and how they

Source: Adapted from Wells (1999, p. 140).

Table 4.1 demonstrates in a very simple way what Wells was getting at. For planning purposes, we might want to add two more columns – one to exemplify the subject vocabulary the teacher would want the students to be using and another for the activities or classroom situations that could facilitate this. Some of the statements from the National Curriculum might help us. For example, the following to be applied during the theoretical or reflection phase:

- Ask relevant questions to extend their understanding and knowledge
- Articulate and justify answers, arguments, and opinions
- Use spoken language to develop understanding through speculating, hypothesising, imagining, and exploring ideas

We may also want to add these, too, from the introductory section:

- They [sic] must be assisted in making their thinking clear to themselves as well as to others, and teachers should ensure that pupils build secure foundations by using discussion to probe and remedy their misconceptions

And this from the non-statutory guidance:

- Should have opportunities to work in groups of different sizes

In an excerpt from a lesson Wells observed (Figure 4.1), we see this approach in action. The teacher mediates curricular requirements, encouraging children to develop their understanding. To use the phrase from Table 4.1, they are 'Considering predictions and interpreting results in relation to theory.' And from the National Curriculum, they are 'articulating and justifying answers and using spoken language to speculate, explore and hypothesise.' They are investigating the question, 'Does mass change when matter changes state?' They are a mixed Grade 4/5 class – nine and ten year olds. They are of mixed Canadian and Canadian Chinese heritage. They are used to this approach to learning, what we call a collaborative community of enquiry, as many of them had the same teacher the previous year. The teacher has decided to change direction in her lesson, as it has become apparent that a number of children have not grasped the importance of predictions. When it becomes clear that this is the case, she decides to initiate a discussion on predictions, so she begins by appealing to the boy Philips, who she remembers has made a prediction.

Teacher:	**Please, guys, it's important that you do some prediction. . . . Now, those people who say 'decrease,' why do you think it decreased? Philips. That day you offered some reasons. Why do you think it would decrease when it changes state from solid to liquid - the ice?**
Philips:	Um. because like when it's - ice has some air in it, and when it's melted, the air will go, so it's, um . . .
Teacher:	**Uh-huh. So the air - there's air that's trapped in the block of ice that will escape as the ice melts, and therefore, you think the mass will decrease, right?**
Philips:	Mm . . .
Teacher:	**Any other reasons behind those who say it will decrease? Yes, Benjamin?**
Benjamin:	I said that it would decrease because there was a little bit of air inside the ice and it would um -um it would melt, so the . . . more than . . . greater than air.
Teacher:	**You said it would decrease but then it would mass MORE? I didn't follow. Can you repeat what you said, Benjamin?**
Benjamin:	Um. When - it decreases because the air comes out, and that means it would weigh less *(softly)*, mass less -
Teacher:	**Are you agreeing with Philips or disagreeing with Philips?**
Benjamin:	Agreeing.
Teacher:	**You're agreeing with Philips that it would decrease? Now, Mr. Wells also raised the point - now, when the ice melts, say we froze that water again. What would you predict?**
Angeline:	I have two things to say. The first thing is, if you left it long enough while it was melted, some of the water could evaporate and then, when you froze it, it would um - it would probably have more air left, then it might be slightly different or it might be - er, it might increase . . . depends if you left it long enough for the water to evaporate
Teacher:	**Uh-huh. Good point! Very good point!**
Jessica:	I think that if - if the ice melted, and then we froze it again, the mass would increase because of the dust and particles in the air that might, like, get captured . . . um, onto the ice or into the ice that might -
Teacher:	**Into the water**
Jessica:	Yeh, so it might, um - the mass might increase.

Figure 4.1 Developing scientific understanding (Wells, 1999, pp. 210-211)

In the lesson, children and teacher use talk together to navigate the curriculum. It is clear that there is a climate of trust. The students are willing to take a risk and are not worried about not giving the right answer – a problem which can forestall discussion in classrooms. The teacher also shows a genuine desire to hear what they think. In an interview with Wells about the lesson, she explains that her intention is for students to learn that Science is a form of enquiry, not just the memorisation of facts. She wants them to understand that the process by which the solutions to problems are arrived at is progressive and involves an interplay between theory and evidence (1999, p. 213).

The children show varying degrees of language facility. They are not all using correct scientific terms, and the teacher is not insisting on this as the 'entrance fee to knowledge,' as Barnes so memorably expressed it (1987, p. 129). The pupils Angeline and Jessica do, using words such as 'evaporate,' 'mass,' and 'particle,' whereas Philips provides his explanation in 'everyday' terms. He talks of the ice having 'some air in it' and 'when it's melted, the ice will go.' The teacher rightly focusses first on his reasoning, not insisting on the correct scientific vocabulary. Use of the correct vocabulary is no measure of the child's powers of understanding. But she does then model the correct vocabulary by rephrasing what he says – 'therefore, you think the mass will decrease, right?' This is something that we saw called 'elaboration' when referring to how parents help develop young children's understanding through talk in Chapter 1. The term 'reformulation' is used by one of the best writers on children's talk, Neil Mercer (as we shall see in Chapter 5). Whatever we call it, and it doesn't really matter what name is ascribed to it, it is a good example of a teacher actively listening, probing a child's understanding, and supporting their next steps in concept development by modelling the correct vocabulary.

A powerful feature of this kind of discourse is that by witnessing their peers reason aloud, and in some cases using the correct language, children will learn. This 'witnessing' of learning is something we will return to later. It is a powerful form of social learning which is currently much under-used in education but illustrated in all the lesson outtakes used in this book. We all learn from observation. It is what Rogoff describes as 'cognitive apprenticeship' (1990), and what Lave and Wenger identify as a 'legitimate peripheral participation' (1991): this stage involves more observation than action until the novice reaches a level at which they feel ready and able to play an active role. It is very common in language learning. And, coincidentally, for a significant number of children in the class observed, English was the second language.

To summarise, the excerpt from the discussion earlier shows:
- Children using firsthand experience in a social context to construct meaning together – much of the discussion develops from experiments they have previously conducted in school and prior experiential learning inside and outside of school
- Children thereby developing agency and confidence in their ability to share ideas and reason
- The use of theoretical or disciplinary (scientific) vocabulary by some, but not all, children
- A teacher who genuinely encourages children to explain the reasons for their ideas but does not make the use of correct vocabulary the criteria for reasoning
- Children learning by witnessing their peers reasoning and being challenged by the teacher to account for their reasoning

One aspect of the discourse which children in this lesson are not yet confident with is building on each other's ideas. They offer reasons for their predictions, demonstrating a developing ability to show accountability to reason – one of the three accountabilities used by Michaels, O'Connor and Resnick (2007). But they do not, as a matter of course, refer to each other's ideas, showing agreement or disagreement. However, at a certain point, the teacher asks Benjamin directly 'Are you agreeing or disagreeing with Philips?' as an attempt to encourage them to begin to use this discourse norm, which we will find out more about in Chapter 7 when we look at Philosophy for Children.

In this excerpt, we have seen how the curriculum can be planned to accommodate opportunities for exploratory talk. Of course, a curriculum need not be subject-focussed or discipline-specific, and the current orthodoxy of approaching curriculum in England through a series of subjects for younger children, and even for those into the early years of secondary education, is by no means the only way to plan. In Scotland, for example, the *Curriculum for Excellence* takes the approach of including some subjects under a common heading. Social Studies include History and Geography and allows the opportunity to look at the interface between these subjects when studying something like the local community. Scotland's curriculum consists of eight curriculum areas: Expressive arts, Health and wellbeing, Languages (including Literacy in English), Mathematics, Religious and moral education, Sciences, Social studies, and Technology. Crucially also, there are in addition three separate strands, entitled Health and Wellbeing Across Learning, Literacy Across Learning, and Numeracy Across Learning. The Literacy strand does include several pages of advice and example statements of progress in skills within listening and talking. Wells believed also that it was possible to organise 'almost any curriculum unit' in such a way that it provided opportunities for collaborative learning to occur (1999, p. 156).

Talk as pedagogy

But is talk curriculum, or is it pedagogy? Or is it both? As Alexander points out, it arguably 'makes little sense to specify a curriculum for speaking and listening which lists the requirement for one of the parties to classroom talk but not for the other, but that is exactly what successive versions of England's National Curriculum have done, and the same applies in many other countries and jurisdictions' (2020, p. 27). He proceeds to challenge the assumption that talk can be considered as curriculum in isolation from talk as pedagogy.

We have seen in the classroom discussion earlier the successful inclusion of opportunities for talking about ideas which is vital for children to build upon their existing knowledge – what Piaget termed 'schemata.' Indeed, we would argue that this is only possible where there are opportunities for discussions about these ideas and where language is put to a theoretical use (thus, rendering many classroom activities in which children work independently a waste of time). But this approach requires a teacher with a certain set of skills and, crucially, a certain disposition. And this is where the pedagogy comes in. For although you can plan for class or group discussions, it takes belief and understanding, as well as time, energy, and commitment, to teach children the ground rules of discussion and enquiry and for your classroom to develop into a genuine community of enquiry of the sort we have seen so far in this book. The teacher needs to have a genuine interest in their pupils and want to hear what they have to say. They need to be able to facilitate discussion without telling, although, of course, as in the example in Figure 4.1, they need to be persistent in their interrogation of students' ideas and encourage them to listen to and agree or disagree with each other.

So, what do we know about this pedagogy? As with the National Curriculum for England and its limited advice on spoken English, sadly there is very little evidence of any useful advice on talk pedagogy in the statutory documentation. The Teachers' Standards (DfE, 2011) do not mention talk (or the related word oracy) at all. In fact, the only place in which a term associated with talk gets a look in is in one section of Standard 3 ('Demonstrate good subject and curriculum knowledge') where there is the statement, 'Demonstrate an understanding of, and take responsibility for, promoting high standards of literacy, articulacy and the correct use of standard English, whatever the teacher's specialist subject' (DfE, 2011). In the *Initial Teacher Training Core Content Framework* (2019) – a sort of curriculum for teacher education – there is slightly more. But considering this is a document of some forty-seven pages, it is a shame to find only this statement 'Learn that high-quality classroom talk can support pupils to articulate key ideas, consolidate understanding and extend their vocabulary' followed by 'include a range of types of questions in class discussions to extend and challenge pupils (e.g. by modelling new vocabulary or asking pupils to justify answers).' And frankly, this is a request or a command and does not really provide insight in how to go about it.

So, where can the teacher go to find useful advice? In the next chapter, we discuss dialogic approaches which take the view that all subject learning must be mediated through talk. But a useful way of consolidating some of the themes we have come across so far, and introducing some which will recur later in the book, we could do worse than to turn to the *Bullock Report*. Although written nearly fifty years ago in the 1970s, its advice is still entirely relevant today. The committee which produced the report was set up in 1972 by Margaret Thatcher, the then education secretary, with the brief to 'inquire into the teaching in the schools of reading and other uses of English' (1975, p. v). Sadly, its impact was limited, although some of its recommendations surrounding what we would now call English as an Additional Language had a positive impact. The tenth chapter, entitled 'Oral Language,' contains a mine of useful advice on pedagogy.

References

Alexander, R.J. (ed.) (2010) *Children, Their World, Their Education: Final Report and Recommendations of the Cambridge Primary Review*. London: Routledge.

Alexander, R.J. (2020) *A Dialogic Teaching Companion*. Abingdon: Routledge.

Barnes, D. (1987) *From Communication to Curriculum*. London: Penguin Books.

Bullock, A. (1975) *A Language for Life: Report of the Committee of Enquiry Appointed by the Secretary of State for Education and Science under the Chairmanship of Sir Alan Bullock, F.B.A.* London: HMSO.

Carter, R. (1990) *Knowledge About Language and the Curriculum: The LINC Reader*. London: Hodder and Stoughton.

Department for Education (DfE) (2011) *Teachers' Standards*. Available at: https://www.gov.uk/government/publications/teachers-standards (Accessed: 12 April 2024).

Department for Education (DfE) (2013) *National Curriculum in England. Key Stages 1 and 2 Framework Document*. London: DfE.

Department for Education (DfE) (2019) *Initial Teacher Training (ITT) Core Content Framework*. Available at: https://www.gov.uk/government/publications/initial-teacher-training-itt-core-content-framework (Accessed: 12 April 2024).

Department for Education and Employment (DfEE) (1999) *The National Curriculum for England*. London: DfEE.

Department for Education and Science (1988) *Report of the Committee of Inquiry Into the Teaching of English Language* (the Kingman Report). London: HMSO.

Edwards, A. and Furlong, V. (1978) *The Language of Teaching*. London: Heinemann.

Freire, P. (1970) *Pedagogy of the Oppressed*. London: Continuum.

Galton, M., Hargreaves, L., Comber, C., Wall, D. and Pell, T. (1999) Changes in patterns of teacher interaction in primary classrooms 1976–1996. *British Educational Research Journal*, 25(1), pp. 23–37.

Galton, M., Simon, B. and Croll, P. (1980) *Inside the Primary Classroom*. London: Routledge.

Halliday, M.A.K. (1993) Towards a language-based theory of learning. *Linguistics and Education*, 5, pp. 93–116.

Lave, J. and Wenger, E. (1991) *Situated Learning: Legitimate Peripheral Participation*. Cambridge: Cambridge University Press.

Michaels, S., O'Connor, C. and Resnick, L. (2007) Deliberative discourse idealized and realized: Accountable talk in the classroom and civic life. *Studies in the Philosophy of Education*, 27, pp. 283–297.

Reese, E., Haden, C.A. and Fivush, R. (1993) Mother-child conversations about the past: Relationships of style and memory over time. *Cognitive Development*, 8, pp. 403–430.

Robinson, K. (2015) *Creative Schools: Revolutionizing Education from the Grassroots Up*. London: Penguin Books.

Rogoff, B. (1990) *Apprenticeship in Thinking: Cognitive Development in Social Context*. Oxford: Oxford University Press.

Sinclair, J.M. and Coulthard, R.M. (1975) *Towards an Analysis of Discourse: The English Used by Teachers and Pupils*. London: Oxford University Press.

Smith, F., Hardman, F., Wall, K. and Mroz, M. (2004) Interactive whole class teaching in the national literacy and numeracy strategies. *British Educational Research Journal*, 30(3), pp. 395–411.

Tyack, D. and Tobin, W. (1994) The grammar of schooling: Why has it been so hard to change? *American Educational Research Journal*, 31(3), pp. 453–479.

Wells, G. (1999). *Dialogic Inquiry: Toward a Socio-Cultural Practice and Theory of Education*. Cambridge: Cambridge University Press.

5 Talk as a tool for thinking

Thinking aloud

Schools are places of communication. In fact, they are probably the only environment uniquely dedicated to communication, with the possible exception of the courtroom. Talk plays a major role in learning. But there is an inherent paradox: in teaching, you are providing pupils with the opportunity to build their own individual understanding in a social context. But the individual alone has access to their own picture of the world. Only they will be able to ask the right questions to build on their current state of knowledge and understanding. It is part of the teacher's role to identify their pupils' achievements and misconceptions. Much will be manifested through what a pupil says and by feeling able to ask questions and make statements. But for a child to feel able to talk in this way, to try out their ideas, the teacher has to build a 'culture of talk' and an environment where it feels safe to do so – as we have seen in the previous lesson excerpts. This is not easy. Pupils will only be prepared to take the risk of expressing their own ideas where they feel there is a receptive and non-judgemental audience. *The Bullock Report*'s advice was to start in the small-group situation. This may well be a useful first step, although group work is not a panacea and needs careful planning. In a small group, some children, and particularly those who may be more nervous or hesitant to articulate what they think, will feel less pressured. Pupils need a teacher – and indeed peers – who attribute value to what they say.

Research has consistently revealed that the way teachers behave towards their pupils is closely linked to their own beliefs about the nature of the knowledge they are teaching (Barnes and Shemilt, 1974; Boyd and Markarian, 2011; Gurton, 2022). Those who see teaching as simply the transmission of knowledge are not likely to encourage pupils to explore through expressing their ideas. They are also more likely to blame the child for not 'getting it,' rather than reconsider their own approach to teaching. We often find pupils forget information from one lesson to the next. This is usually because the way the material has been presented to them has no connection with their models of the world. This is why teachers need to make links with children's knowledge and experience, and this includes the language they may use to describe what they know from outside the classroom. If they are not encouraged to articulate their understanding through talking about it, then the process of learning has already encountered a significant obstacle.

DOI: 10.4324/9781003451044-7

Exploratory and presentational talk - performance mode and co-operative mode

Barnes distinguished between two types of talk in the classroom - 'exploratory' and 'presentational.' There is value in both, but he felt that much of the time, teachers call upon pupils to use presentational talk when they are not yet ready for it. Presentational talk involves 'having to order ideas and present them explicitly to an audience' (2008, p. 7). He believed this mode was often used when children weren't quite ready for it and were still at the stage of digesting and assimilating new ideas. Exploratory talk, by contrast, is used to explore ideas and make suggestions. It is characterised by questions to confirm understanding and tentative statements like those we use in conversation - 'So, does that mean that?' 'Am I right in thinking?' 'So, what if?' The verbs are often conditional or modal - the coulds, shoulds, mights, and oughts. This kind of talk is hesitant and uncertain, and children, like adults, will only use it in situations where they are confident they will not be judged for making a mistake. Barnes believed that most class work should focus on exploratory talking and writing to enable pupils to relate 'old ways of thinking to new possibilities' (2008, p. 7). Using a presentational approach too soon can lead to confused thinking and only partial understanding. It is easy to understand how it can become commonplace when teachers are often encouraged to seek 'results' from their pupils and the whole system is tilted towards measurable outcomes. I (Paul) remember when I first started teaching, my mentor who was a very experienced infant teacher and had worked in the Inner London Education Authority where there was a major focus on talk in the 1980s, and she was always stressing the importance of 'consolidation' in young children's learning, whether in reading or another area of the curriculum - 'you have got to give them time to practise and let the learning really take root, before you move on to the next thing,' she would say. It is good advice to any teacher at any phase of education. The pressure of covering the curriculum can too easily lead to shallow learning.

Christine Howe's research identifies two different modes of interaction in the classroom - 'performance mode' and 'co-operative mode' (Howe, 2010). Performance is associated with a pupil answering teacher questions in whole-class settings and is very common. It is characterised by children 'bidding' for teacher attention (by having their hands up) and the rest of the class being audience to the response. Teacher feedback is often, but not always (See Wells, 1999 on 'the third move'), a form of judgement of the answer and, by implication, of the child. This is the exchange often called IRE or IRF ('Initiation, Response, Evaluation/Feedback') after the work of Sinclair and Coulthard (1975). If practised traditionally, this approach just reinforces the social distance between the child and the teacher. Performance mode could also take in Douglas Barnes' idea of presentational talk, not because it is using talk to make an ordered presentation of information but because of the nature of response that it elicits. We quite often ask children individually or in groups or pairs to engage in this kind of talk to present an experiment or piece of research they have done or a design they have made. Sometimes they are presenting to others in a class or even in an assembly. But it is not used to discuss or develop our understanding, and it is not characterised by pupils asking questions or making hesitant assertions to try out ideas such as are found in exploratory talk.

Co-operative mode, by contrast, is when pupils experience their peers differently, not as an audience but as a source of contrasting or complementary ideas. It can take the form of asking for help in which a child asks a peer for help. Or it could be a debate or discussion. In this circumstance, children experience their peers as respondents to their own ideas and sources of alternative ideas to which they can respond. The roles are relatively symmetric – they have both got something to give. But pupils can also help each other to further their understanding through explanations where the roles are asymmetric – as one gives and the other receives. In neither situation do pupils experience the same degree of social distance as they do in conventional or traditional classroom situations. Howe draws attention to Piaget's theory of what happens when children encounter different ideas. Although he believed that young children could not see another's point of view, Piaget thought cognitive growth depended on existing beliefs being coordinated with contrasting perspectives (1932, 1985). Children were more likely to engage conversationally with their peers, coordinate the views expressed by their peers, and, when different opinions were detected, comment accordingly. This comparison with alternative views was more likely to promote cognitive growth. It was less likely to occur between an adult and a child because of the contrasting power relations. Because adults are more powerful, children tend to assimilate their ideas unthinkingly and are less likely to engage with them or challenge them. Although he proposed this theory, most empirical testing of these ideas did not occur until after his death. But there is now a significant body of evidence supporting the value of children's progress in learning of exchange of opinion in peer group interactions. Most has been at group level. The group studies range across different curriculum areas – e.g., Literacy and the Arts (Miell and Littleton, 2004), Mathematics (Damon and Phelps, 1988), and exploratory talk (Barnes and Todd, 1977). One of the most popular contexts has been Science. There have also been two at whole-class level, both using 'Philosophy for Children' (Trickey and Topping, 2004; Gorard, Siddiqui and See, 2015). There is pupil progress in all of these studies, but it is particularly strong where differences in opinions are expressed in group work without adult or teacher involvement, supporting Piaget's initial hypothesis. The value of peer interaction in learning is not a golden bullet. But used well, it can be a powerful means of children growing in knowledge and confidence. It empowers them to feel that their thinking is valuable and thereby develops their sense of agency. And because it positions them as active agents in their own learning, not passive recipients, subjects rather than objects, if you like, new knowledge and understanding will take root in a meaningful way.

Dialogue

Much of the literature associated with using talk to develop children's knowledge, skills, and understanding uses the word dialogue or its associated adjective 'dialogic.' Dialogue, a Greek word meaning a conversation, is probably most commonly associated with the dialogues of Plato, the great works of Greek philosophy that exemplify the spirit of enquiry through the characterisation of the philosopher Socrates. In these works, which are written to be accessible to a general reading public, we can follow the steps that Socrates takes to establish what we mean by the concepts that matter in life – *friendship, love, courage, beauty*. etc. The call to live the 'examined life' and to be responsible for the management of our own lives is only possible through dialogue when we listen to others and interrogate their ideas.

When we reexamine what we have said and thought in the light of this, we may adapt our thinking accordingly – very much akin to Piaget's argument for the value to cognitive growth of encountering different ideas. Some approaches to using dialogue to develop children's thinking, particularly in Philosophy for Children, use a method heavily influenced by Plato. We shall be focussing on Philosophy for Children later in this book as a useful underpinning pedagogy to support children learning through talking (see Chapter 7 and Part II).

Language forms and the dialogic stance

The adjective 'dialogic,' when used in teaching, is a broad term encompassing a variety of similar approaches – e.g., *Dialogic Instruction* (Nystrand et al., 1997), *Dialogic Inquiry* (Wells, 1999), *Dialogical Pedagogy* (Skidmore, 2000). Maybin draws a distinction between the word 'dialogue' as a synonym for conversation and 'dialogic' which she sees as a 'constant ongoing process of interactive and recursive meaning-making amongst children' (2006, p. 24). This meaning making thrives in conditions where there are contrasting perspectives, as outlined earlier, where cognitive growth depends on existing beliefs being coordinated with contrasting perspectives (Barnes and Todd, 1977; Piaget, 1932, 1985) – what Wegerif (2011) calls the 'dialogic gap.' Important techniques of a dialogic approach are seen to be teachers' use of authentic questions; uptake, where a teacher incorporates student responses into subsequent questions; and the extent to which the teacher allows a student response to modify the topic of discourse.

Much is made of the use of questioning in dialogic teaching. Open questions are often, and often rightly, seen as preferable to closed. But as Mercer argues in a passage entitled 'the trouble with questions' (1995, p. 27), it is not the verbal techniques *per se* that a teacher uses that are critical in their classroom talk. People do not reliably use the same grammatical forms of speech to pursue the same purposes. Likewise, Barnes and Todd believe 'Forms are shaped to the purpose of the speaker and not vice versa' (1977, p. 116). It is this belief also that leads Boyd and Markarian to hypothesise what they describe as a 'dialogic stance.' This disposition is not dependent on the use of any particular language form (2011). They argue that the use of certain talk structures is not necessarily indicative of the underlying dynamic of learning in the classroom. A teacher may use open questions, following up with 'why?' or 'do you believe?' but 'only truly care about how closely the student's response aligns with some school-sanctioned or teacher-predetermined position' (2011, p. 517). Indeed, they believe that the dialogic stance permeates the 'illocutionary force' of the talk and the discourse space (Linell and Markova, 1993). In other words, it is how we say what we say and also how we listen and how we are disposed to hear what we hear from pupils, not the types of language structures we use. They expound these ideas by reference to a series of classroom observations of a teacher they call Michael in an American elementary class of nine-year-old (fourth grade) pupils, who actually uses closed questions throughout his classroom discourse with his pupils in discussion of a piece of literature. Michael's relationship with his class is close and his disposition is one of humanity. He is convincingly shown to mobilise the pupils' everyday knowledge by first listening carefully to their contributions and then anchoring his questions and comments in these contributions. Using talk in this way, he is able to negotiate school knowledge and connect it to what students already know in a meaningful exemplification of mediating between school and everyday language – Bernstein's horizontal and vertical discourse (2003).

A 'dialogic stance' is reliant on a teacher's ability to listen to students' real voices – the everyday language and experiences they bring to class – in order to 'translate' this into school learning (Boyd and Markarian, 2011, p. 519). Many writing about dialogic teaching make a distinction between teachers who adopt monologic or dialogic stances. In this context, both terms are drawn from the work of the Russian literary theorist and philosopher Mikhail Bakhtin, whose work *The Dialogic Imagination* (1981) is focussed on the nature of language and knowledge. A teacher who adopts a monologic stance believes that if a student listens carefully enough to the dissemination of school knowledge, he or she should be able to understand, retain, and apply what the teacher has said. They believe teaching is just about transmitting knowledge. A dialogic teacher, by contrast, takes the onus of careful listening upon themselves. They do not assume that a student's lack of comprehension is evidence of not listening and is rather of not being able to make the link between everyday knowledge and the new school knowledge the teacher is asking them to learn. Rather than telling the student to listen harder, the dialogic teacher will try to listen better, to seek out a better way to make links between the student's current knowledge and what they are expecting them to learn (Boyd and Markarian, 2011).

So, we can see that dialogic teaching represents a broad set of concepts and values rather than merely a repertoire of talk moves. But what unites all approaches is the commitment to democratic participation in which the interaction between pupils and teacher relies on careful listening by all participants; questioning which is not limited to the IRF/IRE exchange; and students at times determining the direction the learning takes. The teacher may also provide useful links between pupils' life experiences and school knowledge – a constant theme in the writings of John Dewey and something that is central to the message of this book. The 'dialogic stance' is generally associated with a classroom environment which encourages exploratory talk involving discussion and debate between pupils with contrasting ideas with or without the presence of the teacher. It is a pedagogy committed to developing the agency of the child and seeing them as playing an active role in their own learning – a subject, not object, of their education. Whilst many trace the use of the word dialogic to the work of Mikhail Bakhtin, others, such as Boyd and Markarian (2011), associate it with Paulo Freire (1970, 1974) and a political stance leading to the development of individual agency and emancipation.

A key feature of dialogic teaching common to all approaches is the importance of the relationship between teacher and pupils and amongst pupils. The relationship which develops requires an atmosphere of trust and reciprocity, a genuine sense of community. Teacher and pupil are both seen as engaged as subjects in acts of cognition, not agent and object in an act of transferral of information.

Reasoning

Several approaches to developing students' reasoning focus on the use of talk within a framework that supports co-operation, respect, and accountability. Two are American in origin – 'Philosophy for Children' and 'Accountable Talk' – and two are British – 'Thinking Together' and 'Dialogic Teaching.' We start here with the two British approaches which both build upon the work of Barnes and others in the 1970s. We look in more detail at Philosophy for Children later in the book for its relevance to the pedagogic approach suggested.

Thinking Together

The Thinking Together programme (2024) grew out of the work of Neil Mercer and colleagues on the relationship between pupils' talk and thinking. The project, which now includes Oracy Cambridge (2024), focusses on the use of exploratory talk across the curriculum. Associated publications include research and activities in books published by Mercer, Lyn Dawes, and other colleagues which provide resources for teachers to get started using 'ground rules' and 'talking points.' The focus throughout is on making children's reasoning visible through talk, developing and sustaining collaboration, and balancing the competitive and cooperative elements in group work (Dawes and Sams, 2004).

Mercer, whose work on language as a crucial tool for learning now spans more than three decades (see Mercer, 2019), coined the term 'interthinking' to identify how humans have evolved the ability to transform individual experience into shared knowledge through language. We can represent our experience in a shared communication space and then take it apart again and reconstruct it using the medium of language, he says. And one of the beauties of language is that it is flexible and allows recombination, making it possible to introduce new ideas and renegotiate meanings (2000, p. 168). Mercer's work is accessible because he makes links between the way we use language in everyday situations with how it is used in education. This allows us to see how, as teachers, we are not merely deliverers of parcels of knowledge but are engaged in another form of conversation, one which uses many of the same techniques we will use when conversing with friends or family to communicate information, share or negotiate views and opinions, and persuade – or, as a parent, elaborating a young child's utterance. For Mercer, language is the preeminent tool for building on prior learning and should be used as a joint tool for making sense of experience. Education will have failed if it consists of little more than listening to the teacher's voice and answering the questions a teacher asks (2000, pp. 55–56).

Mercer identifies five techniques, common in the classroom, that teachers use for building on prior learning and supporting children to develop their understanding, skills, and knowledge, readily recognisable to all teachers:

Recaps - often used for setting the scene or reviewing prior learning in the subject/theme

Elicitations – asking questions to recap or consolidate prior learning. Often used together with recaps

Repetitions - when a teacher repeats what a pupil has said used either as an affirmation after a pupil answer to a question or with a questioning tone, indicating that more detail may be required

Reformulations – Similar to 'elaboration' (see chapter 1). Teachers will often expand upon and (instinctively) remodel a child's utterance, affirming what they say, and keeping the momentum of the learning conversation

Exhortations – when a teacher urges children to 'think back' or to 'remember' prior learning or experience

Five Teacher Techniques, adapted from Mercer (2000, pp. 52–55)

Teachers commonly use all of these techniques. But Mercer's point is that it is how they use them and to what purpose that counts. When they are used to pursue a line of logical thinking, it really begins to make a difference. He is unambiguous: 'Children need to be enabled to become active users of the tool of language, and this means giving them opportunities for use of the tool of language in less didactic conversations' (2000, p. 56).

Mercer argues that group work in schools can be a waste of time if pupils do not communicate effectively. This can happen if they have past 'history.' Maybe they have worked together before uncooperatively, or they just simply do not get on. In this case, the 'interpersonal' function of language gets in the way of discussing the issue or problem that requires cooperation to come up with ideas to solve or work through (what Halliday terms 'the ideational function'). But this is not the only reason that developing children's co-operative reasoning skills can be a challenge. If they have had no past experience of working cooperatively, then they will not be skilled in listening to each other, building on each other's ideas, or disagreeing respectfully. Such non-productive talk he calls 'disputational.' It is often characterised by simple utterances, short amounts of discussion, and an individual or pair taking control and making all the suggestions or doing all the work.

The Thinking Together programme (2024) much like Dialogic Teaching (see what follows) or Philosophy for Children aims to enable pupils to build the cooperative skills described earlier to enable more productive interactions. These can involve 'cumulative' talk, where they build up a picture of something in a mutually supportive way, their contributions adding detail. This type of talk is not critical, but is used to 'flesh out' understanding. The third type of talk he identifies is 'exploratory' using the term coined by Barnes to describe

> that in which partners engage critically but constructively with each other's ideas. Relevant information is offered for joint consideration. Proposals may be challenged or counter-challenged, but if so, reasons are given and alternatives are offered. Agreement is sought as a basis for joint progress. Knowledge is made publicly accountable and reasoning is visible in the talk.
>
> (Mercer, 2000, p. 153)

He gives an example from work developed for computer-based group discussion by Wegerif relating to citizenship education called Kate's Choice (Mercer, Wegerif and Dawes, 1999). Kate's friend has stolen from a shop. His motivation is unselfish, and she promises not to tell on him. But gradually, as the pressure tells, she begins to question herself. In an excerpt from a group discussion in a lesson, Mercer shows how children begin to grapple with the ideas and start to give each other space for proper discussion. Although they may not reason well yet, they are taking their first steps. He singles out a child named Gavin for mention. He gives a reason, introduced by the word 'because.' Kate should tell on him, he says, *because* if he steals, he's not worth having as a friend. The use of the words 'because,' 'if,' 'why,' and 'I think' are identified by Mercer as being consistent with pupils accounting for their reasons and being engaged in critical constructive discussion. Reason giving, like this, is a key indicator of all aspects of dialogic learning.

Dialogic Teaching

Like Mercer, Robin Alexander's research spans several decades. Alexander was the leader of the largest independent research review into primary education since the *Plowden Report*, the *Cambridge Primary Review - Children, Their World, Their Education* (2010). He also led a major cross-national research study comparing primary education in five countries - England, France, America, Russia, and India - a work published as *Culture and Pedagogy* (2001). And it was out of this that his interest in using talk and dialogic pedagogy developed.

Dialogic teaching grows out of Alexander's contention, originally published in the *Cambridge Primary Review* as one of the twelve core aims of public education, as 'Enacting dialogue':

- To help students understand that learning is an interactive process and that understanding builds through joint activity between teacher and student and among students in collaboration and thereby to develop students' increasing sense of responsibility for what and how they learn.
- To help students recognise that knowledge is not only transmitted but also negotiated and recreated; and that each of us in the end makes our own sense out of the meeting of knowledge, both personal and collective.
- To advance a pedagogy in which dialogue is central: between self and others, between personal and collective knowledge, between present and past, between different ways of making sense. (2020, p. 129)

Alexander uses a number of definitions and categorisations to describe the different aspects at work in his model of dialogic teaching. They are detailed and can feel complex, but they are there for a reason. He includes, for example, a list of justifications for those intending to adopt a dialogic stance in their teaching, principles that underpin and guide the planning of classroom talk, and repertoires that work in combination to assist teachers to put talk in its pedagogical context.

Alexander's six principles of dialogic talk bear comparison with some of Mercer's concepts. Dialogic talk should be:

Collective - meaning undertaken as a group or class
Supportive - meaning students should feel able to express ideas freely without fear about hesitation or 'getting it wrong'
Reciprocal - meaning participants share ideas, listen to each other, and have opportunities to air alternative viewpoints
Deliberative - meaning participants discuss and seek to resolve different points of view, evaluating arguments, and work towards reasoned positions
Cumulative - meaning students should build on their own and each other's contributions to develop coherent lines of thinking and understanding
Purposeful - meaning that classroom talk can be open-ended but should work towards specific learning goals.

Six Principles of Dialogic Talk, adapted from Alexander (2020, p. 131)

Central to dialogic teaching is the idea of repertoire. It is built upon an understanding of teaching as being about judgement and choice. As Alexander points out, teaching is about judgements and choices which are both considered and planned in advance and those taken in the moment. We include a fuller discussion of this aspect of a teacher's *'praxis,'* or 'acting wisely and carefully in a particular situation' drawing upon Kemmis and Smith (2008), in Chapter 12.

The eight repertoires cover forms and functions of talk. They include such elements as patterns of classroom organisation and pupil grouping; norms for talk, including student attitude and relationship to others; 'moves' such as questioning and extending; and lastly, discussion and argumentation (2020, p. 136). Alexander is insistent that it is how the so-called 'third turn' (the feedback in the cycle of initiation, response, and feedback) is used that is crucial to dialogic teaching. This is because feedback can either close down or extend thinking. His sixth repertoire, 'extending,' for which he draws on the work of Michaels and O'Connor and Resnick (2007), encourages students to be able to share and build on each other's ideas through careful listening, evaluating, and giving reasons.

The final two repertoires, 'discussing' and 'arguing,' have aspects in common with Mercer's exploratory talk. They focus on talk that involves careful reasoning and can entail critical thinking. Discussing can take place in whole-class or group situations. It can take different forms and pursue different purposes and is therefore distinct from arguing which, Alexander states, 'follows a particular trajectory and incorporates generally agreed elements' (2020, p. 157). Discussions, he argues, are beneficial because they allow the full range of desirable learning talk to be engaged. But there is a caution to those beginning on the journey. Children who are not used to this approach and are only used to the teacher asking questions will not automatically begin to ask questions themselves. They will need time to adapt. Likewise, the forms of discourse used in public argumentation (arguing is the repertoire) will need direct teaching, as many children will not be familiar with this sort of communication – as we see also with Philosophy for Children. Phrases such as 'So, are you saying that . . .?' or 'What is your reason for saying that?' or 'Can you explain why you disagree? can be used for presenting and supporting a position, claim, or hypothesis. They help us explore different perspectives and clarify, evaluate, and use logic in making connections (2020, pp. 161–163).

The Thinking Together programme and dialogic teaching share a number of distinctive features which set them apart from the commonplace of classroom interactions. To work, they require a supportive classroom environment that fosters interactions amongst students as well as between teacher and student(s). They both require children to be given the time and space to follow a line of reasoning – even up a blind alley, if necessary. And they both need children to be equipped with the discourse norms of discussion, reasoning, and respectful disagreement – something which will be differentially available to them depending on their home background. Some may be used to having discussions of this sort at home, and so when the approach is introduced, it will not seem alien. But many will not, and they will need time to adjust. Learning to listen to each other, discuss issues without personalities getting in the way, and use the appropriate language – the 'ifs,' 'becauses,' 'what ifs?' 'I thinks,' and 'can you give me a reason for that?' – takes time, teacher patience, and skill, as they bring past experience to bear on new knowledge.

The human factor

One thing lies at the heart of all the approaches outlined earlier. That is the relationship between a teacher and their class and among the pupils themselves. Without a teacher who can model reasoning skills and fallibility, or show themselves to be a good listener and a caring human being, dialogic teaching is not possible. Paulo Freire said, 'Dialogue cannot exist without humility' (1970, p. 71). The disposition requires an understanding that teaching is not about asserting your power nor about believing that you are the dispenser of all knowledge. You need your pupils to see you can get it wrong! Showing humility, however, does not mean your classroom is not a respectful and disciplined place. Children who really respect staff – and each other – will not want to upset, offend, or hurt each other or the teacher. But they will not automatically understand a dialogic approach, and it will take time to familiarise them with its discourse norms – especially if they have been subject to a home background where authority is equated with discipline and punishment.

But what of the students themselves? What are the benefits of learning to reason out loud to them? Whilst many writers on the dialogic approach promote the cognitive benefits to students, there are also other powerful reasons for this approach being adopted. Becoming articulate leads to confidence and self-belief. Students who are more articulate are more likely to be able to express what they feel as well as what they think, if indeed the two are disentangleable.

But the area which seems to elude many writers on dialogic teaching is that of pupil agency. In learning to discuss and reason, people realise that their thoughts, beliefs, and values are of importance. They learn that they can play an important role as citizens in their community. The ability to evaluate and scrutinise what is around you, not least what you are 'consuming' through social media, is consciousness-raising. Instead of taking what we read and see around us 'at face value,' we become able to use the lens of critical awareness to evaluate what is presented as fact – a really important skill in an age of the 'counterfactual.' Being the subject in your own learning is likely also to increase your chance of social mobility, happiness, and healthiness. In Part II, we look at the value of a dialogic approach and opportunities for children to develop critical reasoning skills to apply them to everyday experiences that stretch from mental health issues and cyberbullying to contentious topics such as racism, sexism, religious intolerance, and radicalisation. But first we need to look at how to plan for this approach. In the following chapter we consider whether planning which lists sets of preordained objectives and measurable outcomes is appropriate for lessons which focus on enquiry. Or is there another path teachers can take?

References

Alexander, R.J. (2001) *Culture and Pedagogy: International Comparisons in Primary Education*. Oxford: Blackwell Publishing.

Alexander, R.J. (ed.) (2010) *Children, Their World, Their Education: Final Report and Recommendations of the Cambridge Primary Review*. London: Routledge.

Alexander, R.J. (2020) *A Dialogic Teaching Companion*. Abingdon: Routledge.

Bakhtin, M.M. (1981) *The Dialogic Imagination*. Austin, TA: University of Texas Press.

Barnes, D. (2008) Exploratory talk for learning. In Mercer, N. and Hodgkinson, S. (eds.) *Exploring Talk in School*. London: Sage, pp. 1–15.

Barnes, D. and Shemilt, D. (1974) Transmission and interpretation. *Educational Review*, 26(3), pp. 213–228.

Barnes, D. and Todd, F. (1977) *Communication and Learning in Small Groups*. London: Routledge and Kegan Paul.

Bernstein, B. (2003) *The Structuring of Pedagogic Discourse: Class, Codes and Control*, Vol. 4. London: Routledge.

Boyd, M. and Markarian, W. (2011) Dialogic teaching: Talk in service of a dialogic stance. *Language and Education*, 25(6), pp. 515–534.

Damon, W. and Phelps, E. (1988) Strategic uses of peer learning in children's education. In Berndt, T.J. and Ladd, G.W. (eds.) *Peer Relationships in Child Development*. New York: John Wiley and Sons, pp. 135–157.

Dawes, L. and Sams, C. (2004) *Talk Box: Speaking and Listening Activities for Learning at Key Stage 1*. London: David Fulton.

Freire, P. (1970) *Pedagogy of the Oppressed*. London: Continuum.

Freire, P. (1974) *Education for Critical Consciousness*. London: Bloomsbury.

Gorard, S., Siddiqui, N. and See, B.H. (2015) *Philosophy for Children: Evaluation Report and Executive Summary*. Durham: Education Endowment Foundation.

Gurton, P. (2022) *Teacher Talk and Pupil Talk: A Case Study of a Thinking Skills Approach to Learning in an English Primary Academy*. University of Wolverhampton. http://hdl.handle.net/2436/625068.

Howe, C. (2010) *Peer Groups and Children's Development*. Oxford: Wiley-Blackwell.

Kemmis, S. and Smith, T.J. (eds.) (2008) *Enabling Praxis: Challenges for Education*. Rotterdam: Sense Publishers.

Linell, P. and Markova, I. (1993) Acts in discourse: From monological speech acts to dialogical inter-acts. *Journal for the Theory of Social Behaviour*, 23(2), pp. 173–195.

Maybin, J. (2006) *Children's Voices: Talk, Knowledge and Identity*. Basingstoke: Palgrave MacMillan.

Mercer, N. (1995) *The Guided Construction of Knowledge: Talk Amongst Teachers and Learners*. Clevedon: Multilingual Matters.

Mercer, N. (2000) *Words and Minds: How We Use Language to Think Together*. London: Routledge.

Mercer, N. (2019) *Language and the Joint Creation of Knowledge: The Selected Works of Neil Mercer*. Abingdon: Routledge.

Mercer, N., Wegerif, R. and Dawes, L. (1999) Children's talk and the development of reasoning in the classroom. *British Educational Research Journal*, 25(1), pp. 95–111.

Michaels, S., O'Connor, C. and Resnick, L. (2007) Deliberative discourse idealized and realized: Accountable talk in the classroom and civic life. *Studies in the Philosophy of Education*, 27, pp. 283–297.

Miell, D. and Littleton, K. (2004) *Collaborative Creativity*. London: Free Association Books.

Nystrand, M., Gamoran, A., Kachur, R. and Prendergast, C. (1997) *Opening Dialogue: Understanding the Dynamics of Language and Learning in the English Classroom*. New York: Teachers College.

Oracy Cambridge (2024) *The Hughes Hall Centre for Effective Spoken Communication* [online] Available at: https://oracycambridge.org/ (Accessed: 13 April 2024).

Piaget, J. (1985) *The Equilibration of Cognitive Structures*. Chicago, IL: University of Chicago Press (Original work published in 1932).

Sinclair, J.M. and Coulthard, R.M. (1975) *Towards an Analysis of Discourse: The English Used by Teachers and Pupils*. London: Oxford University Press.

Skidmore, D. (2000) From pedagogical dialogue to dialogical pedagogy. *Language and Education*, 14(4), pp. 283–296.

Thinking Together Project (2024) [online]. Available at: https://thinkingtogether.educ.cam.ac.uk/ (Accessed 13 April 2024).

Trickey, S. and Topping, K.J. (2004) Philosophy for children: A systematic review. *Research Papers in Education*, 19, pp. 365–380.

Wegerif, R. (2011) Towards a dialogic theory of how children think and learn. *Thinking Skills and Creativity*, 6, pp. 179–190.

Wells, G. (1999). *Dialogic Inquiry: Toward a Socio-Cultural Practice and Theory of Education*. Cambridge: Cambridge University Press.

6 Learning without objectives

For John Dewey,

> Child and curriculum are but the two limits which define a single process. . . . It is a continuous reconstruction moving from a child's present experience out into that represented by organized bodies of truth we call studies.
>
> (1902, p. 129)

The crucial word in this quotation is *reconstruction*. We have seen how, to develop knowledge and understanding, children need opportunities to try and articulate what they have understood. To assimilate new ideas, they need to be able to try out what it means within the scope of their current models of the world. In Chapter 5, we explored how a dialogic approach to pedagogy is based on a listening teacher – one who can hear what a child is trying to say and reformulate it, maybe using some of the terms or grammatical constructions that the child is using. In this way, the teacher affirms and corrects at the same time, showing respect in their relationship with the pupil but extending their understanding by posing a question or elaborating. Of course, the challenge in a class of thirty is greater than a parent one to one with a child, but teachers do regularly use the approach. In the classroom excerpt in the Introduction to this book, the teacher listens carefully to the feedback from a group and asks 'Are you talking about the concept of influence?' The teacher suggests; she does not insist. This way, the children are more likely to take on board the new word. Paulo Freire attempts to explain the partnership between teacher and pupils as they build understanding together in the following way:

> [the teacher] does not regard cognizable objects as his private property, but as the object of reflection by himself and his students. . . . The teacher presents the material to the students for their consideration and reconsiders her earlier considerations as the students express their own.
>
> (1970, pp. 61–62)

Here, as with Dewey's words in the opening quotation of this chapter, the ideas of re-creation and co-creation, of reflection and reconstruction, frame teaching and learning dialogically. This provides a much more fluid and symbiotic language than the rather rigid concepts of delivery, objectives, and measurable outcomes which are the stock in trade of didacticism. Freire regards dialogic teaching as liberating. His problem-posing approach encourages the individual to question why things are as they are, not just take them as given.

DOI: 10.4324/9781003451044-8

But there is a significant problem faced by those who adopt a dialogic stance in their teaching today. Teachers are principally answerable for their pupils' exam results, whether this is SATs in a primary school, or GCSEs or A levels in a secondary school or sixth form college, and, sadly, often at university, too. And exams and tests are only part of the story. To ensure that their pupils get good results, teachers must teach to the test and 'cover' the curriculum. If not, the school will suffer in league tables and Ofsted judgements. Pay is linked to 'performance' in education, and schools are judged by their results. And there is one sure way to do your best to ensure that your pupils get the best results (and your pocket doesn't suffer), and that is by adopting a didactic approach. Many teachers privately know that teaching in this way does not engage children or necessarily develop thinking skills, and they are very frustrated by this delivery model. But they feel they have little choice. And, of course, there are plenty of skills that do lend themselves to an approach focussing on instruction rather than discussion. But by no means all. Other teachers, like some we will meet and have already met in this book, are brilliant mediators of learning by subverting the orthodoxy and teaching in a way they know works best, despite the challenge of covering the curriculum. But most teach didactically, as it is the only way they know how. It is how they have been taught and how they have been shown how to teach. Notions of pace, delivery, and performance have held sway for many decades now, coupled with what can often be a superficial approach to learning subject content. But as this book shows, there is another way which encourages deeper thinking and develops independence of mind.

Language use, measurement, and hegemony

There is another reason why we find it hard to see beyond a didactic approach to teaching - and this lies in the language we use. We are trapped in a particular view of the world influenced as we are by the vocabulary of efficiency, effectiveness, and what Biesta has called 'learnification' (2010). The language we use forms a prism through which we see the world. It affects the way we think, and it seems like common sense. The Italian political philosopher Antonio Gramsci named this effect 'hegemony.' If we could bring back someone from a past era - a teacher from the 1970s, for example - they would view the world differently and would use a different vocabulary to describe some of our everyday experiences in education. The language we use in education today (key stages; programmes of study; learning objectives) came about as part of the *Education Reform Act* (DES, 1988). It brought with it concepts from business such as SMART targets and payment by results, previously unheard of in education. It was all part of larger societal changes which occurred as a direct result of the economic policies of monetarism introduced by Margaret Thatcher in the UK and Ronald Reagan in the USA, now commonly known as neoliberalism.

At the heart of this discourse is the concept of measurability. Everything is reduced to what is measurable in quantitative terms. But, of course, not everything is. Social, emotional, and moral development are largely forgotten or ignored, as they have no measurable performance value (Ball, 2016). The change in discourse has had a profound effect on what can be said and thought in education. Kelly (1995), for example, suggested that it has brought about a shift in the intellectual categories with which we are able to debate and plan educational provision:

> The moral category has been replaced by the mechanistic; the social by the political; the ideal by the expedient; the cooperative by the competitive and . . . education as a 'human right' by education as a 'national investment.'

> (1995, p. 166)

At the heart of this hegemony in education for teachers is a curriculum which conforms to what is termed a behavioural objectives model. Knowledge is regarded as something to be selected and distributed, the curriculum divided into a set of subjects, and pupils to be assessed on how much they have assimilated its content. The impact of these changes on educational discourse is profound. There is less room for the teacher to respond to the needs of the learner and even to individual sense making. Little significance or credit is attached to creative or 'left-field' responses, as these are not listed within the 'assessment criteria' or mark schemes (Pring, 2004). Challenge is discouraged or at least not invited. Exam results become the be all and end all, the *raison d'être* of the whole system. And written individual attainment is nearly always what is measured. Yet ironically, the individual as a whole person is ignored. They become merely the object of instruction in receipt of a deposit of knowledge (Freire, 1970). There is very little opportunity in this model for the individual pupil to become subject of action and responsibility, with self-determination, and a chance for their voice to be heard.

The behavioural objectives model – an educational panacea?

The behavioural objectives model is used in most Western curriculums at every level of education today. In England, it is the basis of the Foundation Stage Curriculum, the National Curriculum, GCSE, and A level exams and is used extensively in curricula adopted in universities and higher education institutions. Its origins lie in Ralph Tyler's book *Basic Principles of Curriculum Instruction* (1949), and by the 1960s and 1970s, the approach was in widespread use in the USA, as it has been in the UK since the first National Curriculum in 1988. The procedure of identifying learning objectives and then selecting and organising content, individual learning activities, and modes of assessment is one we are all very familiar with. We use it as the basis for long-, medium-, and short-term planning. And it can be really useful. But it carries with it significant risks. It is essentially a means-end, input-output model, reducing all areas of learning to one simple, though persuasive, approach. And the truth is not all areas of learning are amenable to this treatment. It can, and often does, result in trivialising and actually limiting opportunities for learning. It encourages taxonomies of educational objectives which are often contradictory, unnecessarily hierarchical, and that tie teachers and students in knots. Moreover, as we have said, the dominance of this paradigm has resulted in the marginalisation of other important aspects of learning such as social, emotional, artistic, and moral development, as they do not have measurable performance value. In fact, the problems we are facing as a society in areas such as mental health may well be in part exacerbated by a model of schooling that objectifies the learner, depriving them of agency and their teachers of humanity. Most people reading this book will, in their own education, have had experience of some of its shortcomings, and if they have escaped them, that will be due to the excellence of individual teachers. Have you, for example, throughout your education, had target grades set for you? Have you as a student written assignments in which the structure has been determined by an attempt to meet all the learning outcomes, and this has hampered your ability to fully explore a subject or an argument? Have you as a teacher felt constrained in the middle of a fruitful discussion or learning experience by feeling obliged to move on to another lesson or activity, although you knew it would be beneficial to your students to spend more time on the matter in hand? Or have you been held accountable for the progress or lack of it of some of your students when significant elements are beyond your control?

The behavioural objectives model formed the basis of a lively debate in the 1970s between an American educationalist, W. James Popham, and Lawrence Stenhouse, founder of the Centre for Applied Research in Education at the University of East Anglia. Stenhouse is best known for his view of the teacher as researcher, for which he became nationally and internationally famous. Stenhouse felt that there were significant strengths to a behavioural objectives approach to curriculum planning, but he was alive to its shortcomings. The blanket application of theory without sufficient evaluation through research and testing troubled him, as did the

> vein of advocacy and certitude of some of its proponents. . . . Many people believe that the more systematic a theory is, the more likely it is to be correct. In curriculum studies, though not, perhaps, in the physical sciences, the reverse is likely to be the case. . . . We must beware of believing that in the objectives model – or any other model or theory – we have a systematic solution to our curricular problems, much less an educational panacea.
>
> (1975, p. 71)

Stenhouse and others listed eleven shortcomings of the objectives model, usefully summarised by James (2012, p. 66) here:

1) Triviality, because trivial learning behaviours are easiest to make operational and measure
2) Pre-specification prevents teachers from taking advantage of unplanned learning opportunities
3) Neglecting wider objectives than pupil behaviours, e.g., community values
4) Difficulties with measurement which becomes mechanistic and dehumanising
5) Being undemocratic because it prescribes how learners should behave
6) Insisting that teachers should specify their goals in terms of measurable behaviours, which is unrealistic
7) Ignoring the difficulty of defining measurable behaviours in the Arts and Humanities
8) Making most educational goals innocuous, if stated precisely
9) Turning measurability into accountability by encouraging the judgement of teachers by outcomes their students achieve, which may be affected by factors beyond the teachers' control

10) Underestimating the difficulty of teachers generating objectives unless they are given a bank of them to choose from

11) Making teachers inattentive to unanticipated but important results

Many of Stenhouse's criticisms proved prophetic. He was critical of payment by results approach which leads to teaching to the test and the propensity to contract out to 'profit-making learning system companies whose profits depend on their capacity to achieve objectives pre-specified in terms of the children's performance on standardised tests' (1975, p. 69). He would shudder to see what has happened to education in the UK now, were he still alive.

Stenhouse's critique of the behavioural objectives model

1) It mistakes the nature of knowledge itself

Stenhouse's principal objection to the objectives model was that it is based on a flawed understanding of the nature of knowledge and how to improve practice, and it can only account for part of what education should aim to achieve. He set out four processes of education - 'training, instruction, initiation, and induction' (ibid, p. 80). Only two of these - training and instruction - concerned with prespecified skills and information (often based on memorisation and retention) - fit the behavioural objectives model. The other two - initiation and induction - do not. Initiation involves being socialised into the practices and traditions of a community - the norms and values of society - and is often absorbed through the hidden curriculum, so difficult to evaluate. But for Stenhouse, the one crucial area for which the objectives model was a poor fit was what he termed induction into thought systems - what we may call the discipline of different subject areas. Stenhouse's own definition of curriculum was

> an attempt to communicate the essential principles and features of an educational proposal in such a form that it is open to critical scrutiny and capable of translation into practice.

> (his italics) (1975, p. 4)

He believed in the importance and value of disciplinary knowledge but that subjecting propositions to critical scrutiny needed to be at the heart of the process. Knowledge was not something given from on high without being subject to constant revaluation. Otherwise, how would progress be possible? Students would grow in understanding of 'the best that might be thought and known' by subjecting propositions to testing for bias and error against logic and experience (James, 2012, p. 64). Thus, in a classroom, students learn both facts and processes, and both child and teacher are involved in the learning process - teachers challenging their own assumptions and the classroom becoming a scene of research for the teacher in building a better understanding of how to teach. Knowledge was not just a set of facts to be memorised but the imparting of structures and concepts. Knowledge with meaning could only be discovered gradually. Here, drawing on an analogy initially used by Dewey, he likens knowledge to a map. It has changed over time, and it can be projected differently. This is both true for the individual child as they grow and mature in understanding as it is for humanity as it has expanded knowledge and understanding. His view was that

> key procedures, concepts and criteria in any subject – *cause, form, experiment, tragedy* – are, and are important, precisely because they are, problematic within the subject. They are the focus of speculation not the object of mastery.
>
> (1975, p. 85)

This articulation of disciplinary knowledge as not being an 'object of mastery' is crucial in our understanding because it so clearly goes against the concept of measurability which we have become accustomed to. It has particular resonance today as the word 'mastery,' initially coined in an educational context by Benjamin Bloom (1968), has become prevalent in its usage, especially in the area of mathematics teaching, where it has been adopted (after the widespread introduction of an approach favoured in Southeast Asia) as a key term. Pretending that you are, as a teacher, the fount of all knowledge is encouraged by the objectives model. Stenhouse gives an example of how prespecified objectives in the area of 'historical causation' can distort knowledge. Suggesting that there is a limit to the identification of causes of the First World War, for example, and only marking the exam paper accordingly is, he argues, arbitrary. There is no 'limit' to the concept of historical causation, no 'generally acceptable and pre-specified answer' (1975, p. 86).

2) It can lead to an abuse of power by the teacher/school by setting arbitrary limits to speculation

Another significant concern for Stenhouse was the very real abuse of power relations between pupil(s) and teacher that the behavioural objectives model can give rise to.

> The translation of deep structures of knowledge into behavioural objectives . . . gives the school an authority and power over its students by setting arbitrary limits to speculation and by defining arbitrary solutions to unresolved problems of knowledge. This translates the teacher from the role of the student of a complex field of knowledge to the role of master of the school's agreed version of that field.
>
> (1975, p. 86)

Note how he sees the teacher as a student, albeit a student with much more knowledge than the pupils but a student nevertheless. The temptation for the teacher to pretend to know more than they do because the learning outcomes have been prescribed (the observable behaviours by the students all listed) or to be the possessor of all knowledge diminishes the act of learning itself. It presumes there is always a definite goal that can be achieved, de-valuing speculation or what we have earlier called exploratory talk. It sets the teacher in direct opposition to the student. They become the 'owner' of the knowledge – an act of oppression and domination, to use Freire's words (1970) – negating the aspects of wonder and questioning that education should arouse but also acculturating the student into the acceptance of a passive place. It encourages quite the reverse of an open and approachable attitude in a teacher as someone on a journey with their students, modelling the desire to want to find out more and be open to student suggestions and reinterpretations. It makes the teacher less likely to be attuned to student attempts to articulate their understanding and students less likely and willing to have a go.

3) It is designed as a tool for summative assessment and not suited to critical appraisal, formative assessment, or self-assessment

The objectives model itself arose from concern at the subjectivity of marking and a desire for objective tests, the criteria for which (statements of objectives) could not be misinterpreted. Indeed, Stenhouse is unequivocal of the danger posed by bad teachers:

> The capacity of the limited teacher to limit us is the price we pay for the price of the profound teacher to extend us. But since grading counts for so much, we want to be assured that the limitations of our teachers do not seriously penalise us in examinations.
>
> (1975, p. 95)

This statement is a backhanded justification of the objectives model. But should the quality of learning experience offered be sacrificed because of the variability in teacher expertise and judgement? It has, indeed, often been argued that the adoption of the National Curriculum in England and the introduction of the Ofsted inspection regime has resulted in a homogenisation and 'dumbing down' of education – doing away with the very good teachers along with the very bad. What Stenhouse suggests as an alternative, the 'process' model, offers a different sort of marking altogether. It places the teacher as 'critic, not marker' (1975, p. 95). And by this, Stenhouse clearly means what we would nowadays call formative assessment. He talks of 'appraisal,' which clearly improves the students' capacity to work to the criteria (not objectives or outcomes) by critical reaction to work done. 'In this sense,' he states, 'assessment is about the teaching of self-assessment' (1975, p. 95).

The 'process' model – an enquiry method

Stenhouse went about the process of proposing an alternative to the objectives model by setting himself the following questions:

- Can curriculum and pedagogy be organised satisfactorily by a logic other than that of the means-end model?
- Can there be principles for the selection of content other than the principle that it should contribute to an objective? (1975, p. 84)

His search for an alternative to the objectives model drew inspiration from the work of Jerome Bruner, whose assertion 'any subject can be taught effectively in some intellectually honest form to any child at any stage of development' (Bruner, 1966, p. 33) was a cornerstone of his alternative approach. And it was Bruner's curriculum project, 'Man: A course of study' (MACOS), that formed a basis for his justification of his own approach, which he called a 'process' model. It had specified content for the student and specification of what the teacher was to do in terms of principles of procedure, but it did not specify outcomes. Indeed, one of the appeals of the process model (elsewhere called enquiry or question-raising approach) is that, unlike the objectives model, it contains more pedagogical advice.

'Man: A course of study' was shaped around three recurring questions:
- What is human about human beings?
- How did they get that way?
- How can they be made more so?

The concept of the teacher as 'senior learner' required a philosophical understanding of the subjects they were teaching, the deep structures and rationale. But crucially, it placed the learner in an active role, expected to raise questions, take part in discussion, and construct hypotheses. The pedagogical aims as identified by Hanley et al. (1970, p. 5) were:

1) To initiate and develop in youngsters a process of question posing (the inquiry method)
2) To teach a research methodology where children can look for information to answer questions they have raised and use the framework developed in the course (e.g., concepts of the life cycle) and apply it to new areas
3) To help youngsters develop the ability to use a variety of firsthand sources as evidence from which to develop hypotheses and draw conclusions
4) To conduct classroom discussions in which youngsters learn to listen to others as well as express their own views
5) To legitimise the search; that is, to give sanction and support to open-ended discussions where definitive answers to many questions are not found
6) To encourage children to reflect on their own experiences
7) To create a new role for the teacher, in which he (sic) becomes a resource not an authority

These process (rather than product) goals, expressed in an evaluation of the project, which sums up the aims in its title, *Curiosity, Competence, Community,* are at the heart of the approach we recommend in this book as a basis for building a curriculum and pedagogy centred around talk and children's experience – hence, *Bringing Talk to Life*. They are very close to the aims of Philosophy for Children, which interestingly arose at the same time in America. They also exemplify the principles which Stenhouse went on to apply to his own Humanities Curriculum Project (HCP), but with a crucial difference, which he was keen to point out. MACOS had a body of disciplinary knowledge – a framework of criteria and principles of procedure (1975, p. 93). Like MACOS, the HCP crossed curricular boundaries. It also needed teachers with a 'good grasp of quality in each of the subject fields involved' (1968, p. 27), or it would 'run the risk of degenerating into incoherence.' But although it drew upon knowledge from different disciplines, it did not have a discipline at its base.

The Humanities Curriculum Project

The Humanities Curriculum Project (HCP) ran from 1967–1972 and was an experimental Humanities project across forty schools, arising from the need to re-engage disaffected students of 'average and below average' academic ability in the light of a projected rise in the school leaving age to 16 years. It was novel in its attempt to tackle controversial issues. The topics selected were based on their enduring importance and reflected the aims stated in 'Raising the School Leaving Age, School's Council Working Paper No. 2.' These were intended to enable adolescents to gain '. . . some access to a complex cultural inheritance, some hold on his personal life and his relationship with the various communities to which he belongs, [and] some extension of understanding of, and sensitivity towards, other human beings' (1965, p. 14). Some of the topics were 'The Family,' 'Relations Between the Sexes,' 'People and Work, Law and Order,' and 'Education.' Students were intended to develop an understanding of human acts, social situations, and the controversial issues they raise. Teachers needed to remain neutral despite the fact that they would hold views on some of the issues under discussion. They were certainly not meant to 'use their position of authority in the classroom to advance their own views or perspectives' (Stenhouse, 1975, p. 93). The model was intended to have 'discussion rather than instruction at its core' and should 'protect the divergence of views amongst participants' (1970, p. 8).

The choice of issues which divide people was deliberate, and the teacher's role was to 'teach the dispute rather than the truth as he (sic) knows it' (1975, p. 93). The approach was one of enquiry and question raising. The choice of themes was deliberately those that raised questions of value. The tendency at the time to plan learning that integrated several areas of humanities, so-called topic-based curricula, was becoming popular. But Stenhouse clearly distinguished between such topics as 'transport, water and local government' (1968, p. 28), which he felt dealt with 'facts and techniques' from those which lent themselves to controversy. The approach presented significant challenges for teachers, as Elliott, one of those involved at the time, attests. Teachers were unprepared, struggled with facilitating discussions and not letting their personal biases restrict pupils' ability to explore ideas. 'The principles that defined classroom procedure . . . did not prescribe the concrete actions of teachers' (2012, p. 89). But there was a plan for this. The difficult areas of protecting divergence and facilitating discussions formed part of the development phase of the project, and hypotheses were drawn up by teachers from their own action research designed to deepen their understanding. The empowerment of teachers in this way was a critical aspect of the whole design. There were video recordings, observational and interview data. Elliott gives examples of some of the questions raised in the self-training procedure:

- Reflective discussion can be slow-paced and contain sustained silences. What proportion of these silences are interrupted by you? Is your interruption ever simply a matter of breaking under the strain rather than a real contribution to the task of the group?
- Do you press towards a consensus e.g., 'Do we all agree?' If so, what is the effect of this type of question? Compare this with the effect of 'What do other people think?'
- To what extent do you confirm? Do you, for example, say 'An interesting point' or 'Well done'? What is the effect of this on the group?
- What prompts you to provide the group with a piece of evidence? Was the piece of evidence in practice helpful to the discussion?
- Are you neutral on controversial issues? (Further questions ask teachers to reflect on explicit ways they may explicitly and implicitly bias the discussion, e.g., 'Do you draw

attention by questions to certain parts or aspects of a piece of evidence which seems to support a viewpoint with which you agree?')

- Do you attempt to transmit through eliciting questions your own interpretation of the meaning of a piece of evidence such as a poem or a picture? (Elliott, 2012, p. 93)

These prompts, which could as well come from the Philosophy for Children approach (P4C), were designed to move teachers from the mindset of 'just tell us what to do' (all too common in today's system, too) to a recognition of their own agency in the process. As Elliott remembers from his role as a coordinator, Stenhouse was resistant to recasting the questions as hypotheses to test in their classrooms because he thought they would be interpreted as rules set by HCP. Stenhouse stressed one thing above all else:

> The major weakness of the process model of curriculum design will by now have become apparent. It rests upon the quality of the teacher. That is also its greatest strength.'
>
> (1975, p. 96)

References

Ball, S.J. (2016) Neoliberal education? Confronting the slouching beast. *Policy Futures in Education*, 14(8), pp. 1046–1059.

Biesta, G.J.J. (2010) *Good Education in and Age of Measurement: Ethics, Politics, Democracy*. London: Paradigm Publishers.

Bloom, B. (1968) Learning for mastery. *Evaluation Comment, Los Angeles, University of California Center for the Study of Evaluation of Instructional Programs*, 1(2), pp. 1–12.

Bruner, J.S. (1966) *Toward a Theory of Instruction*. Cambridge, MA: The Bellknap Press of Harvard University Press.

Department of Education and Science (DES). (1988) *The Education Reform Act*. London: HMSO.

Dewey, J. (1902) *The Child and the Curriculum*, reprinted in Garforth, F.W. (1966) *John Dewey: Selected Writings*. London: Heinemann.

Elliott, J. (2012) Teaching controversial issues, the idea of the teacher as researcher and contemporary significance for citizenship education. In Elliott, J. and Norris, N. (eds.) *Curriculum, Pedagogy and Educational Research: The Work of Lawrence Stenhouse*. London: Routledge, pp. 84–105.

Freire, P. (1970) *Pedagogy of the Oppressed*. London: Continuum.

Hanley, J.P., Whitla, D.K., Moo, E.W. and Walter, A.S. (1970) *Curiosity, Competence, Community: Man: A Course of Study, An Evaluation*, 2 vols. Cambridge, MA: Educational Development Center Inc.

James, M. (2012) An alternative to the objectives model. The process model for the design and development of the curriculum. In Elliott, J. and Norris, N. (eds.) *Curriculum, Pedagogy and Educational Research: The Work of Lawrence Stenhouse*. London: Routledge, pp. 61–83.

Kelly, A.V. (1995) *Education and Democracy: Principles and Practices*. London: Paul Chapman Publishing Ltd.

Pring, R. (2004) *Philosophy of Educational Research*. 2nd edn. London: Continuum.

The Schools Council (1965) *Raising the School Leaving Age Working Paper No. 2*. London: HMSO.

Stenhouse, L. (1968) The humanities curriculum project. *Journal of Curriculum Studies*, 1(1), pp. 26–33.

Stenhouse, L. (1970) *The Humanities Project: An Introduction*. London: Heinemann.

Stenhouse, L. (1975) *An Introduction to Curriculum Research and Development*. London: Heinemann.

Tyler, R. (1949) *Basic Principles of Curriculum Instruction*. Chicago, IL: University of Chicago Press.

7 Philosophical talk

Making learning meaningful

Enquiry learning

In Chapter 6, we saw how the behavioural objectives model of curriculum design can lead to an overemphasis on measurable outcomes, resulting in a prescriptiveness that can stifle individual thinking and sense making, depriving learning of meaning. This approach can also reinforce an authoritarian teacher-centred view of classroom life that creates greater social distance between teacher and learner, making it difficult to develop a learning community or a shared sense of enterprise – the feeling of being on a journey together that secures a bond of trust between learners and between teachers and their classes. Lawrence Stenhouse's alternative approach showed that curriculum design need not be dictated by objectives and measurable outcomes but could be enquiry based. Enquiry learning involves the teacher applying criteria and using processes to develop understanding in lessons and pupils playing more of an active part. This does not mean that there is no place for didactic teaching of specific skills and teacher modelling, just that this need not be the default approach to teaching. Some areas of learning, like specific skills of multiplication or division in Maths, for example, require a didactic approach, but crucially, once children become confident and familiar with the enquiry approach, they find it does not impose a ceiling on their learning. In fact, speculation and hypothesising are encouraged.

An enquiry approach develops a community of learners who are more invested in their learning because they get to raise questions relevant to their own experience. Their agency and academic motivation increase because lessons are relevant to them and their life experience, and they can discuss it with their peers. It is not surprising, really, if you think about it. We are all more motivated and engaged when we can see the meaning of what we are doing. Research from a meta-analysis by Watkins (2005) posing the question 'What do we know about classrooms as learning communities?' found that

- the opportunity to have their questions addressed in authentic collaborative enquiry increased student productivity
- cognitive engagement increased where public dialogue centred on discussions of students' own experiences
- questions and intellectual processes that follow were found to be of a higher order than text-based questions produced after reading for secondary aged children (Scardamalia and Bereiter, 1992), and primary school students are able to follow their questions in greater depth (Hakkarainen and Sintonen, 2002)

DOI: 10.4324/9781003451044-9

At the heart of a shift from didactic to dialogic teaching is the need to make education meaningful and relevant to life. The relationship between education and meaning should be inviolable. As Matthew Lipman and colleagues so admirably express it,

> Schools that consider education their mission and purpose are schools that dedicate themselves to helping children find meanings relevant to their lives.
>
> (Lipman, Sharp and Oscanyan, 1980, p. 13)

But for many teachers, making the link between what is in the curriculum and children's experience does not seem obvious. The pressure of meeting targets and covering the curriculum is too great and it is much easier, though correspondingly less fulfilling, to adopt a delivery mode of teaching. If we ask ourselves how often we get to know our students and allow them to share life experiences and ideas, we are likely to admit that it is seldom, if we are being truthful. Yet, to paraphrase Dickens' criticism of Mr. Gradgrind in his arch satire of a recitation culture in education in his novel *Hard Times* (1989), 'if only we tried to cover a little less, how infinitely better we might teach much more.' As Stenhouse suggested (1975), taking this alternative approach requires you to be a much better teacher.

Philosophy for Children

One method dedicated to making learning meaningful to students' lives is Lipman's own approach, known as Philosophy for Children (P4C). Founded on principles of communality and the development of reason, it has Community and Enquiry at its heart. P4C is all about students of almost any age – it has been used in community settings and old people's homes and pubs, for example – sharing their views and building their understanding of concepts. And it is this pursuit of concepts that gives it its distinctive feel. Many schools worldwide have adopted P4C, either having Philosophy lessons as discrete classes where children are given a stimulus – a story, videoclip, piece of music, or something similar – and then develop a discussion based around a question or questions which they want to pursue or integrating the approach into their teaching of other subjects or both. It is the approach used by the case study school in Part II of this book.

In P4C, students choose the questions they want to discuss and take turns, choosing each other to deepen their understanding in philosophy and other curriculum areas through a philosophical approach. P4C is not a scheme or an 'off-the-shelf' teaching resource. It does not consist of a series of graded lessons produced by a limited company. It does not have a copyright. The organisations that advocate P4C are cooperative and charitable. In the UK, SAPERE (The Society for the Advancement of Philosophical Enquiry and Reflection in Education) a non-profit society, was set up in 1992 to promote the use of P4C in schools through training teachers and an accredited award scheme. It is not 'difficult,' in any conventional sense of the word. It does not involve direct teaching of ideas, and children do not learn the history of philosophy. Instead, they explore philosophical concepts such as *justice* and *equality, freedom* and *adversity*, but always in a way and at a level that is appropriate to their age. Questions observed in a class of six year olds from the Education Endowment Foundation Study (EEF), for example (Gorard, Siddiqui and See, 2015), were based on a story about a bird that could not fit into other families of birds. They ranged from 'Why do we need to have a family?' to 'If you look different, does it also mean you are different on the inside?' It is an approach which develops habits of mind and behaviours that encourage active participation and equal opportunities to speak. All those engaged, teachers and pupils alike, show respect for each other by a process known as 'appreciative enquiry.' Studies have shown that there are significant social benefits, such as the development of resilience and teamwork, empathy, and confidence in questioning and reasoning (e.g., Siddiqui, Gorard and See, 2019; Trickey and Topping, 2007). The expectations of a teacher who facilitates, encourages children to explore their understanding, and build on and challenge each other's ideas in a supportive environment thus satisfies many aspects of the dialogic stance.

Lipman, along with his colleague Ann Margaret Sharp, dreamed up P4C in the late 1960s when he was a Philosophy lecturer at Columbia University, New York. He went on to found the Institute for the Advancement of Philosophy for Children (IAPC) in 1970. It was a time of great social upheaval with students across the West rebelling against the *status quo*. Divisions in society were, in some respects, similar to what we find today. It was a time when reasonableness was in short supply! There was a concern amongst educationalists that children were becoming passive and being told what to think, something that sounds familiar, heightened as it is today by the influence of social media. In a climate of intolerance and competing values there was then, as there is now, a pressing need for people to think for themselves, and Lipman felt his students were poorly equipped to articulate what they thought and apply logic and reasoning to their arguments. He believed that education in reasoning should start earlier in school. The resultant approach was based on the Socratic notion of dialogue and influenced by the American pragmatic philosophers Charles Sanders Peirce and John Dewey. He envisaged a community of enquiry – a caring, critical, creative group of collaborators (the 4 Cs of P4C) of children and adults – who could together raise questions and pursue answers through dialogue. Philosophy seemed the ideal medium as it was an existing discipline that

- promotes questioning and open-mindedness
- requires precision in language use and thinking
- can make meaningful connections between an otherwise disconnected-seeming curriculum
- creates links between the conceptual foundations and assumptions in different disciplines
- allows us to explore the relationship between facts and values in the context of our life experience
- makes individual thinking accountable to a community of peers

Developing a disposition to question

From a young age, children are curious and disposed to ask questions. Why does the sun move across the sky? Why does it rain? What happens when we die? Humanity has forever been seeking to answer questions. We want to know the reason and the cause for everything we see and do. It is such a human trait, maybe distinctly human, to have developed tools and then used them in novel ways. We invented language to communicate wants and needs, but it opened a whole new dimension when we started using it to analyse, reflect, and evaluate.

Provisional answers derived from religion and supposition have, in some cases, given way to more exact answers derived from science. But many scientific answers have had to be revised and will continue to be so. We construct whole civilisations and cultures based on very provisional and often quite wrong explanations or reasons, the obvious example being the belief that the Earth lay at the centre of the universe, the so-called geocentric view. But our facility to use reason is also a basic human trait.

Given that children are prone to ask questions and speculate as to why things are as they are, it seems perverse that our education system defines intelligence as the ability to answer, rather than question or to solve problems rather than recognizing and formulating them. As Lipman ruefully remarks, 'the intellectual progress typically credited to children occurs, not when they learn to think for themselves, but when the content of their thought has begun to approximate the content of our own - when their conceptions of the world begin to resemble ours' (1980, p. 60). Yet, given the opportunity, children can show enormous creativity and originality in their thinking. In the passage in Figure 7.1, for example, children from a Year 6 class speculate on the concept of number.

	There is much animated talk in this first part of the enquiry. Children talk to their partners, and then the teacher draws them to a stop.
Teacher:	**Good stopping, Matthew. . . . Joseph! Now, let's think about the question! Do numbers exist?**
Evan:	I think they do.
Teacher:	**Why?**
Jamie:	They do and don't - because you can see them, but you cannot touch them.
Nasreen:	I want to build on Jamie's point. You may choose bigger or smaller, but they are made up of other numbers.
Holly:	I think numbers don't exist because you can't touch them. . . . We made them up.
Catherine:	What do you mean by exist? To humans or to everything? *(Challenges the teacher)*
Teacher:	**What do YOU take it as?**
Jeffrey:	They do exist. They are in our world, so they do exist.
Abdulpreet:	They are just things we write down.
Joseph:	Numbers don't exist because they weren't originally on the Earth. We made them up . . . coming back to Holly's point . . . we are the only animal that uses numbers . . .
Grace:	I think exist means, like, unicorns don't exist but numbers do.
Teacher:	**Can anyone think of a concept we cannot see but is there?**
Holly:	Wind?
Arjun:	It's like kindness. It exists, but we cannot always see it.

Figure 7.1 Extract from the enquiry 'Do numbers exist?'

In a very short time, the children raise some interesting questions. Can you touch a number or is it a concept? Did humans invent the concept of numbers, or is it there in nature? How does the abstract notation for numbers relate to numbers themselves? The teacher keeps out of the discussion apart from on two occasions, letting the children air their 'first thoughts' – a typical stage in an enquiry. But there is plenty to come back to. Notice, too, how a child in this enquiry questions the teacher about what she means by the statement. This is something novel in most classroom learning situations but not in P4C, emphasising again the greater social equality between teacher and pupil. The children, now familiar with the conventions of this sort of public discourse, are able to engage with each other, building on previous statements, using phrases such as, 'I want to build on Jamie's point' or 'coming back to Holly's point.' This opportunity to share thoughts together through talk is liberating, giving rein to children's natural sense of fascination and wonder and allowing them to begin to suggest reasons for why things are as they are. The lesson may at first seem to be a stand-alone one, but it is followed by a video which demonstrates some of the number sequences evident in nature – looking at the golden ratio – and then the Fibonacci sequence – and the example of the ammonite's shell which perfectly exemplifies this. We can see how this is a way of contextualising and giving meaning to learning about numbers and may even pique the interest of some children who are not keen on mathematics.

Learning to think using concepts

Philosophy for Children takes a different path to a conventional curriculum. The purpose is to train children to think. Yes, 'to think' – that verb so rarely used in curriculum! It is conducted through a group and/or a class talking together in what is usually called an enquiry. It enables children to explore concepts that we may broadly call philosophical but can fall into realms as diverse as Religious Education, PSHE, History, Geography, and Sociology. They are the concepts that Vygotsky called 'scientific,' as we saw in Chapter 2: such concepts as *justice, fairness, identity, progress, belief, change, resilience, power, discrimination, prejudice,* etc. Having words for these concepts enables students to articulate ideas with examples from experience. And they are easily relatable to areas of the curriculum. So, for example, when a class explores the concept of *adversity* through a topic entitled 'Does adversity make you stronger?' as we see in Chapter 10, it becomes relevant in the context of geographical learning – a community which lives on the side of a volcano or in an earthquake zone. It also becomes relevant to History, PSHE, or Religious Education. So, why is it so rare to find such themes explored in school curriculums, and why are these concepts not routinely included as part of the curriculum?

The step from an example of a concept in narrative form to naming it is part of an adult's role. When a child talks of how they had to withstand pain in a certain situation and the parent or the teacher names their behaviour as *bravery* or *resilience*, we are providing a sort of mental peg for the child to hang the experience on. It is the linguistic and cognitive step we take which, as we have seen, different authors have used different terms for (Vygotsky's 'everyday' to 'scientific,' Bernstein's 'horizontal' to 'vertical,' Freire's move from 'vernacular' to 'dominant' syntax, and Halliday's 'grammatical metaphor' stage). The noun allows them to sort and classify their experience in the same way as the concrete experience of a sorting exercise with objects and their properties in a nursery or a reception class – it's just that it happens in the head. In a recent study (Gurton, 2022, p. 91), a teacher engaged in using P4C in their school explained how children become able to use concept words gleaned from P4C lessons in other curriculum areas:

> Probably I'd say they had very rarely used the word 'bias' in any other context apart from P4C like they used it today . . . and really that's not something that's prompted, I'm not kind of forcing that into the conversation, but they are naturally bringing up concepts that they link with other things.

Her comments are developed by another teacher, who suggests that such language initially used in a P4C context becomes part of the children's vocabulary and means of expressing themselves:

> That's definitely one of those concepts or themes that comes up in P4C a lot, so those bigger more difficult, sort of more grown-up ideas do come out, and then we talk about them, then you clarify different bits within them, then it becomes sort of part of what they will start using around school. They can talk to each other about it.

One teacher also suggested that when he used the word 'concepts' with his students, it was like activating a muscle or approach that enabled them to think differently:

> I use the idea of drawing out concepts all the time, and I actually feel like as soon as I use the word concepts, they're actually much more successful. Like sometimes, if we are doing an RE lesson, well it could be anything really, and it's not as, like, deep a conversation as I want, I say, 'You need to think about this in a P4C way. You need to think about the concepts.'

Along with the classification principle which we see in action with the use of concept words, Lipman identifies two other aspects of relationships or connections as being of major importance in education. Philosophers would call them 'instance-kind relations,' They are 'cause-consequence' relations and 'part-whole' relations. Cause-consequence relations are the ones we are most familiar with using (examples of these abound in practical situations but also in science and technology teaching in school). But part-whole are equally important because, as he points out, we need to understand how the parts relate to the whole in many situations in life. The given example is that of an art class in school, where an understanding of the properties of different materials and how they can be used contributes to a more effective and satisfying end product (Lipman, Sharp and Oscanyan, 1980, p. 57). If we neglect part-whole, because we live in a society which enshrines cause-consequence in the same way as it instantiates input-output, we do so at our peril. We live in an age where the scientific paradigm is dominant. However, in human terms, creativity and imagination and the ability to see the relationship between parts and whole are just as important and enable us to cooperate and innovate.

Creativity

Creativity is at the centre of Philosophy for Children. The approach stresses the importance of the coexistence and mutual sustainability of creative and logical thinking. Unlike a popular view of Philosophy which sees reason as the antithesis of imagination and spontaneity, P4C stresses the fact that creativity can both be fostered by, and can foster, logical thinking. And a talk-based enquiry is not the only way in which P4C learning can be pursued. The use of games, dramatisations, puppetry, 'philosophical play,' and writing or drawing can also be used to explore ideas. Schools practising this approach give pupils opportunities to choose how they record what they have taken from an enquiry using these means. The lesson on *control*, for example, in the Introduction to this book, yielded a whole range of interesting creative outcomes. The children were given the choice of how they recorded their learning at the end of the session – the choices included using paper and paints individually or in groups, argument alley (a group activity where children take positions for and against), or taking part in philosophical play. The majority voted for using paper and pens. Two examples are given in Figure 7.2 of interactions with the teacher.

Miriam

Miriam produced a drawing of a tree with the title 'Is this your choice?'

Teacher:	**Is it a tree?**
Miriam:	Yes, and it will grow blossom. A person can choose if he shakes the tree for the blossom to come off. Otherwise, God or the wind will decide.
Teacher:	**Is that creative thinking?**
Miriam:	Yes, because I have transferred an idea into an image.

Ayesha

Ayesha drew a picture of the brain.

Teacher:	**How has the drawing helped you?**
Ayesha:	It has made me think about feelings and opinions.
Teacher:	**Tell me more!**
Ayesha:	Well. . . . Emotions can affect choice. Even when you think you are just relying on your brain to think things through, your feelings still have an effect.

Figure 7.2 Creative outcomes of an enquiry

The value of error and the development of empathy

Another area which receives some attention from Lipman and colleagues is how valuable it can be to make mistakes. We all know that we learn as much from our errors as our successes, but a climate focussed on attainment and results can also give rise to a 'right answer mentality,' which is anathema to fostering a supportive community learning environment. Whilst acknowledging the importance of 'rigorous, logical thinking,' the originators of P4C shed light on the value of fallacy. Although it might be logically invalid to deduce 'all vegetables are onions' from the statement 'all onions are vegetables,' for example, they argue that an error of this sort may liberate children's imagination and give rise to inventiveness (Lipman, Sharp and Oscanyan, 1980, p. 64). Of course, this may not be the best example of how error can be used advantageously, but the point is well made and applies equally to flippancy and humour. The ability to consider alternatives can also be liberating and open the mind to new possibilities. If we think of the negative of an idea or concept, it may give us pause to sharpen our thinking. A child may state that the opposite of working is not working or they may suggest playing. The ensuing discussion centred about what they regard as the substantive differences between the two will, in itself, be interesting and will lead to a clearer definition in a child's mind about what he/she means by using certain words. It may also lead to a consideration of whether the two concepts are mutually exclusive, an exercise which could be repeated with many different concept words. Having time to explore meaning through alternatives is another way of opening the mind and developing intellectual capacity which is surely at the heart of what education is for.

The relationship between the development of cognitive and non-cognitive skills is a much under-researched area in education. The term non-cognitive is, of course, a catch-all which covers what are sometimes called social and emotional skills, emotional literacy, self-efficacy, etc. The term *affective*, meaning to do with the emotions, is also often used. But in an education system which is principally focussed on academic achievement, the emotional is often relegated to a level of secondary consideration. In fact, those children who display disruptive behaviours, often as a result of poor family relationships, experience of bullying, or a sense of failure, can also be the victims of conscious or unconscious bias from teachers, keen for their pupils to achieve the outcomes that have been set. There is also a growing expectation for schools to tackle the problems arising from social media - whether that be cyberbullying, exposure to extremism and radicalisation, or grooming and potential sexual exploitation. The difficulty for children nowadays to quite literally turn off, and the relentlessly addictive quality of social media, has seemingly led to a rise in issues related to social isolation, low self-esteem, and poor mental health.

Philosophy for Children, like Stenhouse's Humanities Curriculum Project discussed in Chapter 6, gives an opportunity for children to talk about such issues in a safe space which can help to dispel myths and demystify sensitive issues. Children encounter new ideas and learn to share views with others, to agree and to disagree. The permission to do so in a classroom setting, and respectfully, and the words themselves - I agree and I disagree - are perhaps the single biggest non-cognitive benefit that this approach brings. Permission to voice your opinions and to state formally what you think using these discourse norms - rather than an informal 'you're right' or confrontational 'no, that's rubbish' - is like opening a door to another world. Suddenly, it's possible to realise that you can disagree with an idea without needing to show animosity towards the person who expresses it. This opportunity to engage with each other, brought about through talk - to begin to understand each other's personalities, values, beliefs, and biases (even if at an early age they are merely parroted) - is possibly the greatest gift of this kind of classroom talk. Children will then develop sensitivity to each other, a prerequisite for social development. These are the foundations for empathy.

Studies of Philosophy for Children have also shown many non-cognitive benefits such as improved self-esteem, participation, motivation to learn – especially amongst disadvantaged children (e.g., Colom et al., 2014; Siddiqui, Gorard and See, 2019; Trickey and Topping, 2007). Teachers' own qualitative feedback often reports improved listening skills, ability to resolve conflict independently, willingness to listen to different opinions, improved reasoning skills, ability to research and consider issues and concepts in new and original ways, and understanding that there isn't always a right (or single) answer to a question (e.g. Siddiqui, Gorard and See, 2019; Gurton, 2022). Such views are often corroborated by students themselves, reporting statements such as 'I like to hear people's opinions and problems' and 'we can say our own opinions on what we think, and the teacher helps us build on each other's opinions. And after school, I go home and speak to my parents about the things we done in P4C' (Siddiqui, Gorard and See, 2019, p. 158), as well as such negative comments as 'I don't really like talking so I get bored when other people talk,' 'I don't like sharing my ideas in case others disagree,' and 'it is boring things to talk about, and we sometimes say personal things' (ibid, p. 158).

The combination of an approach which feeds cognitive and affective development together in a holistic fashion in pupils, developing intellectual and emotional confidence, creates the conditions for what Brighouse termed 'flourishing' (2008). Schools are, after all, places where we should be laying the foundations for fulfilment in life, much of which is gained through cooperation as well as competition. Developing self-esteem, enjoyment of the company of others, and learning how to contribute in society are attitudes of lifelong relevance. The opportunity for children from different social, ethnic, and religious backgrounds to cultivate empathy, respect for others, and learn appropriate behaviour is at least as important as a focus on individual attainment in its own right, and this should be reflected in school curricula. Part II of the book demonstrates this approach in action in a school. A concept curriculum underpinned by a pedagogy encouraging enquiry enables children from diverse backgrounds to bring their life experiences to bear on their learning.

References

Brighouse, H. (2008) Education for a flourishing life. *Yearbook for the National Society of Education*, 107(1), pp. 58–71.

Colom, R., Moriyon, F., Magro, C. and Morilla, E. (2014) The long-term impact of philosophy for children: A longitudinal study (preliminary results). *Analytic Teaching and Philosophical Praxis*, 35(1), pp. 50–56.

Dickens, C. (1989) *Hard Times (The World's Classics)*. Oxford: Oxford University Press.

Gorard, S., Siddiqui, N. and See, B.H. (2015) *Philosophy for Children: Evaluation Report and Executive Summary*. Durham: Education Endowment Foundation.

Gurton, P. (2022) *Teacher Talk and Pupil Talk: A Case Study of a Thinking Skills Approach to Learning in an English Primary Academy*. University of Wolverhampton. http://hdl.handle.net/2436/625068.

Hakkarainen, K. and Sintonen, M. (2002) Interrogative model of inquiry and computer supported collaborative learning. *Science and Education*, 11(1), pp. 199–220.

Lipman, M., Sharp, A.M. and Oscanyan, F.S. (1980) *Philosophy in the Classroom*. Philadelphia, PA: Temple University Press.

Scardamalia, M. and Bereiter, C. (1992) Text-based and knowledge-based questioning by children. *Cognition and Instruction*, 9(3), pp. 177–199.

Siddiqui, N., Gorard, S. and See, B.H. (2019) Can programmes like philosophy for children help schools look beyond academic attainment? *Educational Review*, 71(2), pp. 146–165.

Stenhouse, L. (1975) *An Introduction to Curriculum Research and Development*. London: Heinemann.

Trickey, S. and Topping, K.J. (2007) Collaborative philosophical enquiry for school children: Participant evaluation at 11 years. *Thinking: The Journal of Philosophy for Children*, 18(3), pp. 23–34.

Watkins, C. (2005) Classrooms as learning communities: A review of research. *London Review of Education*, 3(1), 47–64.

PART II

What is possible when you engage your students in dialogue

8 Establishing first principles

Aims, meaning, and purpose in education

Every school faces the same questions:

- What do we want our students to be able to know and do?
- How are we going to go about it?

But no school is an island. Each school exists in a social context. So, there are two more questions that need to be considered when fashioning responses to the first two:

- What is particular to our school in its social, cultural, religious, ethnic, linguistic, and environmental context?
- What current issues are there in the country and the world which are significant factors in the lives of these children?

Local considerations are of vital importance to take into account. But in a world where children are increasingly made aware of global issues such as climate change and species extinction; where they may arrive at school one day shocked and perturbed by a piece of news like a terrorist attack that they come into contact through the media; and where they are vulnerable to manipulation, cyberbullying, and various forms of coercion or persuasion via social media, schools need to devise ways of responding. Indeed, it may be that a national or international issue is of relevance to the school community.

Your school will doubtless have a statement of its vision for the children. You may as an individual be committed to seeing social and environmental change. But to what extent are you able to realise it within your classroom and your school? Schools have policies on E-safety and safeguarding and incorporate these into the curriculum. But the pressure of an exam-focussed education system seriously impacts teachers' abilities to address some of these issues holistically. So, too, do their own past experiences and personal and professional beliefs. Rather than review their curriculum and approach to teaching, schools are increasingly adding lessons to address pressing social concerns such as poor mental health and poverty. Lessons in mindfulness and wellbeing have become commonplace.

But is this the right approach to be taking? Or is it time for more fundamental changes to curriculum and pedagogy which enable students to explore their identity and their thoughts and feelings about social issues within the framework of everyday learning? This way, we treat the cause, not the symptoms, of a serious sense of disempowerment which is a contributory

DOI: 10.4324/9781003451044-11

factor to alienation and anxiety. Chapters in the first half of this book outlined the basis of a pedagogy which places talk at the forefront of education, with a curriculum shaped by enquiry and informed by an understanding of the role language plays in transforming experience through concept-formation. But to put this into practice, to be able to answer the questions at the beginning of this chapter, a school and its teachers need to have a clear idea of what their values are and the aims and purposes of the education they offer.

REFLECTION POINT

Can you think of a time when a pupil raised a sensitive issue? How did you respond? How would you like to approach these issues?

Figure 8.1

Philosophers on education

Education is at the heart of what it means to be human, so it has been an important consideration for many philosophers throughout history. Here are some of their ideas along with the titles of their works:

- **Plato** (428-424 BCE) differentiated between education suitable for guardians of the state and for the rulers (who should engage strongly with philosophy). His metaphor of education as 'turning the soul towards the light' has been very influential throughout history (consider the words *enlightenment* and *illumination*, for example, as metaphors for learning). This was coupled with a view of education as knowledge of 'the good.' These ideas were expounded in *The Republic*.
- **Locke** (1632-1704) believed a child's mind was a 'tabula rasa' or clean slate. This sounds similar to Dickens' satirical metaphor of education being about filling children full of facts, like pitchers. But Locke actually believed that children were rational beings. His ideas, which focussed on a view that education was the pursuit of virtue and reason, can be found in *Some Thoughts Concerning Education*.
- **Rousseau** (1712-1778), who wrote *Emile, or On Education*, believed man was born good and degenerated thereafter. He drew attention to what we nowadays term the 'nature-nurture' debate but with a difference. The experience of education, either through enculturation or how we were taught to develop our own potential, could be positive or negative. We could lose some of our essential goodness in the process.

- **Kant** (1724-1804) was a pillar of the Enlightenment, and his motto 'Sapere aude!' - 'Dare to think!' - drew attention to a belief in the capacity of the individual to reason. He saw 'free thinking' as the aim of man's existence. Indeed, he believed that man only became properly human through education. And by human, he meant rational and autonomous - capable of exercising individual and intentional agency. He expressed these ideas in *On Education*.

Despite obvious differences, one of the most notable similarities between these philosophers is the view that education should be focussed on the pursuit of reason and virtue - the 'good.' It is perhaps not surprising that philosophers would prioritise the use of reason, but Kant's addition of free thinking and individual agency is particularly resonant with the aims advocated in this book and with what Biesta calls 'Subjectification' (2015), as outlined later in the chapter.

Educational thinkers

In addition to the writings of these philosophers on what education should aim to achieve, many influential thinkers over the centuries have set up schools and written about how to go about it.

- **Pestalozzi** (1746-1827) believed all children had an equal right to education and that children's faculties ought to be developed in accordance with nature. He recommended the use of familiar and everyday items in teaching, such as apples for counting. He believed that sensory experience and observation were fundamental to learning and was the originator of the idea of learning by doing, taken up by Froebel (see what follows). He and his wife took on and educated children from poor social backgrounds. Today, there are a number of Pestalozzi villages internationally which educate children. He wrote about his thinking in *How Gertrude Teaches Her Children*.
- **Froebel** (1782-1852) stressed the importance of play to learning, fostering enjoyment and wellbeing. He invented the idea of the kindergarten - a child's garden - and was the first to articulate a comprehensive philosophy of education. He stressed the importance of parents in a child's education and the inter-connectedness of life, beauty, and knowledge. His most famous text is *The Education of Man*.
- **The McMillan sisters** had a strong focus on the importance of health, including plenty of outdoor experiences, fresh air, and healthy food. Margaret (1860-1931) and her sister Rachel McMillan (1859-1917) had strong religious and socialist beliefs. They believed that children needed opportunities to run free in the outdoors and explore the natural world. The importance of space and a mission to face the problems of the lives of the poor set the McMillan sisters apart. Margaret McMillan wrote *The Nursery School*.
- **Steiner** (1861-1925) was interested in Spirituality and founded a new religious movement called Anthroposophy. His method (the Steiner-Waldorf) involves a cross-curricular approach to learning at the child's pace with a focus on developing the faculties of feeling and willing. The learning environment is important, as is rhythm and the spoken word, with stories being told rather than read. Steiner believed that many children became demotivated by too much formal learning at a young age. Steiner schools encourage the development of imagination, and reading is not taught until age seven. His most famous work on education is *The Education of the Child*.

- **Montessori** (1870-1952) was the first woman to graduate in Medicine in Italy in 1896. She took a special interest in children who were developmentally delayed and who had special needs. From this, she developed a theory that children needed concrete experiences and materials to understand abstract principles. Her first school, the Casa dei Bambini, was built in a slum district of Rome and designed to get children off the streets as part of a regeneration project. The teachers were told to observe children playing and to not intervene. The Montessori method became so well-known and effective that it formed part of the state education system and was adopted as such in Holland, where she moved later in life. Maria Montessori wrote *The Montessori Method*.
- **A. S. Neill** (1883-1973), like Rousseau, felt that children were innately good. To be happy in life, they needed to be free to follow their own interests. As a school master trained in the harsh discipline of Scottish schools, he rebelled and was strongly critical of corporal punishment. He established his progressive school Summerhill in 1924, where lessons were optional and there was a school council in which pupils and teachers played an equal role. He was critical of what he saw as excessive 'book learning' and felt that children needed emotional education to keep up with their developmental needs. Neill's most famous book is *Summerhill*.

As with the writings of the philosophers, these educational thinkers have some differences, but there are striking similarities in much of their thinking. The focus on play, learning through doing, the development of the senses alongside the intellect – and the departure from formal 'rote' learning which had dominated education for centuries – were all influential in theories of child development which took root in the twentieth century. We can also see a growing commitment to improving social conditions in education and health. Unfortunately, with the advent of mass schooling, some of the old practices of learning by rote were retained and, despite many welcome changes which have to some extent mitigated this approach, we live with the inheritance of the 'industrial model' to this day with many education systems still fixed on using formal methods to teach at a young age. Prescriptive and narrow curriculums, enforced by punitive inspection regimes, have also had a negative effect on the education sector. Sadly, many children are still turned off education, leading them to feel as if they have failed.

So, what is education anyway?

So much for what education should achieve, or how to go about it, but what actually *is* education? The educational philosopher Richard Peters – one of the architects of the degree-level qualifications for teachers in the second half of the twentieth century – sought to bring clarity to the idea of education as a discipline, drawing a distinction between it and concepts such as 'training,' 'socialisation,' and 'therapy' (Carr, 2010). In *Ethics and Education* (1966), he identified three criteria that the process of education must satisfy. It should:

- consist of something being transmitted that is worthwhile in its own right, regardless of its instrumental value

- include some knowing and understanding by the learner with some 'cognitive element' or active awareness of its links to other knowledge and peoples' lives
- not be passed on by procedures like indoctrination that deprive learners of any free will or voluntariness

Peters' criteria provide a useful starting point for us to consider what it is we are about when teaching and what aims and purposes a school should be focussed on. Some may argue that Peters' definitions are no more than value judgements. Who, after all, is to decide what is worthwhile? What is worthwhile to one person may well not be to another. But then, education is a process of making value judgements.

The instrumentalist view is that education should foster economic potential. Education is about providing skills for life, foremost amongst which are those that provide earning potential and allow the individual to enjoy a high standard of living. An alternative view, sometimes called a growth model, maintains that education is important for its own sake and for developing the mind. Peters covers both of these in his first criterion. In fact, he seems to attach greater importance to 'learning for its own sake.'

Central to education is knowledge. Peters' contention is that knowledge that is passed on or 'transmitted,' to use his term, must be able to be activated to be relevant to the individual's life. It must have connections to other areas of knowledge and to the world. This is not something we always see in practice in the classroom. Peters' emphasis on the importance of making cognitive connections, drawing on students' life experience, harks back to John Dewey's belief in the basis of all meaningful education in experience and our contention that the teacher's role is to support children in making the links between their experience and learning, often with a linguistic element (Vygotsky's 'everyday' and 'scientific' language).

And what of this 'passing on,' what we might describe as teaching? It is interesting that Peters defines teaching by implication by what it is not - it is not indoctrination. Yet we know that young children uncritically take on beliefs at an early age. This is a consequence of maturity, but it results in a form of conditioning. The uncritical acquisition of beliefs takes place in all societies, democratic and authoritarian; it is beyond the child's control. John Stuart Mill, writing in the nineteenth century, held that it was legitimate for adults to abridge the liberty of children because children are 'not capable of free and equal discussion' (1910, p. 73). Indeed, Peters himself, elsewhere, states 'the brute facts of child development reveal that at the most formative years of a child's development he (sic) is incapable of [a rational] form of life' (1966, p. 271). Wittgenstein (1969) believed that we communicate cultural values through a sort of training which he called *Weltbild* - meaning world-picture. It is what Stenhouse describes as Initiation - one of the four processes of education which cannot be taught by using a behavioural objectives model but is often absorbed by enculturation, or what some call the hidden curriculum. Biesta (2015) calls this aspect of education Socialisation, as we will see later. Some even argue that strategic structures of communication in teaching are inherently indoctrinatory because children are unable to take a rational position on validity claims (e.g., Young, 1992, p. 53). According to this view, teaching *is* indoctrination.

But if we take the view that education should be about students learning to think for themselves, not just receiving valuable information, and that a central element of thinking is becoming critically reflective, a key question for education must be how can children be taught to become critically reflective? Michaels O'Connor and Resnick (2007) observe that many in education still hold to the view that knowledge is foundational, and so before students can reason coherently, they must acquire a great deal of factual information in any given domain. *The Core Content Framework*, England's curriculum for teacher training, is particularly categorical, holding that, 'In order for pupils to think critically, they must have a secure understanding of knowledge within the subject area they are being asked to think critically about' (DfE, 2019, p. 13). It does not refer to any evidence base for this statement. But surely this is much too simplistic? There are areas of knowledge that cannot be reasoned about until understood, at least in part. But it is also true that engaging with areas of knowledge in a critically reflective way builds self-efficacy, develops understanding, and is a way of practising skills – just like regular practise of an instrument or a sport usually makes you better at it. And you don't need to know music theory perfectly before becoming a proficient player of an instrument. So it is with thinking. Your knowledge base is actually improved by the process of critical thinking – both the declarative or factual 'knowledge that' and the procedural 'knowledge how' – in this case, how to articulate your understanding.

In the introduction to the book, we saw 10 and 11 year olds reasoning about how much control they have over different aspects of their lives. In Part I, Chapter 3, we saw 'Miss W' encouraging her 15 and 16 year olds to draw upon their life experiences to help them empathise with the situation unfolding in the William Trevor book they were studying. And in Part I, Chapter 4, we saw a teacher support and extend her 9 and 10 year olds' scientific reasoning skills. All of these were examples of teachers developing their class's competence and confidence in using talk to articulate their thinking. The second part of the book contains many more examples of classroom talk in which pupils reason together. In each case, the teacher is instrumental in developing students' critical reflections through the use of dialogue. It is precisely through critical engagement, listening to each other and witnessing their peers reasoning, that these children have, to use a phrase beloved of Ofsted, 'made progress in their learning.'

REFLECTION POINT

What does education mean to you?

Figure 8.2

Aims and purposes

In recent years, there has been a notable absence of discussion about what constitutes *good* education. This has been attributed by many to the change in educational language, as discussed in Part I, Chapter 6. Kelly, for example, suggested a shift in the intellectual categories with which we are able to debate and plan educational provision (1995). Biesta identifies this change as what he calls the 'learnification' of education: the transformation of an educational vocabulary into a language of learning (2010). The shift has come about as a new set of metaphors – different ways of describing and evaluating educational activities – repositions the relationship between teacher and learner (Pring, 2004). The teacher has become 'deliverer,' the student being 'client' or 'stakeholder,' and education a series of 'measurable outcomes.' This approach, with its attention to effectiveness and efficiency, focusses on the process of learning at the expense of content and direction, prioritising the individual at the expense of the community. Biesta sums it up, posing the question '[Are we] valuing what we measure or measuring what we value?' (2010, p. 12).

In spite of this absence of discussion, some have devoted time and effort to attempts at defining aims and purpose in education. Two of the writers cited earlier have contributed significantly to our understanding of what we are about when we educate. In carefully tracing the recent history of education in England and Wales since the advent of mass schooling, Richard Pring (2022, p. 152) has recently identified eight 'emerging aims,' which he sees as interrelated. These are:

1) Respecting a common humanity
2) Extending access to the cultural inheritance
3) Promoting practical intelligence and competence
4) Promoting ethical and social awareness and deliberation
5) Preparing for citizenship
6) Preparing for employment
7) Appreciating religious understanding
8) Wider personal development

Pring's aims are drawn from the social and economic changes in society and a developing idea of what it means to be educated. They stress the importance of an education which values the arts and practical skills as well as academic achievements, widening the curriculum to include a broader definition of what constitutes knowledge. He celebrates widening participation and emancipation alongside a recognition of the value of the arts in education and the concept of culture embracing different forms of expression. He draws on influential writers and social reformers. He cites Ruskin, Morris, Arnold, Hirst, notable union leaders such as Thomas Mann, who led the miners and dockers' strikes in the late nineteenth century – as well as more recent writers on craft and working with your hands, such as Crawford (2009) and Sennett (2008). At the heart of these aims is the plea for an education that has as a core value developing a person who is informed, capable, appreciative, tolerant, inclusive, and respectful – of themselves and others. The person thus educated should be conscious of his or her situation and of the possibility of making moral decisions and choices. It is communitarian, seeing individual educated people within a community to which they contribute. The aims of education, according to Pring, using a term oft-used by others and summarised by Kristjanson (2020), are to bring about 'human flourishing.'

Another educational philosopher, Gert Biesta, has over the last two decades made a significant contribution to philosophy of education in three major works which he himself identifies as a trilogy, which together constitute a theory of education (*Beyond Learning: Democratic Education for a Human Future*, 2006; *Education in an Age of Measurement: Ethics, Politics and Democracy*, 2010; and *The Beautiful Risk of Education*, 2013). In these works, he explores ideas about what education is for, using new and arresting vocabulary to explore the ways we come into the world. The word 'weakness,' for example, becomes not something to overcome but 'the very 'dimension' that makes educational processes and practices educational' (2013, p. x). In his final publication in the trilogy, *The Beautiful Risk of Education*, he uses the word 'risk' to signify that engagement in education by both teachers and those being educated should always carry a risk. In a statement that bears comparison with Paulo Freire's concept of education as critical consciousness (1974), he argues that if the risk disappears, education itself disappears, replaced by a process of social reproduction '[which] is not desirable if we are genuinely interested in education as a process that has an interest in the coming into the world of free subjects, not in the production of docile objects' (2013, p. 140).

In a first step to frame discussion about educational aims and ends, Biesta outlines what he sees as the three different domains of educational purpose:

1) **Qualification** - providing children, young people, and adults with the knowledge, skills, and understandings and often also with the dispositions and forms of judgement that allow them to do something, ranging from the very specific (such as in the case of vocational or professional education) to the much more general (as in education preparing children and young people for life in highly complex societies).

2) **Socialisation** - a process of becoming initiated into and part of existing social, cultural, political, professional, or religious communities, practices, and traditions. This can be overt and stated as an explicit aim, as occurs with the transmission of particular norms and values in line with particular cultural or religious traditions, but often occurs as a function of the way subjects are taught or practices take place. This has led to the term 'the hidden curriculum' to define what is communicated through culture and practice, although it may not be 'on the curriculum.'

3) **Subjectification** (sometimes called individuation) - the aspect of education which enables the individual to become the subject of action of responsibility rather than remaining an object of the demands and directions of others. This may be seen as the opposite of socialisation because it is characterised by an orientation towards the process of self-determination and freedom. It has been argued by those belonging to different traditions in educational philosophy (analytical and critical) that any education worthy of its name should always contribute to processes of subjectification, enabling students to become more autonomous and independent in their thinking and acting.

Adapted from Biesta (2015, pp. 73-74)

   This outline framework is an acknowledgment that what makes *good* education is what he calls a composite question combining these three dimensions. They are not separate. Indeed, the different functions can work in synergy or conflict. But they definitely have an impact on each other. Indeed, Biesta encourages us to visualise these different aspects of what makes for a good education as three overlapping areas, a Venn diagram, and gives the following example of interaction:

> Think for example of how an emphasis on exam results might drive up achievement in the domain of qualification but might at the same time 'teach' students that competition is, at the end of the day, preferable over cooperation (a 'message' in the domain of socialisation) and may also contribute to a more self-centred rather than other-centred kind of personality (an 'impact' in the domain of subjectification).

(2015, p. 75)

In Part I, Chapter 6, we encountered a different formulation - Stenhouse's definitions of four processes of education which he termed 'training,' 'instruction,' 'initiation,' and 'induction.' Stenhouse's definition of what he calls 'initiation' is very similar to what Biesta terms 'socialisation,' although he observes that it would be hard to achieve an exact congruence between a school's aims in this area and what a pupil actually experiences, as the influence of community and peer group will also have a significant effect. While it is clear that Stenhouse is strongly in favour of the development of individual consciousness and criticality consistent with Biesta's Subjectification function, he sees this development occurring within what he describes as 'induction,' which falls within both the Qualification and Subjectification domains, according to Biesta. Seeing men (sic) as 'relatively predictable, limited and uncreative,' Stenhouse views the purpose of education as 'to make us freer and more creative' (1975, p. 82). He sees this coming about by induction into the knowledge of culture as what he calls 'a thinking system.' He draws a careful distinction between knowledge and information, the characteristic of knowledge being the fact that you can think with it. Indeed, he goes further, suggesting that the nature of knowledge (as distinct from information) is 'that it is a structure to sustain creative thought and provide frameworks for judgement' (1975, p. 82).

Applying aims and purposes in school

Neither Pring's aims nor Biesta's domains of purpose are prescriptive. Neither tells us how to go about teaching or what to include in the curriculum. And each approach acknowledges the inter-relationship between different areas - whether they be aims in Pring's approach or purposes in Biesta's. But both allow us to reconsider the questions posed at the start of the chapter concerning what a school wants its students to know and do and how to go about it. Of course, certain aspects of Biesta's Qualification function - notably statutory aspects of curriculum - are non-negotiable; the school has to teach a set of subjects by law, and students are entered for exams. This forms part of the answer to the first question, as to what we want students to be able to know and do, but only part. Schools are free to add what they wish over and above the statutory requirements. But what approach the school takes to the

Socialisation and Subjectification functions will greatly influence how they go about their teaching and relationships with the pupils.

In Pring's aims, however, we have some expressions of what curriculum should cover in general terms and some insight into how he sees these aims transferring into practice. While addressing the aim of 'promoting ethical and social awareness and deliberation,' for example, he cites an unnamed primary school where the class had learnt 'rules' for open discussion – sounding very much like the ground rules used in Philosophy for Children, Dialogic Teaching, or Thinking Together. They engage in open discussion, only one person speaking at a time, listening carefully to what each other has said, and saying nothing hurtful to any individual. This ethos of interpersonal support, which he says extends to associations of staff and relations with parents who have their own coffee area within the school, derives from an approach 'which puts the virtue of caring at the centre of its educational programme' (2022, p. 157).

In the chapters that follow, we explore one school's approach to the questions of aims and purpose in light of the discussion in this chapter and the implications this has for curriculum and teaching.

References

Biesta, G.J.J. (2006) *Beyond Learning: Democratic Education for a Human Future*. London: Routledge.

Biesta, G.J.J. (2010) *Good Education in and Age of Measurement: Ethics, Politics, Democracy*. London: Paradigm Publishers.

Biesta, G.J.J. (2013) *The Beautiful Risk of Education*. London: Routledge.

Biesta, G.J.J. (2015) Thinking philosophically about education; thinking educationally about philosophy. In Matheson, C. and Matheson, D. (eds.) *Educational Issues in the Learning Age*, 4th edn. London and New York: Continuum, pp. 64–82.

Carr, D. (2010) The philosophy of education and educational theory. In Bailey, R., Barrow, R., Carr, D. and McCarthy, C. (eds.) *The Sage Handbook of Philosophy of Education*. London: Sage, pp. 37–54.

Crawford, M. (2009) *The Case for Working with Your Hands*. London: Viking (The Penguin Group).

Department for Education (DfE) (2019) *Initial Teacher Training (ITT) Core Content Framework*. Available at: https://www.gov.uk/government/publications/initial-teacher-training-itt-core-content-framework (Accessed: 12 April 2024).

Freire, P. (1974) *Education for Critical Consciousness*. London: Bloomsbury.

Kelly, A.V. (1995) *Education and Democracy: Principles and Practices*. London: Paul Chapman Publishing Ltd.

Kristjanson, K. (2020) *Flourishing as the Aim of Education – A Neo-Aristotelian View*. London: Routledge.

Michaels, S., O'Connor, C. and Resnick, L. (2007) Deliberative discourse idealized and realized: Accountable talk in the classroom and civic life. *Studies in the Philosophy of Education*, 27, pp. 283-297.

Mill, J.S. (1910) *On Liberty*. London: Dent.

Peters, R.S. (1966) *Ethics and Education*. London: Allen and Unwin.

Pring, R. (2004) *Philosophy of Educational Research*, 2nd edn. London: Continuum.

Pring, R. (2022) *Education, Social Reform and Philosophical Development: Evidence form the Past, Principles for the Future*. London: Routledge.

Sennett, R. (2008) *The Craftman*. London: Penguin.

Stenhouse, L. (1975) *An Introduction to Curriculum Research and Development*. London: Heinemann.

Wittgenstein, L. (1969) *On Certainty*. New York: Harper and Row.

Young, R. (1992) *Critical Theory and Classroom Talk*. Clevedon: Multilingual Matters.

9 Bringing it together

Developing a concept curriculum

This chapter begins to explore one school's response to questions raised in the previous chapter as to the aims and purposes of education. It outlines an approach to curriculum and classroom practice which is then explored in more detail in subsequent chapters.

The school

The school is a larger than average primary with around 465 children on roll. It is situated close to the centre of a northern English city, in the second most-deprived ward and serves a diverse community. It is a Christian faith school, but not all pupils are from a Christian background. Many come from the local community and are Muslim. Compared to the national average, a higher proportion of pupils are from minority ethnic groups and speak English as an additional language. There is also a higher-than-average number of children eligible for support through the pupil premium and with special educational needs and/or disabilities. It is a two-form entry school, and in its two most recent inspections (2017 and 2022), it has achieved the highest Ofsted rating (Outstanding).

The school has been on a journey of discovery in recent years. This stemmed originally from a need to improve test results, as the children were falling below the national average. But instead of narrowing the curriculum and increasing their focus on English and Maths, the staff reflected on what they wanted their students to be able to do for themselves and how they wanted them to be. The deputy head teacher articulates their aims as 'giving more ownership of learning . . . and responsibility back to the children.' He talks of children who are now 'efficient learners who have a self-dialogue and agency' and who can 'affect the context of learning . . . to the point where they feel like they are in almost complete control of the projects in some cases . . . not that they actually are. But they feel they are and that's important' (Gurton, 2022).

But it wasn't always like this. The quest to create an approach to empower the children, improving their independence and creativity, took them several years. The school adopted Philosophy for Children (P4C) and took several different approaches to curriculum planning. The initial focus on cross-curricular links to improve creativity and raise expectations in terms of 'quality outcomes' meant teachers were designing learning creatively. However, on reflection, they believed that this was not what they wanted for the children, even though results were improving. The deputy states, 'it was our creative process and it was being delivered at the children. . . . They were passive recipients, and they enjoyed it and were engaged, which is no bad thing, but it was at odds with having creative thinking at the centre of the curriculum.'

DOI: 10.4324/9781003451044-12

Again and again, this point is reinforced. 'We want children to be able to think' (ibid, p. 72), he says, 'which is not a given, when you look at the national curriculum document.'

Things changed when the school finally ditched this approach and based their curriculum around areas identified in a document originally designed for those in secondary education – the *Personal Learning and Thinking Skills Framework* (QCA, 2007). This document aims to develop dispositions and attributes such as 'Creativity,' 'Self-reflection,' and 'Collaboration.' The school's focus switched from teachers planning creatively to encouraging children (and teachers) to make critical connections in their learning. The final decision was to take an approach which was concept-led, reinforced by the pedagogy of P4C. It derived from a belief that it was important for pupils from this community to develop their understanding of social concepts such as *justice, equality,* and *rights*. The deputy head teacher explains that they thought, 'There were always a couple of subjects that were squeezed out, that didn't fit into the topic-based approach (which we had adopted previously) and these were PSHE and RE. . . . And I think that the kind of concepts you can get to through RE and certainly PSHE, it's the stuff that really matters in the world, as opposed to just subjects. You know, there's big things within those two curriculum areas and certainly with the current mental health agenda. I think that actually, if schools are not making certainly PSHE central to their work, they are failing kids, ultimately' (ibid, p. 104).

This final statement, reinforced when seen in context of the practice and beliefs of other teachers in school, articulates a vision of education at odds with current cultural practice. It places a strong emphasis on the domains we saw in the previous chapter described as 'Socialisation' and 'Subjectification' by Biesta (2015) and is consistent with Pring's aims of 'Respecting a common humanity,' 'Promoting ethical social awareness and deliberation,' and 'Preparing for citizenship' (2022).

The choice of approaching curriculum through the prism of important social concepts and the moral tone of the deputy head's words gives a clear message about what the school values. They want their pupils to become the subjects of action and responsibility, independent in their approach to learning, and creatively engaged. This extends this aspect of Biesta's Socialisation into the Subjectification domain, and it is on this axis that the school pivots its curriculum and pedagogy, as we shall see. For to facilitate pupils becoming empowered in this way is not only a curricular choice, but it also necessitates the coming together of a number of approaches previously outlined in this book – respectful classroom relationships; a 'process' curriculum that encourages question-raising; and a dialogic stance amongst teachers, who are open to their pupils and model their fallibility and humanity. Above all, it requires talk: talk that is exploratory, cumulative, and develops reasoning and creativity.

So, what does it look like in practice?

Guiding principles of creating a concept-led curriculum

The National Curriculum (DfE, 2013) can be viewed as a restrictive document, binding teachers to the burden of curriculum content. However, looked at in a different way, it can be used to identify concepts. For example, turning to the second page of the Key Stage 2 History programmes of study and looking at the 'Viking and Anglo-Saxon struggle for the Kingdom of England to the time of Edward the Confessor,' bullet-pointed content readily reveals four concepts: *justice, death, resistance,* and *invasion* (DfE, 2013, p. 191).

Rather than thinking about how these concepts relate specifically to the historical event being outlined, they can be considered historically, geographically, scientifically, religiously, and so on. It is possible to create a curriculum underpinned by concepts which can be drawn from subject areas. Concepts act as the linchpin ensuring that all subjects have a genuine inter-connectedness rather than forced links. Asking questions about the concepts, having discussions about them, and providing space to do this in lessons allow students to draw in their own life experience and prior knowledge and make links between disciplines.

The core principle of creating a concept-led curriculum is to provide learners with the opportunity to develop concept language which encourages independence and bridges the gap between the teacher and the student. In the case study school, each year group focussed on three question-led projects, one planned for the autumn, one for spring, and one for summer. Each project enabled the development of a single Humanities or Arts subject in depth rather than spread across the year. Table 9.1 shows an example of this approach in Year 6.

Table 9.1 Term projects across Year 6

Autumn	Spring	Summer
History	Geography and Design and Technology	Art
Should we accept our place in society?	**Does adversity make us stronger?**	**How can we make our mark?**

The National Curriculum can present an intimidating amount of content. However, a curriculum choice to cover subject content in depth can be achieved when you look at the disciplines through the lens of concepts. The decision for projects to be question-led was a further innovation and taken for several reasons. Planning a unit of work is often dominated by the teacher: they form the connections within and across subjects and ultimately make the final decisions about what the students will learn. Framing a project with an overarching enquiry question provides a starting point and some focus. From the initial question, more questions can be generated by the students which develop into various lines of enquiry. Students can then make their own connections and explore concepts of their choosing, and this promotes genuine creative thinking amongst the learners.

For each project, teachers were provided with an overarching enquiry question and some potential concepts through which the content of multiple subjects could be explored. The subject leaders supported teachers by offering a range of subject-specific stimuli that could expose students to the concepts selected for the project. Teachers were also encouraged to seek out other examples of stimuli. This did not mean a project was restricted to those potential concepts. The route to reach a final outcome was guided by the teacher but developed by the students. Students could bring in concepts throughout the project, many of which reflected their life experiences, and this was actively encouraged. This approach is not about the teacher telling the students what *justice* is, for example, but providing a space for students to think, question, and make up their own minds about it.

At the beginning of the autumn term, the project in Year 6 was 'Should we accept our place in society?' The class explored a range of stimuli: images of historical signage and a news article depicting messaging such as 'Waiting room for coloureds only' and 'First class passengers only' From these stimuli, the students drew out various concepts, such as *respect, power, wealth, cruelty, reality, fairness, difference, acceptance, exclusion, hate, colour,* and *racism*. The concept of *power* was developed into a number of enquiry questions, and the students chose to explore the question 'How much power should everyone get?' This was not a concept mapped out by the teacher but was viable to explore, as the students wanted to question where discrimination stems from with regards to people having 'power' at an individual and institutional level. Figure 9.1 is a transcript of part of the resulting enquiry.

Mary:	Everyone should get equal power, everyone needs to get enough to help others. No one should be better than anyone else.
Ellie:	I agree with Mary. Some may want more because they think they should like it if they have more money.
Heather:	I agree with Mary and Ellie, we all have the right to power. It doesn't matter if you are a king or queen or the police, we all deserve power.
Tom:	I disagree. I think the police save and protect us, the Queen and the government help the poor, so they have more power.
Alex:	He makes a good point, as their job is good and they do good for us. Some people use power to start war and rebel. That's the wrong use of power. We need enough power to survive but not too much to take over.
Mohammed (child facilitator): Who gives you power?	
Evie:	The government gives you it.
Sara:	I agree but also others give us power through voting, they lift us up.
Yusuf:	Where we think we have power . . . we build it ourselves. No one gives us it, and it could be good or bad.
Mohammed (child facilitator): Do you need it?	
Logan:	Yes, some people need it to help others. But others can use it wrong.
Heather:	I agree with Logan. Queen Elizabeth needs it to run England, but some people are dangerous with power.
Eben:	Some countries don't get, erm, what do you call it, freedom. In England, we have a little of power. We voted for the Prime Minister. We have power to use.
Mohammed (child facilitator): Is force linked to power?	
Logan:	If you are a higher rank, force and power become a way you do things.
Teacher:	**Can you give an example?**
Tom:	Hitler uses force linked with power.
Alex:	Hitler used force to get power. Like when the king died, he used force to take his place in power.
Teacher:	**Okay, so this is what I mean by example, and the use of force and power in this example is negative. Can anyone think of a positive force/power link?**
Alex:	Martin Luther King.
Kai:	Winston Churchill.
Alex:	Barack Obama. He was the first black man to become president.

Figure 9.1 Transcript of part of the enquiry from 'How much power should everyone get?'

From this enquiry, we can see that students have begun to think about the concept of *power* from the stimuli provided by the teacher. They are sharing their own experiences and understanding of *power,* referring to institutions such as the monarchy and the government. They are able to listen to each other's thoughts on the concept of *power*: who has it, how much people have, what they use that *power* for. Mohammed is a student facilitator alongside the teacher. He asks questions such as 'Is force linked to *power*?' to develop the use of concept language. The teacher enables the use of the concept of *power* by asking, 'So, what is *power*?

This enquiry demonstrates the role of the teacher as a facilitator. They need to listen carefully for when students try to talk in concepts so they can support the development of the students' concept language. This then leads to the students using concept language throughout their daily learning because the teacher has provided the opportunity to use concepts. Figure 9.2 demonstrates the process in action.

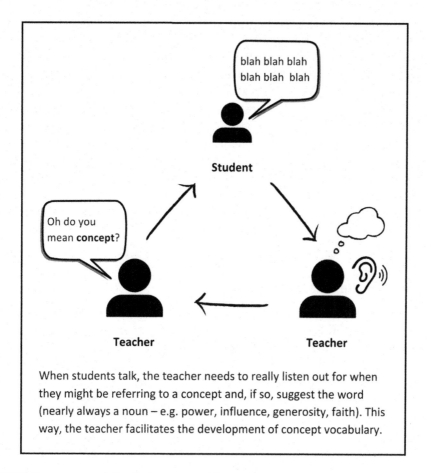

Figure 9.2 The process of developing concept language

The projects would build incrementally based on the stimuli the teacher introduced, but it was essential to allow room to branch off in varying directions based on the concepts that the students show an interest in thinking critically about. For a project to be successful, teachers need to be comfortable with learner agency and pivot throughout the term. As explained in more detail in Chapter 11, being trained in P4C provided teachers with the confidence and skills to implement this dialogic approach to learning.

For this school, a concept-led curriculum was not achieved overnight. It was arrived at over time by teachers thinking about how best to enable children to become independent and how to tap into their natural curiosity and creativity – two aspects which a conventional curriculum tends to squash. The school made some significant choices that supported the implementation of a concept-led curriculum: authentic outcomes, transforming the classroom space, verbal feedback, and peer critique.

Authentic outcomes

Each project was driven towards an authentic outcome, something that students could take ownership of. An authentic outcome does not need to be over-complicated or elaborate. In the next chapter, one project sees a Year 6 class creating a museum exhibition. For this school, this purpose served them well: an underused corridor space was transformed to be reused as a museum every autumn by students – an opportunity for them to make their mark in the school. If you don't have a spare corridor, pop-up exhibitions are an equally authentic option. It is about working out what works well for you and your school. In another example, Figure 9.3, we see Year 4 student costume designs on a moodboard based on various fictional characters: Puck, Maleficent, and the Fairy Godmother. These individual moodboards included design sketches, swatches of materials, and handmade lino print stamps as part of a project called 'Grand Designs.' Authentic outcomes are not only beneficial for the pupils with regards to engagement in learning and pride in their achievement but also in terms of future employment. Entering the world of work is challenging, and to expose young people to real examples of career choices and immersing them in what that work may entail is potentially inspiring. A memorable experience in school drives many of us to our future careers, even if it is only in hindsight that we realise this.

Transforming the classroom space

To stimulate curiosity and encourage the students to ask questions, teachers transformed their physical classroom spaces. This involved removing the traditional tables and chairs and creating flexible spaces of sofas, beanbags, steps, etc. Decoration was also added to create an atmosphere linked to the core subject that was covered during the term. Budget was allocated for this, but it also involved a lot of sharing and passing on items between classes each term to reduce costs and minimise time spent on creation. Many items were made from cardboard, papier-mâché, and plastic bottles. Less is more; you can do a lot with fairy lights and coloured organza!

Primary teachers already spend a lot of time ensuring their classroom space is inviting and engaging. This includes creating and managing display boards. What if the students were actively involved in creating the display boards instead of the teachers? This would free up time for teachers to think creatively about organising the classroom space differently. Providing the students with the agency to add content to displays that is useful to them also supports the teacher in identifying levels of understanding. Enabling students to display their progress throughout a project is more effective than choosing some of their final work

Figure 9.3 A display of costume designs, Year 4

to display. This active involvement provides space to consolidate learning on the students' terms and stimulates discussion amongst the class.

Verbal feedback and peer critique

The flexible use of space for sofas, beanbags, steps, etc., not only contributed to an engaging environment, but it also lent itself to successful verbal feedback and peer critique. As teachers became more dialogic as a result of the pedagogy of P4C, it supported other strategic moves

Figure 9.4 A Year 6 classroom

within the school such as the decision to move away from teachers providing written feedback in books to engage in more purposeful verbal feedback and teaching the students peer critique.

Verbal feedback is effective because it is often given during, or very quickly following, the learning. It offers more opportunity for dialogue between the teacher and students, ensuring that the students understand the feedback, enabling them to respond to it and to action it straight away. Additionally, for the teacher, giving verbal feedback provides an immediate understanding of where the students are, if there are still misconceptions or lack of clarity following the learning or a task. This informs the teacher and enables them to adapt their teaching.

Feedback is vital in teaching; however, over the years, effective marking or feedback has been replaced by disproportionate written feedback that has often been generic. Generic written feedback does not enable students to think critically about where they went wrong. The recommendations of the Education Endowment Foundation (EEF, 2021) focussed on the principles of good feedback, not whether it should be written or verbal. Ultimately, for feedback to be purposeful, it needs to be given at an appropriate time so students can receive, process, and respond to that feedback.

If both teacher and students learn the discourse norms of dialogue, it provides an environment for successful feedback, whether that be written or verbal. As the teacher takes a more dialogic approach to teaching, the exchanges between them and the students become more meaningful. When students are struggling in any lessons, one effective strategy is role reversal: *How can you help me?* If the teacher pretends they do not quite understand and asks the student to assist them in gaining that understanding by talking things through, it can be powerful and effective. Offering the student the opportunity to help the teacher neutralises the imbalance of power. If the correct language is used when giving verbal feedback, it will be non-judgemental and therefore will build students' confidence. This dialogic formative assessment also supports the implementation of peer critique. Peer critique empowers students with the skills to self- and peer- assess. Building in time for students to practise peer critique enables them to identify their own errors and mistakes more readily. Importantly, it contributes to the development of a community of trust amongst students as they learn to give and take feedback from each other, not just the teacher.

A successful concept-led curriculum is not dependent on these other complementary practices outlined earlier; however, these examples from the case study school highlight what is possible. The core principles of creating a concept-led curriculum are to provide learners with the opportunity to develop concept language which encourages independence and bridges the gap between the teacher and the student. The next chapter, Developing agency through talk: a year in Year 6, explores the development of this language in more detail.

References

Biesta, G.J.J. (2015) Thinking philosophically about education; Thinking educationally about philosophy. In Matheson, C. and Matheson, D. (eds.) *Educational Issues in the Learning Age*, 4th edn. London and New York: Continuum, pp. 64-82.

Department for Education (DfE). (2013) *National Curriculum in England. Key Stages 1 and 2 Framework Document*. London: DfE.

Education Endowment Foundation (EEF) (2021) *Teacher Feedback to Improve Pupil Learning*. Available at: https://educationendowmentfoundation.org.uk/education-evidence/guidance-reports/feedback (Accessed: 16 April 2024).

Gurton, P. (2022) *Teacher Talk and Pupil Talk: A Case Study of a Thinking Skills Approach to Learning in an English Primary Academy*. University of Wolverhampton. http://hdl.handle.net/2436/625068.

Pring, R. (2022) *Education, Social Reform and Philosophical Development: Evidence from the Past, Principles for the Future*. London: Routledge.

Qualifications and Curriculum Authority (QCA) (2007) *Personal Learning and Thinking Skills Framework*. Available at: https://webarchive.nationalarchives.gov.uk/ukgwa/20110215111658/http://curriculum.qcda.gov.uk/key-stages-3-and-4/skills/personal-learning-and-thinking-skills/index.aspx (Accessed: 16 April 2024).

10 Developing agency through talk

A year in Year 6

> This chapter is written by Meghan Tipping. Any reference to the first person, I, is a reference to her role as class teacher.

This chapter maps the progress of a Year 6 class across the year as they develop agency and criticality through talk in three question-led projects: 'Should we accept our place in society?' 'Does adversity make you stronger?' and 'How can we make our mark?' Throughout each project, you will see how the various stimuli provide the students with opportunities to be exposed to, develop, and use concept language. The concepts act as threads pulling together the learning in various disciplines to reach an authentic outcome at the end of each term.

To create a space conducive to developing agency through talk, there are several factors to consider. Having high expectations during a project is essential to creating a learning environment where the students want to be proactively involved. At no point did I limit the concepts I thought the students could grapple with. As demonstrated in Figure 10.1, the role of the teacher during the projects is key to the opportunities the students are provided with. It means exposing the students to language they may not have come across before. The teacher has to really listen to what the students are saying to draw out when they may be referring to concepts but not necessarily using concept or abstract vocabulary. It is not a question of didactically teaching vocabulary in a 'now children, today we are going to learn about the word resilience' fashion! Instead, you act as the bridge between what Vygotsky called 'everyday' and 'scientific' or Bernstein called 'vertical' and 'horizontal' language, as we saw in Chapters 2 and 3. Helping your pupils to develop concept vocabulary means they will use it more readily in all conversations. When students ask questions and explore concepts that are meaningful to them, there are more opportunities to raise aspirations.

Creating a space for agency also means planning for opportunities. Planning a unit of work is daunting. Every primary teacher cannot have an in-depth knowledge of all topics they have to teach, such as the Vikings, World War I, World War II, or the Maya, for example, in History. There are so many other subjects to consider. So, in our school, as in many others, subject leaders were incredibly important to the success of projects. Their

DOI: 10.4324/9781003451044-13

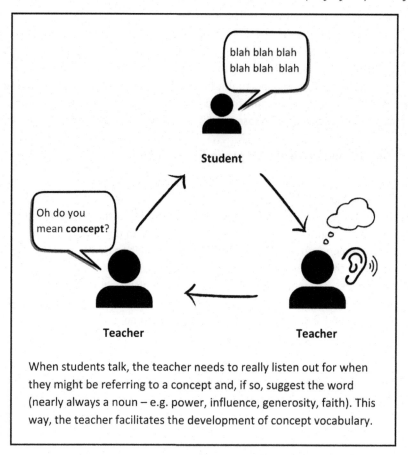

Figure 10.1 The process of developing concept language

expertise provided multiple starting points to develop each project (see Appendix). For example, the Art subject leader was instrumental in offering me examples of artists I had not come across that I could use as stimuli throughout my projects. As History and P4C leader, it was important for me to support all of my colleagues with accurate historical knowledge and concept development.

Although each term 'focussed' on a discipline such as History in autumn, there was a genuine inter-connectedness with other subjects rather than forced links throughout. Using concepts as a starting point meant we were able to interweave the key scripture in religious education, the subject matter in PSHE, and the skills and styles of various aspects of Art. For example, during the autumn term, the key concept of *discrimination* could be referenced in Corinthians 12: 12–17, 21–27, Unity and Diversity in the Body, but the scope of discussion around that concept was led by the students. The geographic location of the passengers on the *Titanic*, the journey, and the fatal event were explored through *class, segregation,* and *rights.* The scientific understanding of icebergs, the design of lifeboats, and the function and reaction of the circulatory system when it encounters freezing temperatures helped the students understand the responses and consequences of the choices that were made and the *fairness* of those choices. The writing in English was also selected to utilise the historical knowledge acquired, enhancing the students' capabilities in the subject. All of this learning fed into and supported how the student teams developed their final outcome of a museum exhibition.

Once a space is established and opportunities are planned for, talk flourishes and students become agents of their own learning: able to influence their own thoughts and behaviour and have confidence in the actions they choose to take.

Autumn – Should we accept our place in society?

The first project of Year 6 immersed students in concepts such as *class, discrimination, justice,* and *rights* within the context of the *Titanic* voyage and the wider Victorian and Edwardian society. A space was cleared in one of the corridors of the school and filled with empty display cabinets and walls primed for curation. Year 6 students would be responsible for the research, planning, and installation of a museum exhibition by the end of the project. Across the autumn term, opportunities were provided to investigate the role of a curator, understand the process of creating an exhibition, gather historical research, analyse and evaluate sources of information, plan and then practise creating objects for the museum space, and to receive feedback before forming the final outcome.

Relevant stimuli

Throughout the project, I chose a range of stimuli to share with the students so they could develop their agency and criticality through talk. Students began the project by offering first thoughts to the overarching enquiry question. As demonstrated in Chapter 9, Figure 9.1, within the enquiry around the concept of *power*, this would identify concepts and lines of enquiry that were meaningful to the students and therefore would indicate possible directions for the project to take. I still needed to find ways to expose them to concepts such as *class* without telling them what it was but offering space to think, question, and make up their own minds. A local artist, Pete Mckee, had exhibited *This Class Works* which aimed to explore and celebrate working-class culture. I used this to introduce the social construct of *class,* and the students created their own portrait in Pete Mckee's signature style. For the projects, I felt it was important to find and bring in stimuli that made a concept relatable. I wanted the projects to be relevant to the students I was working with so they could draw comparisons and make connections more easily. Often, historical events can feel too detached from the here and now due to the difficulty of grasping chronology. Finding current connections through concepts helps to tackle this barrier.

Historical understanding

With some understanding of the concept of *class*, I then introduced the context of Edwardian Britain, exploring the social and economic situation at the time before delving into the historical subject of the *Titanic* voyage. To develop their historical understanding, students explored the various people who were aboard the *Titanic,* building up a picture of the passenger list and the details of individual stories. Some examples were Jack Thayer, a first-class passenger, Eva Hart, a second-class passenger, and Elin Matilda Hakkarainen, a third-class passenger. Rather than just learning the stories, the students actively engaged with them. Over a series of lessons, they explored each passenger's story and selected one to create a portrait of. I chose Chris Ofili's *No Woman, No Cry* as a stimulus to develop pupils' understanding of portraiture. This piece, a portrait of Doreen Lawrence, explores concepts of *discrimination, fairness,* and *justice* as it references the murder of her son Stephen Lawrence in an unprovoked racist attack in London in 1993. The students analysed the art by answering the questions: What can you see? What is it made from? When was it made? What does it make you think about? Why was it created? Ofili's use of collage and layers such as elephant dung were thought provoking. Students thought critically about the consequences of *discrimination* and whether *justice* can be easily established. During the stages of developing their passenger portraits, they chose different mediums and explained why they made those choices. For example, one student chose to collage using newspapers from 1912 that show women and children boarded the lifeboats first (Figure 10.2). They chose this as it symbolised the *injustice* and *unfairness* Jack Thayer experienced because he was not allowed on a lifeboat. They chose to mix blue paint with sand to create a textured wave pattern which symbolised the ocean and what Jack lost that day.

Figure 10.2 A portrait of Jack Thayer

    The project used the microcosm of the *Titanic* to examine the treatment of people in the Edwardian period. Pupils analysed primary and secondary sources to gather information, to understand how historical evidence can be presented and interpreted, and to question the validity of sources. They challenged how some evidence can skew our understanding of the past – for example, the perception of third-class passengers as portrayed in the popular film *Titanic*. Using the sources of information to develop a picture of the past, the students wrote an essay that argued, 'To what extent was the *Titanic* a microcosm of Edwardian society?' This essay incorporated how people were treated in Edwardian Britain and how people were treated on the *RMS Titanic*, as well as some modern perspectives on *class*. Those modern perspectives enabled the students to reflect on their own position, whether they had heard anyone reference the term before. We watched news interviews with individuals impacted by the Grenfell Tower fire and how they referenced *class*. As we talked about Grenfell, parallels with the *Titanic* disaster were drawn out, and this supported the students' understanding of this historical event. We also interviewed our school leaders and university students in school to gather their thoughts on *class*. This then provided the students with the space to reflect: did they see themselves as part of a *class* structure? Could they explain how and why? Figure 10.3 provides an example of a paragraph from this essay, showing how the child is incorporating ideas from the interviews with his own developing thinking about class and society in Britain today. It is insightful and, like many observations made by young children, gives an adult pause for thought and reflection.

In comparison to Edwardian Britain, class has progressed dramatically. I personally have lots of opportunities and rights, and I feel happy. I also feel like my place in society is fine and normal because I think that I am a middle-class person. Even though I do not have the same rights as adults, I still trust my mum to make the right choices for me. One of the university students spoke to us about class, and she said that she thought that she grew up in a working-class family. In modern society, there are quite a few struggles. One of them is if you had no support, or if you have bad influences, you might find work hard. If you want to be successful, then surround yourself with good influences, have self-motivation, and have a strong moral value. Brexit is also a problem because I do not want to leave the European Union. I do not want Brexit to happen because it will be a pain to do a referendum again. I will feel left out because we will not be a part of the European Union. In the future, I hope there will not be discrimination, and everyone will be treated fairly. I want there to be no classes because everyone will have the same amount of money. Money is a hindrance because, nowadays, there are still a lot of poor people and homeless people living on the streets and in various other places. You cannot survive without any money these days, because mostly everything comes with a price. However, if people lend or give you money, you might still have a bit of a chance, depending on how much they give you. Social Media is also a big wall, and you can be sad if someone bullies you. If you want to be successful and have a good life, then you have to be motivated and work hard in your educational life and generally just your own life. You have lots of opportunities and chances if you work hard.

Figure 10.3 Paragraph from an essay *To what extent was the* Titanic *a microcosm of Edwardian society?* written by a Year 6 boy

For myself as a historian, I recognised the importance of bringing in current cultural and news-related links, which are beyond the usual Year 6 diet, if the students were to have a real chance at successfully achieving the skills mapped out in the National Curriculum:

> They should note connections, contrasts and trends over time and develop the appropriate use of historical terms. They should regularly address and sometimes devise historically valid questions about change, cause, similarity and difference, and significance. They should construct informed responses that involve thoughtful selection and organisation of relevant historical information.

> (DfE, 2013, p. 189)

Authentic outcome

Early into the autumn term, a visit to a local museum revealed the authentic outcome of the project. The purpose of the visit was to provide students with the opportunity to identify what makes a good exhibit and to consider how artefacts are chosen and then displayed. Students spoke to the curators to ask questions and establish a 'How to' guide that they could take back to school to prepare them for their own exhibition. Five research areas were given to the class to explore before they voted on the area that interested them the most. From this, the class was grouped into research teams, and these teams would create an exhibit on their chosen theme. We also set an optional homework project that ran the whole term which enabled students to research and create something for the museum exhibit. This offered a layer of additional independence from their group exhibit.

During the term, the students had to plan what would be included in their exhibit following research into their chosen theme, how they planned to create it, the resources they would need, and dividing up the labour amongst the group to achieve the overall goal. The teams had to sketch out their plan and present it to curators invited into the school. Their pitch included what they would create and in which exhibition cabinet they thought it would be best to display it. After the presentation, the teams would receive critique from the curators that they could act upon before working on their exhibit. Students used various art mediums to create replica artefacts, sketched detailed images or portraits, typed text panels, designed interactive elements, and carefully planned how these items would be displayed within their cabinet. The students were given time to share their exhibits with each other at regular intervals so that they were able to talk through the exhibition as a whole when it was opened.

The opening of the museum saw parents and carers in attendance and it would stay in place for a whole year so that the next Year 6 class could use it as inspiration. For the school, it was always important to engage the parent and carer community, especially as many families had English as an additional language. We intended to bridge the gap between school and home life as often as possible. On the opening day, the students showed visitors around the museum and were able to talk about the entirety of it confidently. One year the opening even fell during an Ofsted inspection! The inspector was visibly moved by the whole experience and the children's confidence in explaining the exhibits to him.

This project offered an in-depth approach to the subject of History, and the concepts acted as a thread connecting other subjects. The students acquired strong, substantive, and disciplinary knowledge in history, and the sense of achievement in doing something with that knowledge was empowering. Perhaps even more importantly, with regards to lifelong learning, the students gained a real understanding of what historians actually do.

Spring - Does adversity make you stronger?

The central concepts of the spring project *change, resilience, equality, weakness,* and *strength* enabled students to explore how different communities across the globe were affected by natural and man-made disasters. Although in some instances the authentic outcome of a project was a physical creation like the museum exhibits, in other cases displaying the process could be just as powerful. To develop some understanding of the role of an engineer, the students were tasked this term with designing an earthquake-proof community building. They were not going to physically create a building, but they were going to display their understanding of the design process of creating one on a moodboard. The moodboard was an A3 foam sheet that displayed a collection of technical drawings, designs, and samples of materials the students compiled throughout the project. These were displayed at an 'Engineers Fair,' where other students were able to look at the various design ideas, and the engineers were also invited back to see them.

Relevant stimuli

Stimuli are used to guide the bigger picture of the project to offer opportunities to discuss concepts you want to become part of the students' concept language. I chose some stimuli such as the Christchurch earthquake, the Indonesian Tsunami, and the Sheffield protesters, as I believed they offered opportunities for thought and criticality during this project. However, early on in the term, the children shared their own experiences of where they had encountered *adversity* in their lives or through reading, watching films, or listening to the news. The Lemony Snicket book and film *A Series of Unfortunate Events*, the Manchester Arena bombing, and the Christchurch Mosque shootings featured strongly in their imaginations. Quite often, children are on the receiving end of the same news as adults, but they are not equipped to deal with or understand the events being broadcast or flagged up to them on social or other media platforms. Prejudice is not inherent, but it is something that can become entrenched young if that is the environment you are exposed to. Drawing on current or recent events within the projects was important and provided students with a safe, non-judgemental environment in which to discuss such themes.

Different subjects allowed me to introduce stimuli that we could talk about and provided space for us to think critically about concepts. Students can often have misconceptions about words like *adversity*, so fostering an approach that allows the class, including the teacher, to unpick meanings together is important. As part of Religious Education, I introduced the story of Moses as a stimulus, and we talked about the *adversity* he and his community faced. Through philosophical play, the students unpicked the concepts of *adversity, choice, equality,* and *change*. Philosophical play is a strategy that offers great learner agency. The classroom floor is covered in large sheets of paper, pens, LEGO, string, Play-Doh, anything you can find, and the pupils are given time to talk to each other and the teacher about various concepts. They may choose to simply write or create something. But beware! It is easy for the teacher to slip into judgement if, say, as once happened to me, a boy is creating a Lego aeroplane. What has that got to do with *adversity*? I asked. 'Well, Miss, you know sometimes the pilot doesn't have a choice if the plane is malfunctioning and it is going down, everyone on that plane is facing adversity. The pilot can only do his best to try and save everyone.' The reasoning was immaculate; I had just not seen it. Play is an essential element of human creativity, and can be easily disregarded as a form of reasoning. As outlined in Chapter 7,

P4C stresses the links between creativity and logical thinking; providing opportunities to think creatively paves the way for a lifelong skill of self-agency.

In another session, we discussed the question, 'Should God have sent the plagues?' Rather than simply telling the story, we thought critically about it. A class of 31 stood up and immediately crossed to the side to say 'Yes' to the question, then, following discussion, three changed their mind and moved to 'No.' Throughout the discussion, the children disagreed and questioned each other. They grappled with the gravity of some of the plagues, they asked for clarification, and they justified their decisions. Often, a whole-class exploration of a stimulus, concept, or question would be our starting point. This provided a safety blanket, a safe practice space for students to air their thoughts and develop confidence in what they wanted to say. This was then followed by individual time to respond to hone the student's own agency and criticality. Figure 10.4 shows a student response to the question after the class discussion.

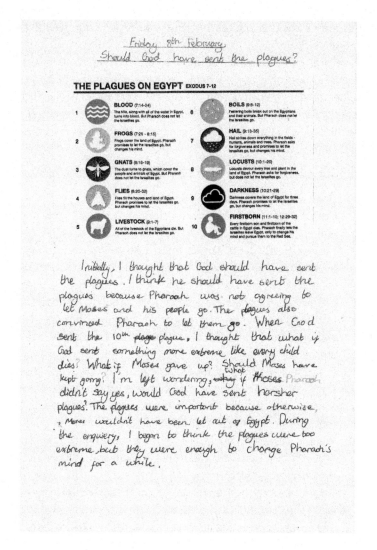

Figure 10.4 Student response following class enquiry on 'Should God have sent the plagues?'

Geographical and technological understanding

As the project developed, the students gained an understanding of countries that were most likely to be affected by natural disasters by analysing data, exploring infographics, and studying maps. They challenged the reliability of the Brandt line, finding out that it was an outdated way of categorising countries based on their wealth. Plotting those countries on a world map enabled them to see how they would be affected by the tectonic plates. The students explored continental drift and created 3D models of the three kinds of plate tectonic boundaries: convergent, divergent, and transform. They learned that tectonic plates were the natural reason that earthquakes occur; however, they also learned that there were some human interventions that can trigger them: fracking, deforestation, and global warming. A news story of three Sheffield protestors being arrested and imprisoned for a peaceful protest about fracking hit the headlines, as it was the first prison sentence of this kind since 1932. This shed light on the controversial nature of fracking and led to discussions around how wealth can contribute to overcoming adversity.

There were several class enquiries during the project. Figure 10.5 is an example of the discussion during one of these. Students activate knowledge of current affairs and geographical understanding gained during the project. Perhaps most significantly, one girl, Logan, feels confident enough to refer to her own immediate experiences of *adversity*. She is, interestingly, the one who rounds off the dialogue, picking up on my introduction of the concepts of *choice* and *control*.

Teacher:	**Does adversity make you stronger?**
Alex:	I think it does because you go through a lot of things and that then makes you stronger.
VJ:	I agree, but it might take a while. Like in the warm up *(game at the beginning of the session)*, after the death of a loved one, you might feel weak first and then get stronger.
Ellie:	I think you will because Indonesia goes through a lot of earthquakes, like even a 9.1 magnitude, and they are still strong. They are, like, used to it now, and they make earthquake-proof buildings so their community is strong as well.
Alex:	I think linking to the attack on 50 Muslims, it was bad, and some people think nothing good came of it, but God wouldn't do anything without reason. Lots of people have converted to Islam, and we have shown so much resilience. The terrorists didn't succeed.
Tom:	What is adversity again? *(misfortune, difficult situation)* What's the group of girls? *(suffragettes)* Yeah, they fought and were stronger, and now women can get jobs.
Logan:	Sometimes it can be like a mask over your head, and like in my church, when we kept getting bricks through the window, we were made to be stronger. The adversity came and made us realise that we needed more security.

Dilkash:	Going back to what Alex said, the attack, like, kind of, backfired because they didn't get rid of them, and now they are stronger.
Teacher:	**Are there any instances where adversity doesn't make you stronger?**
Evie:	Not all adversities make you stronger. It's the way you act upon it.
Farouk:	There are some muscle-wasting diseases that can kill children at a young age, but some are making it past their teens, and this gives hope to others stronger even if it doesn't make them stronger.
Alex:	Stephen Hawking had a disease, but that didn't stop him from being who he wanted to be.
Teacher:	**So, do you have to have hope and choice to overcome adversity?**
VJ:	Yes, you have to choose that you can do it and hope that it will happen.
Tom:	You need both, but it could still go wrong.
Teacher:	**Is that out of our control?**
Tom:	Yes, it can be.
Logan:	You can choose to overcome your adversity, or you can let that adversity overcome you.

Figure 10.5 Extract of a P4C enquiry from the question 'Does adversity make you stronger?'

With this growing knowledge, the class was introduced to engineers, who visited the school and were able to demonstrate what they did for a living. Before this session, we allowed the students to draw an engineer, and very few drew women. It was important for us to dispel the misconception that engineering was a male profession. The students were able to interview the engineers and from this gained an understanding of the importance of design and technology and science in the creation of earthquake-proof buildings. Following the visit, the pupils were grouped into engineering teams and given various examples of earthquake-proof buildings to research to understand what made them effective, such as the importance of foundations. One of the strategies used was 'diagonal struts,' and the class was given the opportunity to investigate the strength of triangles. Using cocktail sticks and gummies, the students were able to plan, make, and test their use of diagonal struts against a brick! It enabled the children to see how triangles can bear weight, therefore providing strength and stability to earthquake-proof buildings. The class also explored gravity and aerodynamics through drawing and annotating a parachute design that would deliver aid to earthquake-stricken countries. The pupils made and tested the parachutes by dropping them from different heights outside, and we replicated the fragility of medical cargo using an egg.

Authentic outcome

To connect students with the purpose of their authentic outcome, I introduced them to the Cardboard Cathedral. The devastating earthquakes in 2011 severely damaged the original cathedral in Christchurch, New Zealand. Following the earthquakes, the Cardboard Cathedral opened. With walls constructed with waves of cardboard, it was one of the very few buildings in the world made substantially of cardboard. I purposefully chose the Cardboard Cathedral as a stimulus because it echoed the concepts of *change* and *resilience*, and the students were not going to create a standard earthquake-proof building; they were going to create a space for a community to gather in times of *adversity*.

Using the Cardboard Cathedral as a case study, the students discussed and gathered different ideas about what they would want their space to look like. They were able to talk about their own experiences of *community* and in some cases their faith building – church, temple, or mosque – was an important space for them. Therefore, their designs incorporated symbols of their faith. For other students, they connected with countries they had researched and decided to create a community building that represented that country's faith.

There were several examples of *adversity* in the news during the time of the project, some of which I raised and some the children had learned about independently. Maybe the most significant and the one the students were most keen to talk about were the Christchurch shootings at a mosque in New Zealand, killing 50 Muslims. They needed to be able to discuss this horrendous example of man-made *adversity* so they could make sense of the difficult news. After discussions, they decided that collective worship was a way they wanted to respond. Regardless of whether the students held a faith or not, collective worship enabled them to sit in groups and talk about something difficult. The steps at our school for collective worship involved deciding how to gather, choosing a piece of scripture from the Bible or some form of word to share, finding a way to invite people to respond, and selecting a final message. Collective worship gave the students a way to channel their thoughts, and in Year 6, they were more than capable of sharing collective worship with the rest of Key Stage 2 in an assembly. Figure 10.6 shows the plan for the collective worship organised by the class.

Summer – How can we make our mark?

The final project designed for Year 6 was 'How can we make our mark?' and I intended to provide the students with the space to reflect on their primary school journey and to create an end-of-year performance that conveyed their experiences. Traditionally, students had performed a Shakespeare play, but although Shakespeare can be used as a great stimulus to talk about word play, I wanted the Year 6 students to leave with something of their own.

Throughout the year, students had become gradually more socially aware. The project on the *Titanic* had introduced them to the concepts of *class, justice,* and *discrimination*, and this had given way in the spring to considering *adversity, resilience,* and *freedom*. Why not give them the opportunity to explore the theme of social justice through the concepts of *identity, dreams, passion,* and *protest* raised by this project? It could be a perfect combination of expressive and performance art. This would be their authentic outcome!

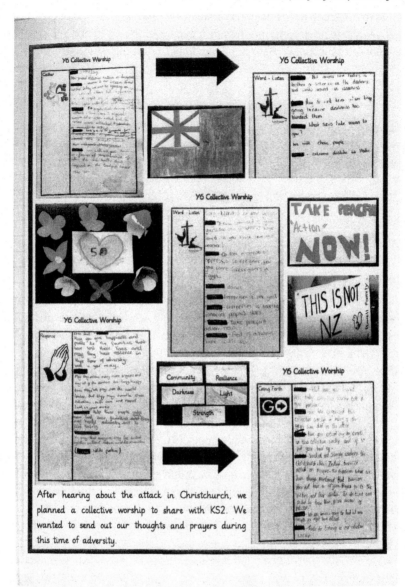

Figure 10.6 Plan for collective worship by Year 6 class

Relevant stimuli and artistic understanding

To explore the key concepts of *protest, passion, dreams, influence,* and *identity,* I introduced the students to a range of local and global artists who created pieces of art as a form of nonviolent protest. From images scattered around the room, the students were given time to select one and to reflect on how it demonstrated protest and what they thought the artist was trying to communicate. In groups and then as a class, we discussed our choices. Figure 10.7 shows one student's response to Banksy's 'I remember when this was all trees':

> I think that this person has made their mark by saying that war and destruction is affecting innocent peoples' lives. I think it means that during childhood, some children like to play outside and climb trees, but now it's been destroyed, their childhood has been ruined. I think the artist is trying to tell us is that war is destroying the world. I think the artist is annoyed and angry and wants to show it.

Figure 10.7 Student response to how artist is 'making their mark'

Jean-Michel Basquiat was the first artist I introduced to the class in detail. We looked at a range of his work and unpicked what we thought were the unique attributes of his style. I chose Basquiat because I believe his work challenges a particular perception of art in schools that I think acts as a major barrier – the idea that the first piece must be perfectly drawn or else you 'can't do art.' I witnessed my students arrive in Year 6, and the vast majority had not grasped that art is a process, one that requires you to be okay with the process being messy. Many students believed that to be 'good' at art meant you should be able to create a masterpiece by the end of the lesson. If not, you were by default 'bad at art.' Basquiat's work, in my opinion, is perfectly imperfect, and the process to achieving a piece that resembled his work seemed immediately more achievable to my class. His final piece does not look like the typical final piece a lot of young people will have been exposed to. We experimented with a range of art mediums creating a self-portrait first on top of an image of the student and then on plain paper. I do not think I have seen so many students respond so positively to creating art. Figure 10.8 shows a student's draft and final self-portraits using Basquiat's style.

We were also studying *evolution*, and Basquiat's work reflected his time in a hospital as a young child and reading *Gray's Anatomy* (1878). We were able to draw parallels between Leonardo da Vinci's drawings and Basquiat's, learning the content of evolution through art. *Evolution* is a subject area that brought up a lot of discussion around who we are, where we come from, and how we come to believe what we do about how the world came to be what it is: our *identity*. I am a huge fan of Oliver Jeffers' work as an artist and storyteller, so when I came across his Dipped Painting Project, I thought it would be a great stimulus to continue exploring the concept of *identity*. After spending time working on self-portraits, we mimicked Oliver Jeffers' dipping ritual and covered the portraits with paint to the point that the students requested. We talked about how it made them feel, what it meant to them to cover some of their face, and why they chose to stop at a particular point. This also led to conversations about *beauty* and *judgement*.

Figure 10.8 Student's draft and final self-portraits in response to Basquiat

Another artist I came to admire through researching the project was Birmingham street artist Mohammed Ali (Aerosol Arabic). I exposed the students to Mohammed's work, and we talked about what he tried to do with his art and the messages he tried to convey. We also used this as an opportunity to talk about the difference between street art and graffiti. I saw how inspired the students were by Mohammed's work, so I chanced my luck by contacting him via social media to explain the purpose of our project and invite him to our school. I was incredibly fortunate that Mohammed had a gap in his schedule, and he was willing to visit our students to inspire and educate them on the power of art in bringing communities together. We also paid for Mohammed's time to offer a tangible experience by creating a backdrop with the students for the end-of-year performance using graffiti art.

On the day of Mohammed's surprise visit, we had asked students to come in painting clothes and explained that the teachers would have a go at some spray painting with them. They were excited, of course, but when they were gathered in the hall to be given instructions for the day, they did not expect Mohammed to walk through the door. Jaws dropped. It was powerful to have a role model come to school to talk about the effectiveness of challenging social issues through art and how art can empower communities – telling their stories. Artists new and old are very willing to connect with young people to share their experiences, teach skills, and inspire budding artists. These authentic experiences are often very memorable. Reach out to your local artists and see what is possible!

Authentic outcome

Throughout the project, art prompted concepts for discussion which were used as a basis for creating spoken word and dance elements for the performance. The students chose three key concepts, *aspire, faith,* and *choice,* to lead their project. They wrote these words in Arabic, inspired by Mohammed's work, using spray paint. They explored different styles of poetry such as acrostic, spoken word, and composite poetry, and they selected songs connected to these concepts to choreograph their dance. The outcome was an hour-long performance of 11 poems written by the students and three dances collaboratively choreographed.

The three key concepts of *aspire, faith,* and *choice* drove the overall outcome. The students learned not to limit their aspirations, to make their own choices and learn from them, and that faith is the truth we choose that brings us together as a united community. The project left a positive last impression of what the young people could achieve, changed perceptions of how they could engage with society on matters that are meaningful to them, and prepared them for a confident start in secondary school. One example that stood out for me was a poem written by an incredibly shy student. They would often struggle to talk out loud, and this was due to their lack of confidence, fearing they might get it 'wrong.' This student wrote a very poignant poem about *comfort zones* (included here in Figure 10.9). In preparation for the performance, students who wrote poems were not necessarily the ones who would perform them. Others could put themselves forward to perform the poem. Using a set of criteria that focussed on intonation, delivery, etc., the class would vote on who they thought should perform their poem. In this case, the student who wrote this poem wanted to read it out to the rest of the class. This was one of those moments – the ones you get during teaching when you think, *this is what it is*

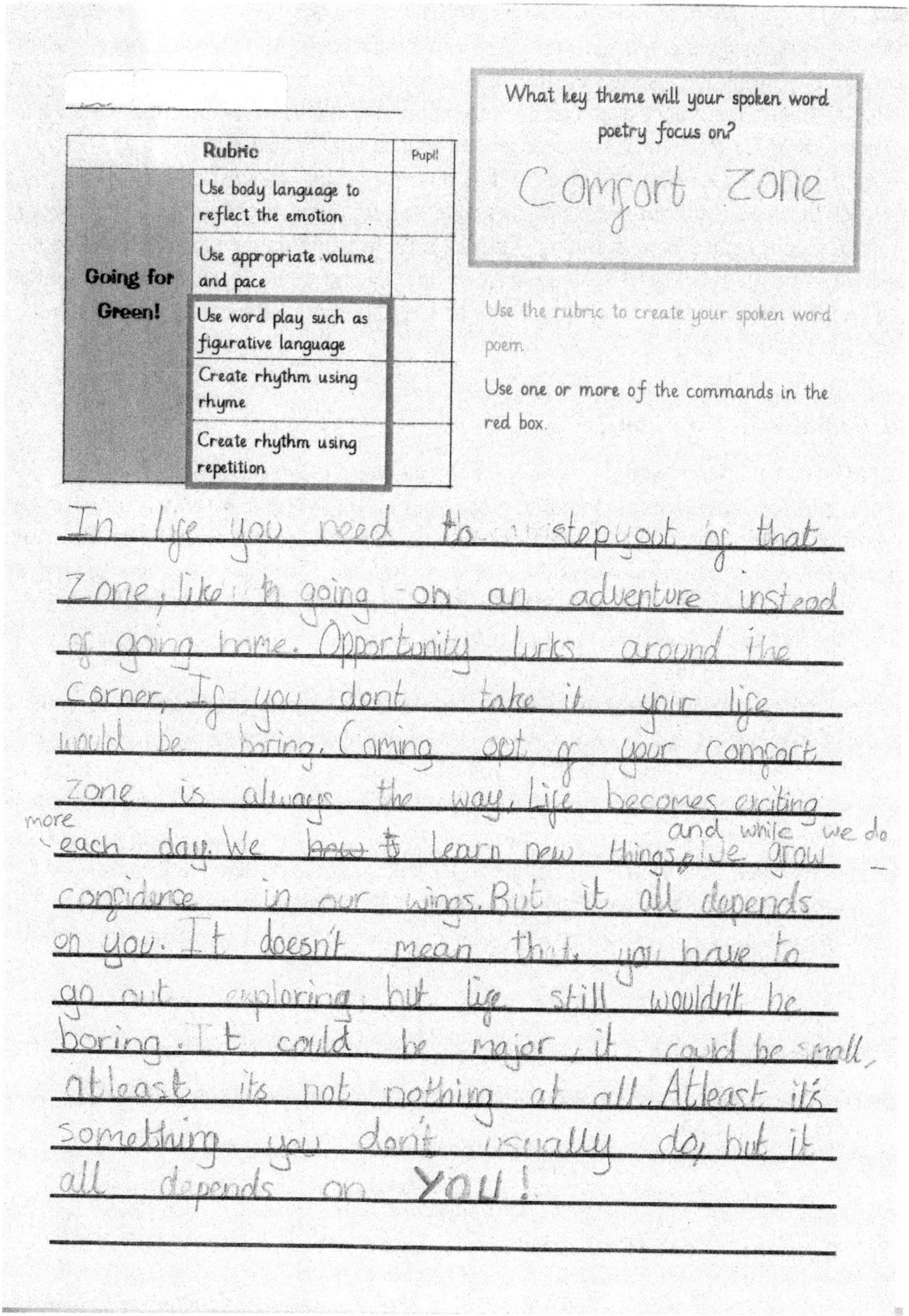

Going for Green!	Rubric	Pupil
	Use body language to reflect the emotion	
	Use appropriate volume and pace	
	Use word play such as figurative language	
	Create rhythm using rhyme	
	Create rhythm using repetition	

What key theme will your spoken word poetry focus on?

Comfort zone

Use the rubric to create your spoken word poem.

Use one or more of the commands in the red box.

In life you need to step out of that Zone, like h going on an adventure instead of going home. Opportunity lurks around the corner, If you dont take it your life would be boring, Coming opt of your comfort zone is always the way, Life becomes exciting more each day. We how to learn new things and while we do grow confidence in our wings. But it all depends on you. It doesn't mean that you have to go out exploring but life still wouldn't be boring. It could be major, it could be small, atleast its not nothing at all. Atleast it's something you don't usually do, but it all depends on YOU!

Figure 10.9 Student poem, 'Comfort zone'

about, this is why I am here and why I do this! The rest of the class was stunned but supportive. Although shaky at the start, the student performed their poem, and the confidence it took to do that was enormous. Despite this, the class voted for another student to read their poem during the final performance based on the intonation they could deliver it with. With only a few weeks left of primary school, this was absolute proof of what is possible.

These projects are examples of how it is possible to use a question-raising approach to curriculum alongside covering core learning expectations for Year 6. A teacher who listens for conceptual understanding and helps their students develop their vocabulary will encourage them to evolve a clear sense of agency and their achievements to highlight their capability. What more could you aspire to offer students before they move on in their education journey?

An elephant in the room?

I can't finish this chapter without mentioning the elephant in the room: SATs.

In spring, Year 6 students are required to sit for SATs. These tests can cause an unnecessary amount of stress. I was, and still am, of the firm belief that tests are part of life. They come in many forms that act as gateways into stages of our lives. Learning to drive a car, getting into university, training to be a mechanic, whatever it may be, they all require us to be knowledgeable and to have that knowledge tested in order to go ahead and progress.

I enjoyed preparing the pupils for their SATs because I held high expectations of all of them. I believed they could all achieve their best and that that would always be enough. My students all aspired to do their best, and this was a powerful self-fulfilling prophecy. I ensured that they knew about the tests we get in life. I normalised nerves by sharing an insight into my own history of tests. How many of us have re-sat something? A GCSE? A driving test? I know I have. The students needed to know that tests do not define them; they are merely a space for you to do your absolute best, and whatever the outcome, it is not definitive. If you want to do better, you can.

Ultimately, SATs do not hinder a child's chances or progress in secondary school – the enormous, unnecessary pressure placed on the child throughout the year does. This pressure stems from Ofsted, league tables and a culture of measurability.

References

Department for Education (DfE) (2013) *National Curriculum in England. Key Stages 1 and 2 Framework Document*. London: DfE.
Gray, H. (1878) *Gray's Anatomy*. Philadelphia and New York: Lea and Febiger.

Appendix

Autumn

Illustrative example of a concept-led project plan

'Should we accept our place in society?'

class, discrimination, justice, rights

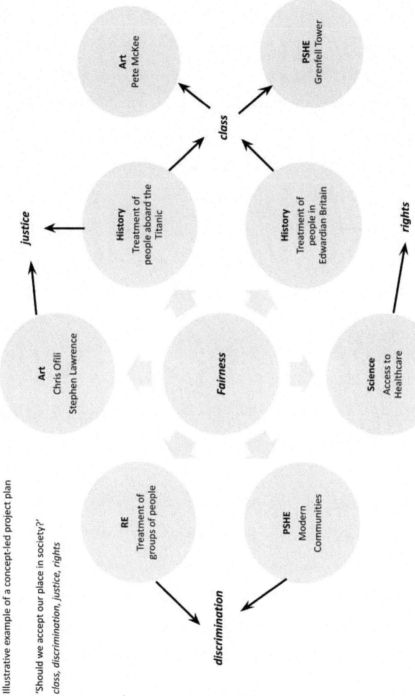

Art
Pete McKee

PSHE
Grenfell Tower

class

History
Treatment of people aboard the Titanic

History
Treatment of people in Edwardian Britain

justice

rights

Art
Chris Ofili
Stephen Lawrence

Fairness

Science
Access to Healthcare

RE
Treatment of groups of people

PSHE
Modern Communities

discrimination

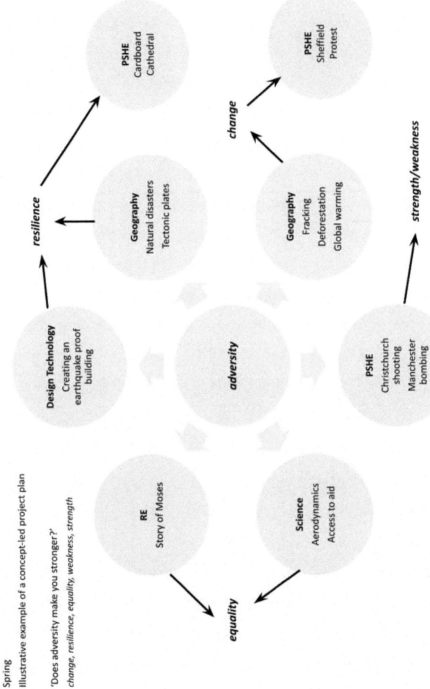

Spring

Illustrative example of a concept-led project plan

'Does adversity make you stronger?'

change, resilience, equality, weakness, strength

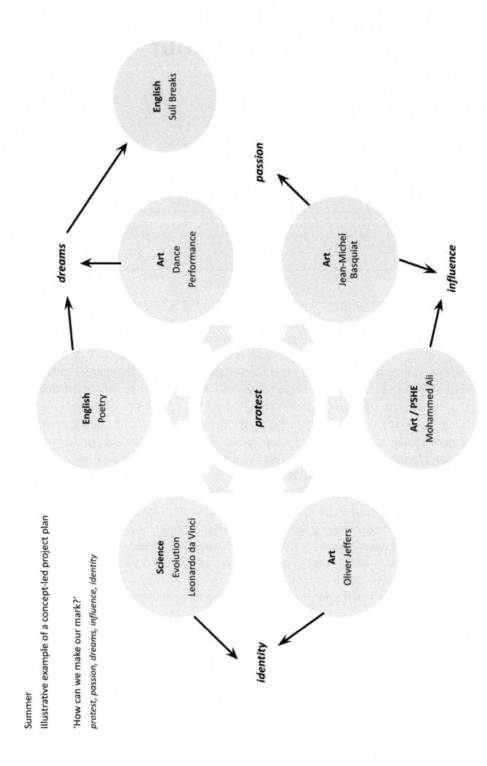

Summer

Illustrative example of a concept-led project plan

'How can we make our mark?'

protest, passion, dreams, influence, identity

English
Suli Breaks

Art
Dance
Performance

Art
Jean-Michel
Basquiat

passion

dreams

influence

English
Poetry

protest

Art / PSHE
Mohammed Ali

Science
Evolution
Leonardo da Vinci

Art
Oliver Jeffers

identity

11 How talking with your class can liberate your teaching

This chapter is written by Meghan Tipping. She reflects upon her changing journey as a teacher and how she took others with her.

Adopting a concept-led curriculum was a major step in our school, providing students with the education we believed they needed to develop independent thinking. Chapter 10 shows just how far children can go with the right curriculum. Crucial to this was the choice of resources, stimuli, and activities. The focus on social class through the story of the *Titanic* and the opportunity to consider the racism in society which led to the murder of Stephen Lawrence enabled the students to begin to evaluate how and why society is the way it is. The chance to curate their own museum in the school building and consider what makes a community, using the Cardboard Cathedral in Christchurch as a starting point, helped grow their independence, sense of self-worth, and pride in what they were able to achieve both individually and cooperatively. But it would not have been possible without other changes too, such as the different approaches to classroom organisation and assessment.

But above all, using a question-raising approach required a considerable shift in teacher mindset which did not happen overnight. Teachers had to learn to be more open to children and allow them to use exploratory talk. They needed to learn to listen to students' thinking aloud in order to develop the use of conceptual language. We worked on this as a school by adopting a dialogic approach to teaching using 'Philosophy for Children' (P4C). In this chapter I discuss how this came about with reflections on my own journey and the role I played in supporting teachers who were only used to a didactic approach to teaching.

2008

Imagine an A-Level English literature class, a group of around 20, studying poetry. In particular, Wilfred Owen's *Dulce et Decorum Est*. This class is a core memory for me. I remember enjoying the sound of the poetry and knowing it was about the First World War which, as I was a passionate history student, was one subject area I was fascinated by.

But I struggled to understand the words within the poem. I did not know what they meant. My teacher asked us what Owen conveyed through his poetry, and because I was displaying an

DOI: 10.4324/9781003451044-14

obviously puzzled look on my face, he may have deduced that I was unsure of the word 'conveyed.' Knowing me as a student, he anticipated that I would quickly follow up that puzzled look with a 'Sir what does conveyed mean?' Fortunately for me, talk is my strength; my inquisitive nature often leads me to ask questions. But perhaps even more significantly, this teacher provided a space where I knew it was safe to talk and to raise questions without fear of judgement. He both provided me with the word and with the space to talk together to make meaning from the poetry. It was a stepping stone to me being able to articulate my ideas using the power of words.

This class is just one example of when I was given the power of words. 'Convey' is now one of those words which makes me smile when I use it because I feel empowered – it feels like a tool I can reach for to articulate myself in this complex world. I am not ashamed to say I lacked vocabulary. Many young people do. For me, it has always been a struggle. To listen to lecturers or just people talking in general, there would be so many words I did not understand. When they say knowledge is power, I believe there are words that provide that power, and without them, you are at a disadvantage.

This is what gave me the drive to become an educator, to enable that agency that I was afforded by the teachers who gave me the words. But when I trained to be a teacher, I found that the route to enabling children to develop their own ability to conjure with the power of words was not a simple step.

Teaching beyond the standards

Becoming a teacher nowadays means meeting a set of standards. In England, these are the Teachers' Standards which in one form or other have been in place for twenty years. The Standards claim to 'set a clear baseline of expectations for the professional practice and conduct of teachers and define the minimum level of practice expected of teachers in England' (DfE, 2011). They are broken down into two parts: part one covers 'Teaching' in eight core Standards, and part two covers 'Personal and Professional Development.' The eight core Standards must be sufficiently met before qualifying as a teacher:

1) Set high expectations which inspire, motivate and challenge pupils
2) Promote good progress and outcomes by pupils
3) Demonstrate good subject and curriculum knowledge
4) Plan and teach well-structured lessons
5) Adapt teaching to respond to the strengths and needs of all pupils
6) Make accurate and productive use of assessment
7) Manage behaviour effectively to ensure a good and safe learning environment
8) Fulfil wider professional responsibilities

DfE (2011)

The Teachers' Standards encourage the promotion of a top-down approach. There are a number of Standards, for example, that indicate that the authoritative voice is the teacher's, and therefore they maintain the overall agency within the classroom. For example, one of the subheadings within Standard 4, 'impart knowledge and develop understanding through effective use of lesson time,' references the traditional delivery model of pedagogy in which a teacher will transmit knowledge to students – commonly known as didacticism. The Standards operate as competencies, detailing what teachers need to do, but with little guidance on pedagogy or how to go about it. Just as the vocabulary of efficiency and effectiveness obscures a proper consideration of what education is actually about, the Teachers' Standards focus on acquiring a set of skills, knowledge, and competencies which limits a full consideration of what teaching is about. Telling teachers what they need to do is not the same as developing their understanding of how they need to be. What does a teacher need to be like? What qualities do they need to develop? What steps do they need to take to go about this?

The didactic approach to teaching, thus encouraged by the Teachers' Standards and reinforced by a behavioural objectives approach to curriculum, is essentially teacher centred. A common interpretation of 'Effective use of lesson time' in fact limits student participation. The expected short, factual answers students respond with inhibit their intellectual activity. This approach is historically what many of us have experienced, what many students still experience, and what many student teachers continue to adopt today, largely because that is how they were taught when they were at school and that is how they were taught to teach at college. This is what has led many to call it a 'traditional' pedagogy (e.g., Cazden, 2001). Two statements within Standard 7 compound the top-down approach to teaching: 'manage classes effectively, using approaches which are appropriate to pupils' needs in order to *involve* and motivate them' and 'maintain good relationships with pupils, *exercise appropriate authority,* and act decisively when necessary' (DfE, 2011). The words in italics have become literal indicators that the teacher is in charge, and the students will be told when their involvement is required, the student perceived as 'object' and not 'subject' of their education. A learning environment cannot foster purposeful talk if the teacher delivers the knowledge and the only exchanges are Initiation, Response, and Feedback (Sinclair and Coulthard, 1975). In these circumstances, students will not become critically engaged; they will not see the value of interaction.

Becoming the teacher I am today

Taking the PGCE route following a History BA meant a year's university course. Most of this time was spent on placement in two different schools. Here, I had the opportunity to hone my practice. Early on as a student teacher, you get to grips with the importance of the 'core' subjects: understanding the National Curriculum requirements, gaining the subject knowledge, and observing what a good lesson is meant to look like. You are also always aware of the need to provide evidence towards meeting the Teachers' Standards. I had two great mentors who commanded the room; they were respected by the students and were motivating. I was able to replicate their approach to practice and performed well against the Teachers' Standards, thereby meeting the requirements for qualified teacher status. But it was all done at such a pace that there was little time to think. During the year, you are not afforded the luxury of reflection to the point where you can recognise that your learning is focussed on performance. The requirement to show progress against the Teachers' Standards and fulfil the delivery model of pedagogy did not provide space for thinking about what meaningful exchanges within the learning environment might look like. Experiences on placement are high pressure and time poor as you try to get to grips with the overwhelming knowledge and skills required to teach, as well as learning how to manage a room full of 30 or more students. This situation has not changed and is now even more focussed on student teachers 'performing' to meet a set of competencies at the expense of using their time to develop an understanding of teaching as a moral enterprise. *The ITT Core Content Framework* (DfE, 2019), essentially a curriculum for teacher training soon to be superseded by another document, the *Initial Teacher Training and Early Career Framework* (DfE, 2024), both designed to supplement the Teachers' Standards, are didactic in approach. They have not been developed by professionals from across the sector but are imposed by the government. As long as the teacher education sector remains highly regulated and assessed based on conforming to Ofsted, the cycle will continue.

It was not until my first year as a newly qualified teacher that I began to understand the significance of exchanges within the learning environment, both amongst students and between teacher and student(s). The Teachers' Standards had been all about me performing and fulfilling competencies, which meant I entered my classroom with only one method of teaching. How was I to know any different? But when I encountered P4C, I realised there was another way. My perspective shifted, and I began my journey afresh, this time with a growing understanding of how much rested on the nature of classroom relationships.

I was first introduced to P4C in 2014, and it was a moment that changed everything for me. I walked into a classroom with 30 children sitting in a circle on the floor. The teacher read a picture book and then asked the children to share their first thoughts. They calmly offered a hand out on their lap to share a word, a phrase, or a question. I would describe those responses as simply surprising. I had never experienced students being afforded the opportunity to share insights into what they thought. To hear Year 3 children identify concepts that were present in the book opened a door into seeing what was possible through dialogue. I returned to the same class on another occasion to observe an enquiry based on a philosophical question they had chosen. The teacher skilfully facilitated the dialogue, taking an unobtrusive yet effective role, as the students engaged in the discourse – agreeing, disagreeing, reflecting, and developing their thoughts. The experience had a profound effect. What I had witnessed was a way to liberate my teaching. It was the start of a journey which led me to become the teacher I am today.

I always wanted the students I taught to feel as though they could talk in the classroom without fear of judgement, and it was important to me that my disposition reflected that. P4C offered a pedagogy that could reduce the social distance to a point where a successful learning community could be established and where students felt that they were engaged in the mutual process of learning. My character helped this. My teacher disposition can probably be described as an 'enthusiastic storm,' and my sense of humour and sarcasm meant I could develop unique relationships with my class which drew us closer. P4C can be delivered as discreet sessions that, at the time I became aware of it, followed a ten-step model. Within those sessions, there was a clear opportunity given to the students to develop the discourse norms of dialogue. Learning how to agree and disagree, explain their reasoning, change their mind, and reshape their thoughts empowered them. Being exposed to abstract nouns, concepts such as *justice, kindness, fairness,* and *guilt* in an accessible way, enabled them to begin the process of thinking critically. These concepts began to restructure their experience (Halliday, 1993). The students developed confidence emotionally and socially and thus could navigate this complex world we live in more readily. The way P4C allowed me to nurture classroom relationships created a climate of trust that is a prerequisite for purposeful dialogue and discussion. Students were no longer vying for attention in a bidding war to respond to a question the teacher was asking but were recognising that each of their contributions was valuable and that another student may challenge their thinking in a way that enabled them to grow. That is when I think my teaching shifted, and the dialogic stance which I had adopted in P4C permeated other lessons, too. Almost without realising it, I used this approach to teaching throughout the curriculum. It became a way of being with the class.

Becoming a dialogic teacher provided me with the skills, knowledge, and the confidence to take back control and restored my professional judgement. Through a process of learning and unlearning, I let go of the need to 'know everything' and I took 'risks' such as simply 'letting go of the reins' enough to offer children the space to develop confidence in their ability to talk. This confidence led to greater student agency, and with time, the classroom environment became richer. I also never restricted access to words. I do not believe that a child cannot understand certain words at certain ages. Why not let them decide? Figure 11.1 demonstrates the journey from didacticism to dialogism that I experienced with regards to the classroom learning community, communication, and relationships between myself and the students and amongst the students themselves.

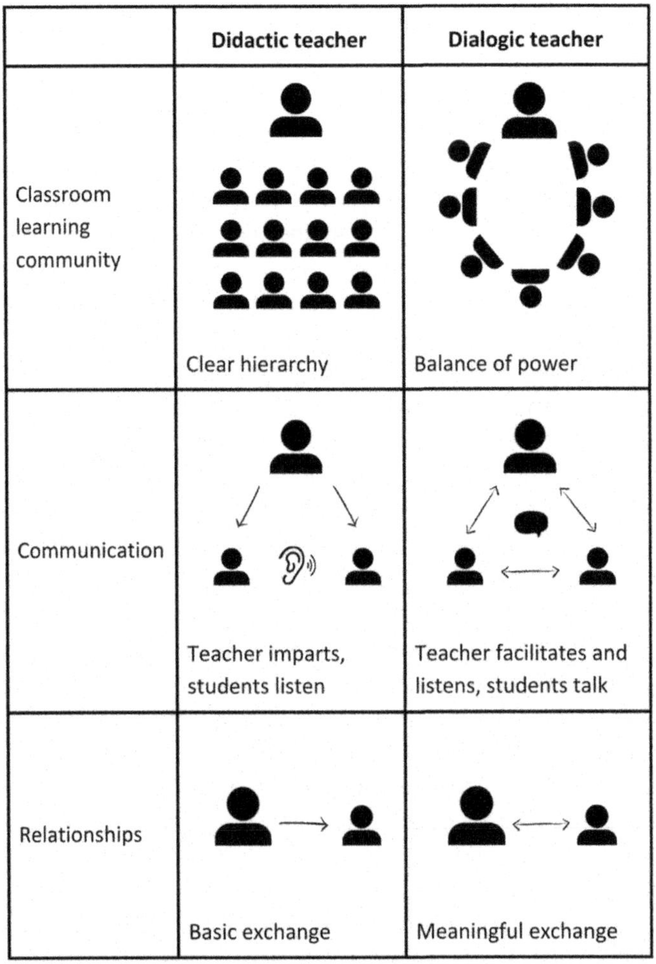

	Didactic teacher	Dialogic teacher
Classroom learning community	Clear hierarchy	Balance of power
Communication	Teacher imparts, students listen	Teacher facilitates and listens, students talk
Relationships	Basic exchange	Meaningful exchange

Figure 11.1 Didacticism and dialogism in three dimensions

Challenges: learning and unlearning

The school had started using P4C a few years before my arrival as a Newly Qualified Teacher. But it was still in the early stages of adoption. The teacher I had observed was the coordinator and a talented practitioner. When she moved on to a new school, I took on the mantle, and with characteristic enthusiasm, I persuaded the headteacher to let me train to Level 3 and embark on embedding P4C within the school using the UK P4C charity, SAPERE's award programme 'Going for Gold,' as a guide. But it was certainly not just about getting an award. I knew how liberating this approach was for the students and how well it enabled the dialogic stance we wanted for our teachers. It aligned with our aims and the concept curriculum. Unknowingly, perhaps, I think that the decision to adapt our curriculum in the way we had had probably grown out of our early experiences with P4C. It made complete sense to adopt this approach. But it was a process, a journey of learning and unlearning, and there were some challenges along the way in developing staff confidence.

Whether teachers trained post-Teachers' Standards or not was irrelevant because the delivery model of pedagogy was widely accepted. The younger cohort of teachers needed convincing that they were not going to metaphorically 'drown' adopting this approach. For older, long-standing members of staff, it was about convincing them that the change was worth it and that substantial support would be provided. We started with everyone being trained to Level 1 in P4C, and I provided opportunities to watch P4C in my classroom as well as for me to lead P4C and/or team-teach in other classes. This was important, as I was able to show teachers that using talk in this way was not something that only Year 6 could do. All Year groups were capable of purposeful talk. However, this did not stop the questions of doubt creeping in:

- What if I choose a bad stimulus?
- Do I stay silent and let them just talk?
- When do I intervene?
- Should I share any personal views?
- How do I know I am facilitating talk well?

This doubt was normal and welcomed. People who train to be educators do it for one core reason – to enable young people to realise their potential. I knew we could not move forward without having an open dialogue, and I addressed these questions in a variety of ways. First, I compiled a list of stimuli with potential concepts that could be explored from them and recommended these regularly to teachers. In continued professional development sessions, I facilitated P4C with teachers and teaching assistants, building confidence in their understanding and practice of facilitation. Another successful strategy of support was giving teachers 1:1 opportunities to talk through lesson plans. This helped me understand how they were feeling about particular aspects of pedagogy and helped them self-evaluate the progress of P4C in their classrooms. Within the first term of P4C practice, teachers were finding their way, and the feedback was positive. I received such comments as these:

> They love to discuss their own opinions, so I have incorporated more activities like this to allow this skill to develop. It has in turn developed some children's thinking, they are now able to listen to others better and use what they hear to add to and inform their choices.

The children are good at offering everyday life examples to clarify their thoughts, and this can allow a number of children to access the discussion better as it is a peer who has offered the support.

Are you curious enough?

Although the teacher feedback was positive, they also recognised this was a journey that both they and their students were on. It was not going to be easy. A teacher trained to be didactic is bound to find the initial facilitation of talk tricky. But once children are given the opportunity to talk, what they come out with usually takes us by surprise. It is their curiosity – they can wonder and imagine – and sometimes as adults, we lose that capability.

Early-years practitioners understand the power of curiosity, and whenever you enter an early-years' classroom, you see how the teachers encourage this so effortlessly. At my school, our early-years teachers implemented Ann Dawson's Rainbow Talk to encourage and facilitate purposeful talk amongst the children. Rainbow Talk fans with the words 'see', 'hear', 'touch', 'smell', 'taste', 'think', and 'feel' written on them were used by the teachers and placed within the classroom to develop the children's vocabulary, questioning and making sense of their world.

It is this curiosity that teachers, who were trained to be didactic, can find tricky to facilitate or encourage. As I explained in Chapter 10, it can be easy to make assumptions about a child who is creatively responding to a concept, but we do not immediately understand. The example I gave was a boy who responded to the enquiry on the concept of *adversity* by making a Lego aeroplane. When Freire stated, 'through dialogue, the teacher-of-the-students and the students-of-the-teacher cease to exist and a new term emerges: teacher-student with students-teachers. The teacher is no longer merely the-one-who-teaches, but one who is himself taught in dialogue with the students' (1970, p. 61), he was trying to get at something that is hard to describe. Perhaps that is why the language appears clumsy, although, of course, we are reading it in translation. He was describing a wonderful zone, created by dialogue, which exists between two people – in this case, the teacher and the pupil – when they are truly listening to each other. The child who explained to me the relevance of the Lego aeroplane to *adversity*, when I failed to see its significance, had let me into his world. But this had only occurred because of my genuine curiosity. After stopping myself short of making a negative assumption (this cannot have anything to do with *adversity*), I showed my curiosity and interest and that I was prepared to listen. And in genuine listening, he took me into his world, and I was 'taught' by him as he explained the relevance (a pilot might have to make decisions that could literally plunge the passengers into the sea if his plane were malfunctioning).

Knowing when to intervene in dialogue and when not to can be daunting. As a facilitator, you need to do more listening, asking questions at times to help clarify or draw out a student's point. You may ask open questions to probe for deeper thought. Ultimately, if you train yourself to listen carefully for the students trying to talk in concepts, you can enable your students to use concept language. It is important not to have preconceived ideas about how you think the dialogue should go. You are providing a space for students to think, question, and make up their own minds about the world.

Wider school community

One other strategy that was important in supporting teachers moving to a more dialogic approach was the way in which we engaged the wider school community. I aimed to engage parents and carers in P4C to provide opportunities to witness the capability of their children when they took part in rich dialogue and also to find ways to continue this dialogue at home. We hosted P4C days which involved choosing a stimulus the whole school could talk about, and encouraged families to come into school to respond with thoughts and questions and to talk about concepts such as *difference, perception,* and *beauty.* These were some of the concepts that arose from the picture book *Square* by Mac Barnett (2019). Picture books are often rich stimuli that can be used across all Year groups. Who doesn't love a picture book? And luckily, the tide is turning on picture books being 'too young' for Year 6. There are many accessible, rich stories within picture books, and they usually refer to concept language. Another book we used for a P4C day was Oliver Jeffers' *Here We Are* (2017). Not only did these days get everyone talking, but we talked about things that were important and that brought us closer as a community.

A parent and carer philosophy group every month or so also provided a space to understand the P4C approach and to pick up the basic skills. Another way to encourage families to engage in dialogue at home was through 'Thinking Thursdays' which was an enquiry question sent out on the weekly newsletter that had space for students and their families to note some thoughts into speech bubbles and bring it back into school if they wanted. I created a display in the school entrance for this and updated it weekly, valuing the responses that were sent in. A home-school P4C book also became popular, and students could request to take it home to fill in a page based on an enquiry question.

The reward

The growth of successful dialogue in our school, through the medium of P4C, enabled children to offer their own life experiences to expand on and link their thoughts to a range of stimuli. In a school with 48 languages, P4C and a dialogic approach to teaching were removing barriers to learning. Many who would not normally contribute to class discussions were doing so. And as talk became the common currency of learning, more students were willing and able to talk. P4C transformed my pedagogy and provided me with the method to fulfil my drive to enable students to experience education differently to me. With the whole school adopting the pedagogy of P4C, children were increasingly able to develop independence and realise agency. It was the perfect medium for us to realise our aims and to put the concept curriculum into action. Children were now bursting into learning and asking questions. We need to allow all children to be those children.

Instruction is part of education. However, the ideology currently is that instruction, the delivery model, is all there is. Verbal contributions are currently less valued than written contributions in education and preordained learning outcomes prevail, diminishing opportunities for creative thinking. P4C with its question-raising approach supports the liberation of teaching. It gives space to children and teachers to think together. When teachers are given the space to let go of the reins and the tools to facilitate talk in lessons, the social distance between the student and teacher is reduced. You feel 'less like a teacher and almost, well . . . more human,' as one teacher said to me.

But it takes patience and trust. Facilitating dialogue is a journey that both teachers and students embark on together. It requires discipline and experience to develop the necessary skills for a talk-friendly classroom. And it involves taking a risk. But it is possible and the reward makes it well worth taking that risk.

References

Barnett, M. (2019) *Square*. London: Walker Books.

Cazden, C.B. (2001) *Classroom Discourse: The Language of Teaching and Learning*, 2nd edn. Portsmouth, NH: Heinemann.

Department for Education (DfE) (2011) *Teachers' Standards*. Available at: https://www.gov.uk/government/publications/teachers-standards (Accessed: 17 April 2024).

Department for Education (DfE) (2019) *Initial Teacher Training (ITT) Core Content Framework*. Available at: https://www.gov.uk/government/publications/initial-teacher-training-itt-core-content-framework (Accessed: 17 April 2024).

Department for Education (DfE) (2024) *Initial Teacher Training and Early Career Framework*. Available at: https://assets.publishing.service.gov.uk/media/661d24ac08c3be25cfbd3e61/Initial_Teacher_Training_and_Early_Career_Framework.pdf. (Accessed: 17 April 2024).

Freire, P. (1970) *Pedagogy of the Oppressed*. London: Continuum.

Halliday, M.A.K. (1993) Towards a language-based theory of learning. *Linguistics and Education*, 5, pp. 93–116.

Jeffers, O. (2017) *Here We Are: Notes for Living on Planet Earth*. London: Harper Collins.

Sinclair, J.M. and Coulthard, R.M. (1975) *Towards an Analysis of Discourse: The English Used by Teachers and Pupils*. London: Oxford University Press.

12 Bringing talk to life
Tackling controversial issues

Previous chapters in Part II of this book have shown what is possible when a school adopts a concept curriculum, placing talk at the centre of learning. We have seen pupils

- listen to each other's ideas, witnessing their friends and peers thinking aloud and developing their understanding through this shared experience. This community aspect of learning bucks the trend of the individualising orthodoxy current in schools where 'work' consists of pupils sitting together in a classroom but completing an exercise or drafting a piece of writing alone.
- become confident in using the discourse norms of discussion which develop their ability to ask questions and challenge the 'given.' Thinking aloud in this way not only provides pupils with social confidence, but it enables them to begin to evaluate what they are often 'on the receiving end of' in life through social media or other experiences. It is the dawning of critical consciousness.
- develop an understanding of concepts which we may call social, philosophical, or religious – such ideas as *class, adversity, power, freedom, equality*, and *resilience* – unavailable to them in a conventional primary classroom.

Teachers in these lessons provide a bridge between the everyday experiences of the child and school learning – Vygotsky's 'everyday' and 'scientific' or Bernstein's 'horizontal' and 'vertical' discourse, as discussed in Chapters 2 and 3. By adopting a dialogic stance (Boyd and Markarian, 2011), they show their openness and willingness to listen to their pupils. When a school moves to using this approach to teaching, lessons are not constrained by having a learning objective or a preordained outcome. Of course, not all lessons are taught this way. There are some skills which require direct instruction and practice and so need well-defined learning outcomes. But enquiry learning, as we have seen, can cross several curriculum areas and be integrated into a teacher's practice so that it becomes a part of their pedagogic repertoire.

Developing the social norms of dialogue and discussion can be alien to some children's life experiences and cultural background and requires time and energy to get right. Children need to adopt appropriate body language, learn to listen to what others are saying, make eye contact, and use 'appreciative' words to engage in this form of talk. Schools need to provide sentence stems such as 'I agree with you when you say X, but I do not agree with it when you say Y' or 'building on what X says, I think Y.' The authors of an American approach to dialogue called 'Accountable Talk' which has many similarities with those discussed in this book, note that 'it

DOI: 10.4324/9781003451044-15

took many months of concerted effort' for children to learn the appropriate verbal and body language to engage in meaningful enquiries (Michaels, O'Connor and Resnick, 2007, p. 295). But when they did, it resulted in 'respectful and grounded discussion' rather than 'noisy assertion and the uncritical acceptance of the voice of authority' (ibid, 2007, p. 286). They acknowledge also that these norms are differently assimilated depending on pupils' cultural and ethnic backgrounds and gender. Some are familiar with such conversational norms from their family settings; for others, it is completely alien. Some are quick on the uptake; for others, it takes time.

Children in our focus school do well in SATs, and it has been judged by successive Ofsted inspections to be 'Outstanding.' But this aspect alone, what Biesta calls the 'Qualification' domain (2015, p. 73), is not the school's sole aim. Their overarching mission to the community they serve is to provide young people with the opportunity to become confident, independent individuals with an understanding that they have a legitimate place in society and a right and responsibility to articulate their feelings and beliefs in the world. They foster and nurture attributes that are not quantitatively measurable and not all about individual attainment: attributes such as creativity, empathy, altruism, cooperation, respectfulness, and a strong sense of independence and individual agency. These qualitative aspects of being human are vital to any culture or society for its wellbeing and self-respect as they are for an individual. Perhaps most importantly, this approach also introduces an element of uncertainty. Pupils learn to understand that it is normal for people to have different views and opinions. They learn that knowledge is contestable – it can be subject to questioning. And they learn that there is much that we do not know. This uncertainty is vital in education. For, as Kelly reminds us, there can be no freedom and no democracy in a society where 'the most important aspects of life, and of education, are treated as a given, as non-problematic and as not themselves subjects of continuing debate nor, as a consequence, open to modification and change' (1995, p. xi). Fallibility is the watchword of this approach. For knowledge is not immutable, and teachers are not infallible. So, the passing-on of knowledge must be open to critical scrutiny, and teachers must learn to challenge their own assumptions.

Talking about controversial issues

At the heart of this school's sense of purpose lies the conviction, as expressed by the deputy head, that 'if schools are not making PSHE central to their work, they are failing kids, ultimately' (Gurton, 2022, p. 70). Time and again, the teachers refer to the benefit of children bringing their life experiences to bear in classroom learning. One teacher talks of the importance of pupils having opportunities to 'explore concepts that are difficult and . . . in other areas of learning and other approaches, they would be untouchable, or you wouldn't have the opportunity to discuss them' (ibid, 2022, p. 70). She is referring to what we might call controversial issues. We have seen in Chapter 10, children developing an understanding of the concepts of *class* and *adversity*. Later in this chapter, we will see another class engage in a discussion on the theme of *terrorism* from the pilot project *Non-Violent Action: A Force for Change*. These topics are planned for because the school believes them to be valuable and important areas for children to research and understand. They are factored into the taught curriculum. Not many primary schools are willing to engage children in the discussion of such topics. Teachers and head teachers are cautious, not wishing to appear to be influencing children, and they are sensitive to the responses they may get from parents. Increasingly, areas such as wellbeing and mental health are taught proactively, but open debate and discussion is not always encouraged. Rather, they often resemble advice clinics.

But often, controversial issues arise spontaneously. Children may have heard about something on social media or listened to their parents or friends talking. In Chapter 10, we saw how Year 6 pupils' need to talk about the Christchurch mosque shootings led to class discussions, followed by the children themselves organising an assembly and sharing acts of worship with the rest of Key Stage 2. Later in this chapter, we will see how Meghan responded when students in her class wanted to talk about the so-called 'Muslim ban' instituted by Donald Trump shortly after becoming president in 2016. Her willingness to enable such impromptu discussions to take place derives from seeing their value and relevance to other areas of learning and 'finding the time' to let the pupils pursue a theme of their choice. There is also the existing structure, developed through the use of P4C, which enables such discussions because the ground rules are understood. But many teachers lack experience in facilitation of dialogue. They may also be fearful children might say things which are hurtful or disrespectful or that what gets reported home might be misinterpreted, so some teachers will not allow such discussions to develop. They themselves, like their pupils, can also feel uncertain. Discussing sensitive or controversial issues may expose them to risk. They or their school may face an online backlash. Adults and children alike can be on the receiving end of abuse sometimes targeted not only at them but at members of their families. This leads them to practise what Chimamanda Ngozi Adichie recently termed 'self-censorship' in her Reith lecture on 'Freedom of Speech' (2022).

Some teachers will give an issue air time because they know it is simply impossible to proceed unless children are given time to let off steam. But often this is merely perfunctory, and an issue is only pursued if the teachers have strong beliefs about the importance of justice and equity themselves (Cassar, Oosterheert and Meijer, 2023). A teacher may also get involved if a student makes a derogatory remark about another student or a general statement that refers to religion, gender, race, or ethnicity which are areas that students perceive to be important to their identities (Tribukait, 2021). In this situation, the teacher may feel a responsibility to intercede to model appropriate behaviour or to make it clear what is and is not acceptable to say and why. There may be no neutral position. But these situations can certainly be emotionally demanding for the teacher.

For teachers who do pursue a discussion with their class when an issue has been raised spontaneously or in a planned way, whether they remain neutral or not in the discussion is complex. Is it right to make clear your own views or feelings or not? Stenhouse's advice in the Humanities Curriculum Project was for teachers to maintain 'procedural neutrality' as students might have difficulties in 'separating the expression of personal viewpoint by the teacher from their authority position in the classroom' (Elliott, 2012, p. 90). To encourage teachers to reflect on how to manage this neutrality, he asked the following questions, as we saw in Chapter 6:

- To what extent do you confirm? Do you, for example, say 'An interesting point' or 'Well done'? What is the effect of this on the group?
- Are you neutral on controversial issues? (Further questions ask teachers to reflect on ways they may explicitly and implicitly bias the discussion, e.g., 'Do you draw attention, by questions, to certain parts or aspects of a piece of evidence which seems to support a viewpoint with which you agree?')

- Do you attempt to transmit through eliciting questions your own interpretation of the meaning of a piece of evidence such as a poem or a picture? (ibid, 2012, p. 93)

More recent research cited by Cassar, Oosterheert and Meijer (2023) reveals one study in which teachers are divided in their views about whether they should disclose their position on an issue or not (e.g., Hess and McAvoy, 2009) and another in which middle and high school teachers categorically rejected the decision to disclose their position on controversial issues (Miller-Lane, Denton and May, 2006). However, this same study revealed a more nuanced position when disclosure was taken to mean disclosure of values rather than a position.

The political dimension of pursuing controversial issues is significant. Some see teaching as 'innately a political endeavour,' as demonstrated by 'any number of routine actions that teachers undertake on a daily basis' (Journell, 2017, p. 112). By this interpretation, even deciding to rebuke a student who makes an inflammatory comment is in itself a break from neutrality and demonstrates a political position. But more generally, schools inevitably reflect the general state of society – and discussions will have personal, current, cultural, and historical dimensions (McAvoy and Hess, 2013). So, discussing controversial issues allows 'students to learn how democracy works' (van Alstein, 2019, p. 4). Some research has seen a clear link between teaching controversial issues and active citizenship. Godfrey and Grayman (2014) found an open classroom climate was related to 'sociopolitical efficacy' and Johnson and Johnson's (2014, 2016) model of 'constructive controversy' bears comparison with P4C. The learners become engaged and socialised in the political discourse of a democratic society. Their work reveals a number of other positive outcomes which resonate with the aims of our focus school. Pupils develop positive self-esteem, improved cognitive reasoning, perspective taking, and interpersonal engagement. Such benefits support areas such as quality of relationships and psychological wellbeing.

Uncertainty, risk, and teachers' practical decision making (*praxis*)

Teachers who believe it is important for children to be exposed to and discuss controversial issues refer to the challenges their pupils face. One teacher puts it like this:

> A lot of our children . . . might, you know, have things talked to them about the news or they might see a lot of things on social media, and addressing those misconceptions is really important because I think they do have a kind of emotional baggage about things almost, from what they read and what they hear.

> (Gurton, 2022, p. 71)

Many refer to the powerful influence of social media and the need to dispel misinformation or other damaging influences children are exposed to. They express concern that a perceived rise in child and adolescent mental health issues, including self-harm and suicide, is not helped by the pressures of the school system, where it is often felt there is not time to discuss such pressing concerns. Those who are committed to discussing controversial issues are driven by a sense of social purpose. Their past life experiences, as well as their sense of moral purpose and commitment to justice and equity, is evident in their actions and decisions in the classroom and in what they say when interviewed (Cassar, Oosterheert and Meijer, 2023; Gurton, 2022). The desire to give students opportunities to understand more fully their life experiences, through discussion, evaluation, and questioning is shaped by a commitment to make lives better and more human and has much in common with the emancipatory pedagogy of Freire (1970, 1974).

Teachers who have this set of beliefs and are committed to enabling discussions which broach controversial issues are doing something special. Their actions are based on a belief system and through these experiences they are honing a disposition that reaches beyond a measurable set of competencies such as the Teachers' Standards (DfE, 2011). The moral conviction that guides their actions in deciding it is valuable to devote time to this aspect of learning, as well as the decision making in the moment, is described by some as *'praxis'* (see Biesta, 2013; Kemmis and Smith, 2008, for examples).

The word *praxis* ultimately derives from the work of the Greek philosopher Aristotle who, in his Nicomachean Ethics (1980), identifies a series of virtues. *Praxis* means a good act or action. In education, we can use it to mean the ability to act wisely and carefully in a particular situation. It is the application of knowledge and understanding in a practical context. According to Kemmis and Smith (2008, p. 7), the teacher whose professional practice derives from personal conviction takes a moral stance which leads them to act in the best interests of their pupils and therefore of mankind. This quality is more likely to develop in teachers who see themselves empowered with the role of decision makers. Some, like Biesta, describe these moments of *praxis* when a teacher has decided to address an unplanned controversial issue, for example, as moments of 'becoming' (2013). Others see the whole person becoming paramount, overriding the subject taught (Cassar, Oosterheert and Meijer, 2023).

To illustrate how beliefs translate into practice and how children, alongside their teachers, can get fully involved in a process of 'becoming,' the remainder of this chapter is devoted to looking at how different teachers react to situations in which controversial issues are a theme and call upon *praxis*, or professional wisdom, to be used. They are all taken from the focus school.

Lesson 1: terrorism

This lesson comes from a sequence. Part of it is reported in Figure 12.1. Here, a Year 5 class compare ISIS to Islam. It shows how the philosophical approach adopted through the use of P4C and a concept-led curriculum enable children to talk about contemporary and controversial issues which have a direct relationship to a curriculum area – in this case, Religious Education. The theme also has a direct bearing upon children's lives, as many of them follow the Muslim faith. The transcript allows us to see into the culture of the classroom through the interactions during the lesson. The excerpt comes from the last twenty minutes of the lesson. Pupils have spent the time before this continuing to research their knowledge of Islam and ISIS. They sit in a circle on the carpet with notebooks or iPads on their laps. They are drawing together what they have learned through research and their own knowledge about Islam and ISIS. The fragmented feel derives from the fact that they are reporting back on their findings.

The classroom, like all in this school, has several sofas, a few low coffee tables, and a worktop with bar stools. There is plenty of space to move around. There is a large painted banner hanging up on the wall reading VOTES FOR WOMEN, and elsewhere in the room, there is a dining table set with silver cutlery and candelabras.

The word TERRORISM is written on the board together with the question 'Who or what is this hatred and violence targeted towards?' There is also an empty grid copied in Table 12.1.

Peter:	Sometimes ISIS shout as if it is associated with Islam.
Shiala:	They try to recruit.
Teacher:	**What do you mean by recruit?**
Jake:	They use guns. They are easier to get than in other countries. Here, there are not as many guns but more knife attacks.
Faz:	One of the countries is Syria . . .
Rueben:	The first two letters in the names are similar.
Zephaniah:	I am not sure if they are a third-world country.
Teacher:	**Are you saying these countries are poorer?**
Zephaniah:	Maybe they come from Yemen or Syria.
Elizabeth:	Linking on from that . . . in Africa, they kidnap and get the family to pay a ransom. They might be forced to join ISIS.
Teacher:	**That's a really interesting point. . . . Can we have more on the Islam side?**
Fatimah:	They are really strict.
Teacher:	**Is that like other faiths?**
Mushraf:	I feel like it's stricter.
Fatimah:	When that terrorist attack happened in New Zealand . . .
Teacher:	**Fatimah, are you building on that point?**
Zephaniah:	Building on Fatimah's point, people might be biased and think that half Muslims are good and half are terrorists. It shows in history . . .
Teacher:	**So, there is, like, a long history with prophets?**
Imran:	Islamic people come from different countries.
Miriam:	Islam is respectful.
Tasneem:	There's lots of discipline. No messing around. You have to be respectful *(This girl, like a number of others in class, is clearly Moslem. She wears a hijab.)*
Teacher:	**So, you are expected not to mess about. There may be another reason why you have to be disciplined?**
Tasneem:	*(Looks up inquiringly. Does not speak.)*
Teacher:	**I am thinking of a thing we watched a video clip about . . .**
Tasneem:	Fasting?
Fatimah:	If you have done something wrong in Christianity, God gives more forgiveness. In Islam, if you do something wrong, you might have to do more prayers . . .
Teacher:	**You mean there are consequences?**
. . .	
Teacher:	**need to pick up on misconceptions here.** *The teacher then refers to a Powerpoint slide on ISIS. There is a series of points. She compares these with what children have come up with to summarise the difference between Islam and ISIS.*
. . .	

Teacher:	**So, that is quite at odds with what people believe.**
Imran:	Yes, he *(Abu Bakr al-Baghdadi)* is using his faith as an advantage. . . . He is portraying himself as God.
Teacher:	**He is giving himself that title. No one has given him that title.**
Imran:	That means he is disrespecting God. People will be ashamed.
Teacher:	**Possibly people will think that.**

Figure 12.1 Year 5 class discussion on terrorism

Throughout the lesson, the teacher fills out aspects of it as she gets some feedback from the children about the attitudes of Islam and ISIS towards the issues listed in the aspect column.

Table 12.1 Comparing Islam with ISIS

Aspect	Islam	ISIS
Murder War and terrorism Suicide The protection of innocent people People of different religious backgrounds Religion and nationality		

The teacher projects her voice clearly, and her manner is quite stern. Her teaching approach is traditional. She stands in front of the seated children and does not sit in the circle with them. At one point, we see her exhorting a pupil to remember prior learning: 'I am thinking of a thing we watched a video clip about.' At another, she directs a child to use language to show appreciation of the contribution of a peer: 'Fatimah, are you building on that point?' (her emphasis). This is not a genuine question but rhetorical – a sort of command to the child to remember to use these strategies. In addition to directing the discussion at key points, she uses questions to enable her pupils to develop their reasoning. She asks, 'Is that like other faiths?' to introduce an element of comparison in response to Fatimah's statement that Islam is 'really strict.' A few seconds later, when she prompts Tasneem to supply the example of fasting as evidence of Islam being 'stricter,' she uses the technique of elaboration (Alexander, 2020; Goswami, 2015) to enable the pupil to justify her statement; the questioning is designed for the children to keep the momentum in their own reasoning. Several other themes are raised, such as the theme of *bias*, which she chooses not to develop at this stage in the lesson. The use of the word itself, however, is a further example of the children's developing sophistication in their criticality. The excerpt demonstrates the extent to which children have become aware, through discussion and research, of several significant recent items of news relating to the theme – like the Christchurch shootings, three months earlier; the Boko Haram kidnappings; the civil wars in Yemen and Syria; and the increased levels of knife crime in the UK. Their awareness of these events, and how they can create possible prejudice towards Islam, provides the basis for their reasoning.

Up until this point, the lesson is nothing out of the ordinary. The interactions between pupils and teacher mainly take the form of the teacher eliciting answers to encourage the children to make comparisons and develop their reasoning. The teacher has an authoritative approach, typical of didactic teaching, and there is a clear delineation of the power relationship between teacher and pupils. The children are sitting and offering responses to the teacher's questions and building on each other's ideas, but the discussion does not flow between teacher and pupil or between pupil and pupil. The teacher is controlling it. However, the subject matter is both contemporary and contentious. It bears upon the children's lives, in their exposure to media, and it is unusual to see it discussed in a primary classroom.

But in the exchange at the very end of the lesson, the atmosphere changes. When Imran states that Abu Bakr al-Baghdadi is 'using his faith as an advantage,' there is suddenly complete silence. The children seem to recognise that something different is going on. Their gaze is drawn towards him. Imran's next statement, 'He is portraying himself as God,' fixes their attention decisively. Imran's tone of voice is questioning, slightly unsure. Eyes are now on the teacher. From their silence, it seems as if the children are waiting to see what she will say. Will she agree with Imran? It feels as if his statement is risky, for them and him, hence his uncertain tone of voice. This is a moment of tension. But she does not agree or disagree. Instead, she confines herself to the facts, stating, 'He is giving himself that title. No one has given him that title.'

The lesson feels like it has entered a new phase. It is now a dialogue between the two. She is looking at him and he at her and, although he is sitting down and she is standing up, there seems to be more equality in the exchange – in the making and taking of meaning. As he grapples and succeeds to explain himself, he uses concepts like *advantage* and *disrespect*. But the teacher does not attempt to influence or even guide him. She is not asking questions to elicit answers and try and support his reasoning, nor is she using an authoritative teacher persona, as we have seen her do before in this lesson. Her manner has changed – her body language and tone of voice have become more engaged, like we saw with 'Miss W' in Chapter 3. Her voice is gentler and her intonation more modulated, more conversational even. She decides to let the dialogue with Imran run its course. She gives him space to reach his own conclusion and does not attempt to influence him – either to agree or disagree.

The next and final exchange follows a similar format. Once again, Imran makes a statement; in fact, he draws a conclusion based on his previous reasoning. He looks down and states, 'That means he is disrespecting God.' Although he is looking down, his voice is not quiet. He falters a moment, looks up, and says with passion, 'People will be ashamed.' The teacher catches his eye as he looks up towards her, but once again, she does not agree or disagree, stating instead, 'Possibly people will think that.' The class remains transfixed. They are witnessing something here. It is not clear whether Imran is breaking new ground in his own thinking, developing his criticality, and altering his view of reality, in Freirean terms (Freire, 1974). That is something we cannot know. He may be. But for the other children witnessing his reasoning and discussion with the teacher, this is a learning experience – of constructing knowledge with others. It has a ripple effect on their own learning. It corresponds to the concept of a learning community in which the goal is to advance collective knowledge and, in so doing, support the growth of individual knowledge (Scardamalia and Bereiter, 1992). By witnessing the reasoning of a classmate, the children are developing shared (and individual) knowledge through this social situation (Watkins, 2005).

In this lesson, it is not clear whether the teacher's practical action is deliberate or instinctive. She could have closed down the discussion. She could have taken a more authoritative stance and suggested Imran discuss the matter with his parents or Imam or said she did not know enough to agree or disagree. But she does not make it personal. Her comments neither reinforce the passion with which he expresses himself nor negate it. She acts merely as a foil for his reasoning, enabling him to proceed to draw a conclusion both by what she says and does not say, all the while enabling the other children to develop their own understanding by witnessing the dialogue. Yet this itself is surely a decision? She has remained neutral but has also decided to allow Imran to pursue the line of reasoning with the resultant effects it may have on him and his peers. It is an emotional moment and will have taken a toll on all involved, but it is a really powerful example of a child reasoning.

Lesson 2: Donald Trump and the Muslim ban, January 2017

What follows is a brief record which Meghan has written about what happened one morning in January of 2017.

I prepared the classroom in the usual way, morning work on the board ready for the students to come in and select a task from. The school bell went, and my teaching assistant was ready to open the door to our class. Within seconds, I could hear a lot more voices than usual. . . .

As I approached the commotion in the cloakroom, I could hear the words 'Trump' and 'World War Three,' and when I arrived to say good morning, I was greeted with a barrage of tense ten year olds, one spilling out the following statement: 'Miss, Miss, Donald Trump is president of America, and he's going to build a wall, and we aren't going to be able to go to America, we won't be allowed!' There were a lot of thoughts and feelings this morning that I knew needed to be addressed. I had a choice: ask the students to calm down, be quiet, and get on with their morning work or ask them to calm down, go into the classroom and sit in a circle on the carpet, and ignore the morning work. I chose the second. Using the strategies of P4C, we sat down to talk about what Donald Trump becoming president of America meant. The students needed the space to air their thoughts, clarify the situation, and it was important that I mitigated this escalating into deeper fear, anger, or anxiety.

When I asked, 'What do you think of Donald Trump?', the students responded with 'irresponsible, unfair, unfit, hatred, rude, disrespectful, crook, idiot, selfish, careless, ignorant, racist, confusing.' We discussed how their thoughts were based largely on the media coverage of Donald Trump. They recognised that they had made some assumptions which could possibly lead to prejudice. We talked about what knowing a person meant and how that was the only way you could accurately judge someone. This led to an enquiry about the media and the impact it has on the way we perceive things. Moments like this were commonplace in my classroom. They are inevitable in school, and they are talked about on the playground if there is no space in the classroom to talk about them.

Meghan's recount of these events gives us a clear insight into her commitment to use her own agency in pedagogical decision making, anchored in a belief that teaching is about giving a good education – and how it can be transformative. Setting aside her personal views about the American president, her commitment was to her class and her moral responsibility to them. She was modelling values fundamental to democracy – tolerance, respect, and the rule of law – the very values that all British teachers are called upon to instil in their students, what have been termed 'Fundamental British Values.'

Lesson 3: control

In the introduction to this book, we saw a teacher facilitating a discussion on the theme of *control*. Children had chosen the areas they wanted to investigate such as 'The food we eat,' 'The friends we make,' 'The dreams we have.' One of these was 'Death,' This would always be a tricky area to discuss with students of any age, but the class wanted to and the group which considered it came up with some interesting points, as we see in Figure 12.2.

Teacher:	**The next theme is 'Death.'**
	The teacher chooses the first child to express an opinion.
Aneesa:	You have some control if you are sick and don't take your medicine because then you might die. Or you might be in a car accident and be really badly hurt and die.
Teacher:	**So, what control would you have then?**
Aneesa:	None.
Tyler:	You can make choices – like whether you wear a seatbelt.
Teacher:	**Are there always things that are preventable?**
Niall:	It might not be preventable if you decide to kill yourself.
Joelle:	I agree. You could decide to kill yourself.
Kiran:	If you just got a disease and died, it would not be your fault.
Teacher:	**If you chose to take your own life, would it be wholly your choice if you had heard something about it?**

Figure 12.2 Year 6 class enquiry 'Is life always within our control?'

At one point in answer to the teacher's question about whether it is always preventable, Niall answers, 'It might not be preventable if you decide to kill yourself,' and Joelle agrees. Instead of agreeing or asking the next group to start discussing their theme – 'Dreams' – as you might expect with such a sensitive subject, the teacher returns to the theme of suicide. In fact, she poses the question, 'If you chose to take your own life, would it be wholly your choice if you had heard something about it?' Although not given explicitly, the reference is to the recent case of the suicide of Molly Russell, a teenager very close in age to these pupils, who took her own life after allegedly reading how to do so on her Instagram account.

In a discussion after the lesson, the teacher confirmed her deliberate choice in taking the discussion further, thereby discussing a serious and difficult issue in a safe space, enabling any misconceptions that children might have picked up from social media to be addressed. She explained how important she considered it to be for children to have these opportunities, which this approach to teaching allows (Gurton, 2022, p. 76).

The decision to refocus the discussion on this contentious issue was, then, certainly deliberate. It may have been that she had planned to discuss it before the lesson. Whether she acted with forethought or she took the decision in the moment, this episode in her teaching corresponds to what we have identified as *praxis*, as she is 'acting wisely and carefully in a given situation' (Smith, 2008, p. 65). She takes a decision to act in what she considers to be the children's best interests. She does so because she believes it is important to be able to discuss it in a safe space to dispel rumours or misconceptions. It is a brave decision, which derives from her convictions, because she is aware that there could be some response from parents, who may consider it an inappropriate issue to be discussed in school.

All three lessons show examples of when practice becomes *praxis* - decisions made when the teacher is showing a commitment to acting truly and justly (Smith, 2008, p. 66). Each teacher pursues what they believe is right in their lesson. In each situation, the teachers encourage the students to subject reality to scrutiny, using reason to attribute causes for why things are as they are (Freire, 1974). And once the decision is made to pursue the discussion, each situation carries with it a certain amount of risk. The teachers do not know what opinions the pupils might express or what situation might arise. However, with experience and by opportunities to take risks, we grow more confident in our *praxis* as teachers. And if we did not take these risks, as Biesta (2013) contends, we may as well regard education as technology, in which there is a perfect match between input and output and where children are objects to be moulded, not subjects of action and responsibility.

References

Adichie, C.M. (2022) *BBC Reith Lecture*. Available at: https://www.bbc.co.uk/programmes/articles/3wc fW2YlJwf8VwD9gOVCc9g/is-free-speech-under-attack-eight-key-points-from-chimamanda-ngozi -adichie-s-bbc-reith-lecture (Accessed: 22 April 2024).

Alexander, R.J. (2020) *A Dialogic Teaching Companion*. Abingdon: Routledge.

Aristotle (1980) *The Nicomachean Ethics*. Oxford: Oxford University Press.

Biesta, G.J.J. (2013) *The Beautiful Risk of Education*. London: Routledge.

Biesta, G.J.J. (2015) Thinking philosophically about education; thinking educationally about philosophy. In Matheson, C. and Matheson, D. (eds.) *Educational Issues in the Learning Age*, 4th edn. London and New York: Continuum, pp. 64-82.

Boyd, M. and Markarian, W. (2011) Dialogic teaching: Talk in service of a dialogic stance. *Language and Education*, 25(6), pp. 515-534.

Cassar, C., Oosterheert, I. and Meijer, C. (2023) Why teachers address unplanned controversial issues in the classroom. *Theory and Research in Social Education*, 51(2), pp. 233-263.

Department for Education (DfE) (2011) *Teachers' Standards*. Available at: https://www.gov.uk/government/ publications/teachers-standards (Accessed: 17 April 2024).

Elliott, J. (2012) Teaching controversial issues, the idea of the teacher as researcher and contemporary significance for citizenship education. In Elliott, J. and Norris, N. (eds.) *Curriculum, Pedagogy and Educational Research: The Work of Lawrence Stenhouse*. London: Routledge, pp. 84-105.

Freire, P. (1970) *Pedagogy of the Oppressed*. London: Continuum.

Freire, P. (1974) *Education for Critical Consciousness*. London: Bloomsbury.

Godfrey, F.B and Grayman, J.K. (2014) Teaching citizens: The role of open classroom climate in fostering critical consciousness amongst youth. *Journal of Youth and Adolescence*, 43, pp. 1801-1817.

Goswami, U. (2015) *Children's Cognitive Development and Learning*. York: Cambridge Primary Review Trust.

Gurton, P. (2022) *Teacher Talk and Pupil Talk: A Case Study of a Thinking Skills Approach to Learning in an English Primary Academy*. University of Wolverhampton. http://hdl.handle.net/2436/625068.

Hess, D.E. and McAvoy, P. (2009) To disclose or not to disclose: A controversial choice for teachers in Hess, D. (ed.), *Controversy in the classroom: The democratic power of discussion*. London: Routledge, pp. 97-112.

Johnson, D.W. and Johnson, R.T. (2014) Constructive controversy as a means of teaching citizens how to engage in political discourse. *Policy Futures in Education 12(3)*, pp. 417-430.

Johnson, D.W. and Johnson, R.T. (2016) Cooperative learning and teaching citizenship in democracies. *International Journal of Educational Research, 76*, pp. 162-177.

Journell, W. (2017) *Teaching Politics in Secondary Education: Engaging with Contentious Issues*. Albany: State University of New York Press.

Kelly, A.V. (1995) *Education and Democracy: Principles and Practices*. London: Paul Chapman Publishing Ltd.

Kemmis, S. and Smith, T.J. (eds.) (2008) *Enabling Praxis: Challenges for Education*. Rotterdam: Sense Publishers.

McAvoy, P. and Hess, D. (2013) Classroom deliberation in an era of political polarization. *Curriculum Inquiry*, 43(1), pp. 14-47.

Michaels, S., O'Connor, C. and Resnick, L. (2007) Deliberative discourse idealized and realized: Accountable talk in the classroom and civic life. *Studies in the Philosophy of Education*, 27, pp. 283-297.

Miller-Lane, J., Denton, E. and May, A. (2006) Social studies teachers' views on committed impartiality and discussion. *Social Studies Research and Practice*, 17(5), pp. 517-528.

Scardamalia, M. and Bereiter, C. (1992) Text-based and knowledge-based questioning by children. *Cognition and Instruction*, 9(3), pp. 177-199.

Smith, T.J. (2008) Fostering a praxis stance in pre-service teacher education. In Kemmis, S. and Smith, T.J. (eds.) *Enabling Praxis: Challenges for Education*. Rotterdam: Sense Publishers, pp. 65-84.

Tribukait, M. (2021) Students' prejudice as a teaching challenge: How European history educators deal with controversial and sensitive issues in a climate of political polarization. *Theory and Research in Social Education*, 49(4), pp. 540-569.

Van Alstein, M. (2019) *Controversy and Polarisation in the Classroom: Suggestions for Pedagogical Practice*. Flemish Peace Institute.

Watkins, C. (2005) Classrooms as learning communities: A review of research. *London Review of Education*, 3(1), 47-64.

13 The place and value of talk in further education

> This chapter is written by Sue Lay.

College is often alive with chatter, but how much quality talk? This chapter takes a look at the place and value of talk with young people in the further education (FE) sector with examples drawn from current work with students in tutorial lessons at Warwickshire College Group (WCG). My experiences working with students as a teacher in FE, a pastoral tutor, and more recently in creating materials for tutorial lessons have informed my practice and understanding of the value of talk for students. In this chapter, I will consider the context of an FE college and the opportunities and challenges for enabling students to take part in meaningful talk. I will then identify specific strategies used to encourage and facilitate quality talk and discussion, and finally I will consider the benefits to the individual and the community when, through talk, a range of skills and thinking is fostered.

Context

Within the FE sector, there are requirements to cover certain themes for students' personal development. Even though some of these are specifically stated, such as equality and diversity, safeguarding, Prevent, physical health, mental health, and careers (Ofsted, 2024), there is freedom to decide how these can be approached and how to get students engaged in important social, political, and personal areas of life. This gives opportunities to develop the skills of talking, listening, and thinking critically alongside gaining knowledge and a deeper understanding of important aspects of society.

There are challenges to face when attempting to incorporate these themes into the curriculum. Some can form part of a main programme of study and be related to the vocational area - for example Construction, Animal Welfare, or Social Care. But others are often put together in a separate scheme of work for 'tutorial' lessons, which at WCG consists of classes of about 15-20 students from the same vocational area. Deciding who staffs these lessons can also be a challenge in FE, and at many colleges, including WCG, the lessons are taken by support/pastoral staff who are not necessarily qualified teachers. Therefore, the confidence and skills to facilitate discussions need to be considered and staff

DOI: 10.4324/9781003451044-16

training and support provided. Tutors, knowingly or unknowingly, model their own thinking and questioning skills. Planning material and lessons to support the pastoral tutors, as well as creating opportunities for students, is key to their success. Many colleges produce material centrally for staff to 'deliver.' Using centrally produced material is always more challenging, and having time to prepare and consider each group specifically is vital to make the concepts come alive and the session truly interactive.

A further challenge is time. Tutorials are usually timetabled weekly for one hour with many subject areas to 'cover' during the year. Even when students really engage in a subject and have good quality discussions, there is rarely the opportunity to develop this the following week. Finally, it is inevitable that some staff will feel more confident and be more skilled at both facilitating discussions and in engaging with some subject areas than others. However, finding ways for students to talk, listen, think critically, and engage should become a central part of the lessons and is certainly well worth striving for.

Choosing content for the tutorial scheme of work at WCG comes from: guidance based on Ofsted requirements and a student's entitlement to have some subjects covered; pastoral staff feedback with suggestions based on what has worked or not worked previously; and some direct feedback from students. This has led to further flexibility and the development of new and changed content over time.

Some of the sessions that naturally have more complex concepts embedded and therefore tend to lead to more interesting discussions are: safeguarding, consent and sexual harassment, democracy, kindness day, Prevent, exploitation (meeting needs and grooming), hate crime (prejudice), Holocaust memorial day, LGBTQ+, international day for the elimination of racial discrimination, gender equality for all, toxic masculinity and femininity, and climate change/ Earth day.

It is important for students to engage in these subjects, as they are aspects of society and culture at a local, national, and international level. For young people to become politically engaged members of society and realise that their agency or apathy can affect life for themselves and others, college needs to try to develop critical awareness, skills of discussion, and agency. Many of these subjects are also very important for confidence and wellbeing at a personal level to support decision making in students' day-to-day lives and personal interactions.

The students we work with are predominantly 16–18 years of age, have left school, and come into classes with lots of people they don't know at a time in life where their self-image can be fragile and changing. It is the curious nature of that time between childhood and adulthood! For tutors, it means finding ways for students to engage actively and personally but not necessarily having them feel too exposed. It's all too easy for the self-conscious teenager to become withdrawn or play the class and not truly stop to consider issues and complex ideas.

Strategies

How to get students engaged, talking, and thinking critically requires skill and careful planning. This section outlines some significant strategies that can help facilitate this.

Questions are often a good way to start a session. They can generate a lot of ideas and concepts to explore and unpack, as well as get students' initial engagement with the subject.

Early questions may include a simple definition of a concept, such as 'What is safeguarding?' or 'What is democracy?' At other times, a more personal lead into a session may be preferable – for example, when looking at exploitation and asking students, 'What are our needs?' 'How does it feel when these are met or not met?' Understanding that we all have needs and that when certain needs are not met we can feel more vulnerable provides an important awareness before looking at grooming in more detail. With all opening questions, it is validating for students to have their contributions drawn on later in the lesson with comments like, 'I'd like to pick up on the point that so-and-so made . . .'

Students are often given a chance to consider questions in pairs or small groups so they don't feel as exposed by needing to answer individually. It gives them an opportunity to talk to each other with a focus. After feeding back to the whole class, there is an opportunity to gain a wider range of ideas than if you just rely on those students who speak up. With smaller class groups, it can be worth going around the whole group and getting contributions from everyone, if this is done sensitively. Students seem more likely to volunteer contributions once they have made one contribution. The tutor can use the process of students talking to each other and taking it in turns to contribute ideas, to facilitate building skills of active listening, and to ask questions to seek further clarification. It is very important that the culture created in the class is one where students don't feel that there is a 'right' answer and that it is a safe place to look at ideas and beliefs and be able to change their minds or to be persuaded by a different viewpoint following further investigation.

Many questions will be open questions, and the tutor can build on students' existing understanding by guiding the discussion to develop ideas expressed for a deeper understanding and higher-level thinking. This may look like first asking for reasons why a belief or opinion is held. The tutor can ask for examples to illustrate how the idea can be explained or shown (supported). Likewise, the tutor can ask for examples of how something might counter the belief or for an idea to show how the idea can be challenged. These simple steps to think critically and analyse an idea or 'argument' show how responses can either support the validity of an idea or statement or can illustrate how the concept may be flawed or more nuanced if examples do not substantiate the original point. When looking at democracy, for example, students may suggest the benefits and shortcomings of this form of government. They could then consider the validity or merits of the claims, along with understanding that all these points for consideration contribute to a greater understanding of democracy, even if they can sometimes be contradictory. In our society, we are so used to seeing life and ideas presented through media and government as binary and over-simplified that this is particularly challenging and important.

When a discussion is successful, it helps students practise testing their thoughts and ideas carefully for accuracy and not jump to conclusions. Where this is a collaborative process, the experience of learning from each other and having time to quietly reflect during discussions is rich and valuable. Students will start to learn the value of this approach and become more independent with their questioning skills and curiosity.

When discussing in this way, it is vital to ensure that it is the ideas, not the individuals, that are being interrogated critically. This should be done by modelling ways of speaking, listening, and questioning. It is also important to set some ground rules for listening and asking for clarification or facts that support a view. These are important skills for developing critical thinking but also for learning how to express personal views and opinions whilst showing respect and tolerance for others who have a different opinion. It is rewarding to see this manifest itself when students do ask each other to elaborate or explain points or have the confidence to say, 'That's a good point, I've seen examples of that in. . .' or 'I've heard what you said and can see why that would be the case in this situation, but what about. . .?' rather than just jumping in with a different view. However, it can take time to build up this culture and skill set in a class with only one hour a week.

Using fictional drama as a way to experience the lives of others has proved to be really useful and enjoyable for students, and so it is embedded into several sessions. In the Prevent material, we use a 25-minute short TV play about two young people who become radicalised and whose paths cross. Being provided with a few questions beforehand to consider and then looking at the motivation, ideology, and behaviour of the main characters, including friends and siblings, is a fantastic vehicle for explaining people's feelings and concepts such as *value, discrimination, prejudice,* and *fear* without needing to reveal personal information. It also gives students a chance to think critically with more empathy about 'choices' people make and the circumstances around these. Once again, asking for reasons for opinions develops students' ability to think critically about the situation and people. As the arts and fiction do so well, it can give a window into a life that is very removed from one's own lived experience. Any attempt to consider different viewpoints and experiences can build tolerance, understanding, and compassion which can only be a good thing.

We also use real-life experiences via short videos or case studies to increase awareness of a section of society that may have some shared experiences – for example, young trans people, refugees, etc. So, when looking at war and conflict for Holocaust memorial day, students were able to respond to open-ended questions about a particular person before generalising from the specific person to what that might mean more broadly. For example, following the account of a refugee who came to the UK, we had a wide-ranging discussion about the concept of *freedom* and what this means.

Getting students moving can also work well to promote engagement with a subject. An example of this was when looking at privilege. Students were given a character on a piece of paper – a single parent, a student with a physical disability, a older male student, a gay student, etc. They stood in a line, and the tutor asked a series of questions. If there was no barrier to education and learning for their character, they stepped forward; if there was a barrier or might be a barrier, they stood still. At the end of the process, they could see how spread out the class was, which visibly illustrated the advantage some people have studying and the extra challenges others have. It also encouraged thinking more critically in a very practical way about differences. This is a good way of getting students who may learn in different ways to access concepts.

Another example of using movement and visual input to provide stimulation for students to consider and discuss concepts is an agree/disagree line. Students imagine a line the length of the room, and one end is agree and the other end is disagree. We used this method to look at racism in a community by using a British Red Cross activity from talking with children and young people about race and racism. Students could individually choose their community for consideration (e.g. the college, youth group, or their local area). They then thought about to what degree they agreed or disagreed with statements read by the tutor and positioned themselves along the line. These statements were:

1. We treat everyone equally
2. We don't value different colours or shades of skin differently
3. We use different words to describe different kinds of people
4. Those words might be hurtful to those we are describing
5. We experience lots of different cultures regularly
6. Most people here think different cultures are a good thing

At each point, the tutor was able to ask why students were positioned in a certain space, and this opened up the complexity of racism. The debate raised ideas and concepts around *institutional racism, subconscious racism, hate, prejudice,* and *intersectionality,* etc. Follow-up questions about why the answers might be different in different communities or within the same community or from different perspectives can add to everyone's understanding and thinking. Once again, getting students to relate to each other's responses is important so that there is peer to peer interaction, not just the tutor drawing out the links from students individually. At its best, this approach also fosters respect and active listening.

Debates have been added to the tutorial scheme of work this year. The need to research a subject before a debate has been beneficial, and opportunities for talk have been rich and varied. Students were given a chance as a class to choose a subject from the following list:

- Disposable vapes should be banned
- Smoking should be banned for anyone who is under 15, and this age will be increased by one year every year to make smoking illegal for the next generation
- The government should recommend a ceasefire in Gaza
- The voting age should be lowered to 16
- Mobile phones should be banned from college lessons
- Healthcare should be free for everyone throughout their lifetime
- Cannabis should be decriminalised
- Playing violent computer games causes violent behaviour
- Climate change as a threat to humanity is exaggerated
- A vegan diet helps the environment
- Sport should remain outside social and political events
- Smartphones should be banned for children under the age of 16
- Banning drivers under the age of 25 from driving passengers who are also under 25 in the first year after passing their test will improve safety

We provided motions in which there may be strong opinions and which were relevant to the students' lives but also broader social issues. Believing in the value of fostering students' sense of being part of society means trying to engage them with the wider world around them and to encourage them to see themselves as having agency. If students have a better thought-through and informed understanding of the issues around them, they are more likely to be actively involved, feeling that they have some ability to shape the world they live in.

Researching facts and distinguishing facts from opinion in articles they read was discussed and practised. Once debating, students found that they appreciated the value of having solid, detailed knowledge to draw on when arguing a point. Holding debates encourages being informed and curious – listening, questioning, and challenging with facts, not just repeating opinions. The need to respond to other people's arguments is probably one of the harder elements of a formal debate, but having secure knowledge and information based on evidence helps. Therefore, being prepared by reading and discussing information and ideas in groups provides a rich opportunity for talk using skills of questioning, critical thinking, and conversation.

There is added value in being explicit about the learning that is taking place and how students are actually learning skills of critical thinking, problem solving, and being able to make informed judgements. Also, it is worthwhile to note how the process is increasing their consciousness of bias, opinion, and fake news when accessing information from various sources – including social media. We will come back to this when looking at benefits.

Debates are one example of group work in which the tutor is not always as actively involved, but it is beneficial for students with the right preparation. Another example is asking for an outcome which necessitates conversation to achieve it – for example, asking a group to decide on 'the top five examples of . . .' This can lead to conversations in which knowledge, thinking critically about the impact, and judgement all play a part. I would suggest it is important for students to practise these skills in groups, both with and without a teacher, to gain independence. If the teacher is always there to facilitate the conversation, students may become too dependent on them, whereas if they have opportunities to do this on their own, they can practise the skills for themselves. Obviously, this is a balance, and both experiences are needed. Like any skill, it needs practice for students to become more proficient and for the behaviour to become a habit.

We use scenarios frequently to engage students with real-life dilemmas and events, so they can creatively problem solve together through talk about what they could and would do in a safe space. When looking at consent and sexual harassment, for example, we have an activity with an imagined text message with a request for nude photos within a relationship, but the person receiving the text feels uncomfortable, and we get students to draft a reply. Thinking about language and using words carefully to assertively communicate a point while respecting someone else is a useful skill in life beyond college.

It is also useful when students have contrasting ideas to illustrate a more nuanced understanding of events and that we have options that have different consequences. It highlights the place of personal choice and responsibility. This type of discussion and awareness should help develop students' emotional sensitivity and intelligence. Some pastoral staff have taken these scenarios into drama-based activities, adding further opportunities for collaboration and talk to complete the task.

Whilst considering strategies to engage students in talk and discussion, the tutor also needs strategies for managing the debate if students get heated. This sometimes happens when discussing controversial subjects. The tutor may need to intervene, perhaps to draw the discussion away from the anger at that moment and take time to consider why we all care so much about the topic. A strategy may be to empathise with the feelings and look at what has caused them – for example, injustice or prejudice. When coming back to the issue, the tutor could ask students to look for the facts that lie behind the opinions we hold and see if we can find any which are indisputable. Another approach may be to look at why the subject leads people to such different opinions or beliefs. It can be interesting to examine what part the media has played in how we've formed our beliefs. It may be possible to look at whether the views held are 'received wisdom' or whether we have come to these views after researching information and thinking critically and carefully to challenge our own prejudices. The use of the word 'we' can show students how we all grapple with these things – and we need to!

When some students get heated, those with differing views may at times feel inhibited from expressing their ideas. Therefore, for the tutor, being aware of ways to look at subjects from different perspectives is important. They can, for example, draw on previous comments and state 'Some people think X. Let's look at what we know. What are the facts and ideas which support this view?' Then, they might encourage students to look at the facts and ideas which challenge this view. Students can be asked to express these whether they believe them or not to hopefully calm a situation but continue with important challenging discussion.

At times, students may express views which are against the law, and a tutor must provide non-judgemental but calmly presented factual information about what is legal or illegal and why, along with the consequences. I can recall a student who thought it was acceptable to take physical action as revenge towards a hypothetical relative after a wrongful act. As a class, we discussed where these actions may lead and the resulting issues with vigilantism, etc. However, the student wasn't convinced, and a clear, calm statement about physical violence and the law needed explaining to the whole class, obviously without singling out the individual. Other recent examples have concerned trans rights with the need to remind students about the Equality Act and Hate Crime laws. Some tutors fear these situations due to the challenging nature of these kinds of conversations and to the necessity of being mindful of safeguarding concerns. However, it's important tutors have the skills and confidence to give students the opportunities to explore difficult ideas and views in a safe space where they can reflect, make mistakes, gain understanding, hear different views, and change their minds.

Benefits

There are significant benefits from having opportunities for talk and discussion for students and tutors. It builds a community in the class, as everyone can offer ideas and opinions or share examples from their lives where appropriate. Depending on the make-up of the class, this may help some students become aware of the issues others are facing based on social and cultural differences. It is also a time when all students should have something to offer and feel valued for their contributions in a judgement-free way. This takes time to achieve and needs ground rules and plenty of opportunities for practice and getting it wrong.

Tutorial discussions also have the benefit of helping students understand how they are part of a community beyond college and that they have some agency as citizens. For example, considering personal actions such as ways to behave to reduce bullying or to challenge stereotypical language which contributes to prejudice. There are times when students have discussed how they can more actively support their desire for change. In a session for the international day for the elimination of racial discrimination, for example, students spent time considering what action they could take as young people to promote awareness and to build a fairer future.

Likewise, for Earth day's theme of plastic pollution, students were encouraged to think about what actions could be taken both personally day-to-day and more broadly.

Some subjects and discussions have enabled students to understand situations in their own life through a new lens - for example, recognising abuse or grooming. When discussing potentially triggering subjects like this, it is vital that tutors clearly explain the range of support available to students at the start and at the end of a session. Tutors may also want to check in with students during the session. When a student recognises a situation for what it is, it is often extremely difficult, but with appropriate support, it can be life changing.

When focusing on welfare themes, students can learn from the information presented but also through talking about this information and sharing ideas to potentially make small changes to their lives which can improve their wellbeing.

Another benefit of talk and discussion is when students bring their existing knowledge and experience to a complex subject and through discussion with others, they may gain a broader perspective and it may open up or add to what they know and understand. Conversations like this can help students to begin to form stronger beliefs and personal values acquired through a broader awareness and a more critical and careful approach to their thinking.

Discussions may also help develop new concepts through the introduction of new vocabulary. When looking at Prevent, students were asked to consider beliefs and values in relation to the concept of *ideology*. Having access to this concept enabled them to formulate their knowledge and understanding in a new and more precise way. Using higher-level language such as this facilitates being able to synthesise and generalise their understanding and apply it to new situations. This is an area where tutors have a very important role both in introducing students to concepts and in helping them apply these concepts, making links between lessons to keep the language and ideas alive.

Holding discussions helps students develop useful academic skills of critical thinking, questioning, and problem solving. These are both helpful to academic study and to enable them to think critically in a world that has increasingly more information available - from instant searching on the web and 24-hour news to relentless social media feeds. The ability to identify fake news, bias, prejudice, and opinion is vital to engage with the world meaningfully.

Explicitly explaining to students the process of critical thinking as a tool to gain greater understanding of a subject, along with an awareness of how they are learning, is of benefit. Students can apply their understanding to new and different situations. With practice, they may look at a statement or opinion and be able to:

- ask questions about what assumptions are made
- judge the validity or probability of a statement or argument by considering examples to support or challenge it
- identify if they can see opinion, bias, or prejudice

When looking at a problem, they are more likely to follow this process:

- consider what all the possible options are
- consider the advantages and disadvantages or probabilities of each option
- make a more carefully thought-through judgement or decision

Obviously, students need courage and self-confidence to achieve this, but the process and time to practise at college can help them develop these skills.

Another benefit is the opportunity to help young people become more able to express themselves in a clear, respectful way and to relate to each other. This is helpful in a student's personal life, and employers also often cite communication, problem solving, and teamwork as skills they value and require in prospective employees. Tutorial lessons provide an opportunity for students to develop these attributes with talk playing a crucial role.

As an educator in FE, I believe we are there to give all students, whatever their life experiences so far, chances to access education and broaden their life opportunities, whether that is personally, socially, or through the opening of new doors into education or employment. I believe providing opportunities for all students through talk to develop skills for learning, thinking, and better social interactions is the right thing to do. Facilitating lessons and discussions to work towards these benefits is challenging but vital for our next generation.

Reference

Office for Standards in Education (Ofsted) (2024) *Further Education and Skills Inspection Handbook.* Available at: Further education and skills inspection handbook – GOV.UK (Accessed: 22 May 2024).

14 Using talk to demystify critical thinking in higher education

> This chapter is written by Hilary Wason.

Explicitly teaching critical thinking within disciplinary curricula can effectively support educators and students to become aware of how they are reasoning within their subject context (Abrami et al., 2015, cited in Heron and Wason, 2023, p. 2)

Introduction

Thinking through talk can support students to develop their critical voice and enhance educators' confidence and competence to teach it (Cui and Teo, 2023). This chapter aims to provide higher education (HE) educators with some practical examples of how dialogue can be used to support teaching critical thinking. It draws on some of the frameworks of dialogic education (Cui and Teo, 2021) which enable teachers to use a common language of critical thinking and support students to access the concept through classroom dialogue (Heron et al., 2021). As such, it views oracy as a *process* in which students use talk as a vehicle to learn about their discipline and to develop their criticality within it (Heron, 2019). In this chapter, teachers from different disciplinary contexts illustrate how dialogue supports their students to be critical. We see how talk narrows the social distance between teacher and student, develops their agency and self-determination, and addresses some of democratic deficits arising from didactic approaches to teaching.

Critical thinking is 'a defining concept of the modern university' (Barnett, 1997, p. 2). It is crucial for students' academic attainment and employability (Teo, 2019). The teachers' reflections we encounter in this chapter show how dialogue forges the partnership between student and student and student and teacher and demystifies the complex phenomenon of critical thinking. Educators have sought to create democratic inclusive learning environments which encourage the expression of different perspectives and allow students to appraise untried concepts and materials in order to develop their criticality (Brookfield, 2013). Through modelling their own critical thinking by using dialogue, teachers support students to think critically themselves (Brookfield, 2015).

DOI: 10.4324/9781003451044-17

Critical thinking can be difficult to define and challenging to teach (Janssen et al., 2019). In this chapter, we see teachers using a range of tools from a *Critical Thinking Skills Toolkit* (Wason, 2016) in different teaching contexts to stimulate the application of critical thinking through questioning, argumentation, clarification, discussion, and justification. The tools are designed to develop Facione's (1990) set of critical thinking skills of interpretation, evaluation, inference, self-regulation, explanation, and analysis, underpinned by purposeful self-reflective judgement. Each tool has a name and logo in order to develop a common language of critical thinking. Dialogue between teacher and student and amongst students supports the application of these tools to their learning. This explicit approach to embedding critical thinking teaching within disciplinary content supports the quotation at the beginning of the chapter. It illustrates how both educators and students use dialogue to develop their metacognition and self-awareness of what critical thinking means to the learning of their discipline.

The learners in these teaching examples are mostly from widening participation backgrounds, often from traditionally under-represented groups and with a wide range of prior learning experiences, demographics, and cultural backgrounds. The richness of learning brought through cultural diversity is something to be valued, and culturally responsive dialogue and respectful interaction can enhance the learning experience. By teaching critical thinking within their curriculum, educators make the concept more accessible to students, regardless of their prior learning experiences, cultural backgrounds, and demographics. This enables a fairer and more equitable approach than relying on the development of critical thinking outside the curriculum. Furthermore, to overcome the argument that dialogue could privilege those who have prior experiences of interactive and dialogic teaching environments (Bali, 2015), the teaching episodes are modelled by the teachers to show how they use talk to develop critical thinking themselves.

In each example which follows, colleagues from a range of disciplines start to recognise the value of dialogue to develop both their own and their students' awareness and metacognition of what it means to teach and learn critical thinking. Francesca, a science educator, shows her own growing awareness of the value of dialogue to her critical thinking teaching: 'And those oracy skills –well, that was amazing. Oh, this is a new level of critical thinking with oracy, this is a new thing.'

Educators purposefully plan structured discussion around a particular learning outcome, often a tool from the *Critical Thinking Skills Toolkit* (Wason, 2016). They encourage talk using a range of dialogic moves and techniques (Cui and Teo, 2021). This helps them develop their own dialogic stance and recognise the value of talk to develop students' disciplinary understanding and how to be critical about their discipline (Heron, 2018). The data is drawn from Wason (2023) which uses a case study in a UK university to explore how educators are learning how to teach critical thinking in their disciplinary contexts. Three teaching examples from science and business have been chosen to illustrate the different contexts in which dialogue has been used as a tool to develop critical thinking. The quotations have all been taken from interviews. Each teacher has been given a pseudonym.

'Lecturing didactically is not enough'

So says Francesca, who is frustrated with the more traditional, didactic approach to teaching science. Embracing the principles of critical pedagogy, her dialogic approach challenges the 'banking concept' of higher education in which knowledge is prescribed to students (Freire, 1998, p. 4). This is particularly important, as she teaches in large HE classrooms which could potentially create distance between her and her students. In addition, she teaches a widening participation cohort with a wide variety of prior knowledge, educational experiences, and cultural backgrounds. The curriculum is heavy with scientific concepts, which she is keen to make accessible, relevant, and meaningful to students. Francesca illustrates this when she says:

> So, with me it's about the dialogic aspect of it. It's really trying to develop this because of the widening participation cohort that I teach. You have got to get them engaged, because it's a level of information that they have never experienced before. I find that didactic teaching alone just does not work in Science. There is nothing worse than having a situation where you are lecturing to a class and there is nothing coming back. What I am trying to instil in these students, particularly in light of where we are in the world, is that you have to invite discussion, you have to remain open-minded, because that is ultimately what Science is.

In this extract, Francesca illustrates her commitment to using dialogue to widen participation in learning and to support access to and understanding of disciplinary concepts (Mah, 2016). She also creates an open, supportive, and dialogic environment which sets the foundations for the critical thinking teaching goals which follow in her next episode (Cui and Teo, 2021).

Using scaffolded discussion around the questions from The Source Tool from *The Critical Thinking Skills Toolkit* (Wason, 2016), Francesca helps her students become aware of agenda and bias, belief versus fact, and to consider the credibility, reliability, and appropriateness of how statistics are used in science. The Source Tool is designed to support students to develop search terms, then find, critique, and reference information from a range of practitioner and academic sources, learning how to discriminate between these. The tool contains an adaptable worksheet with the following questions which students fill out and then use as a basis for a class discussion:

- What question does the source aim to answer?
- What type of source is it? (Academic? Practitioner? Other?)
- How is this source relevant?
- How recent is this source?
- How credible is this source?
- Will you use this source? Why? Provide an explanation.

In the next extended extract, Francesca reflects on the process of asking students to critique a short article about HIV denial in a magazine. Students are asked to question their own opinion about the article and whether or not their opinion can change through classroom dialogue:

> So, you start off by saying, 'Is everyone allowed an opinion?'
> And the class say 'Yes.'

And you work through the Source and the inflammatory article. You pick out emotive language and then you ask, 'Do you still think everyone is allowed an opinion?'

And they say 'Yes.'

This is the theme for the hour.

Typically, by the end of the hour, 100 percent of these students say, 'No way, this is not a balanced argument.'

You then question that and ask, 'But you said that everyone's allowed an opinion.' It makes them think. We were able to have a proper discussion.

They said, 'No, no, no, you are wrong.'

So, you as the lecturer say, 'Let's discuss this and any repercussions.'

You then talk through the article, and at the end, you look at the repercussions of the person who wrote it. You discuss the range of statistics used to back up the arguments and whose research it was based on, any counter-arguments, any inaccuracies in the data and the dates. The other thing to note is that this article is in a high-brow magazine that has had politicians and prime ministers as editors. You say, 'Tell me who is reading this? So what does it mean to be reading a legitimate source? Is this a legitimate source?' And it really gets them thinking about the potency of language, who is speaking, who is saying what. The lesson really was a game changer. It was so good. It was so good it gives you goosebumps talking about it.

By structuring the dialogue around a set of questions, based on The Source Tool, Francesca encourages students to rationalise their own thought processes. The talk focusses on getting students to reflect on why they have a particular opinion and how their thinking is developing during the hour of the session. Using a series of dialogic moves (Cui and Teo, 2021), Francesca elicits students' views at the start of the session by asking them a challenging question to get the discussion started. She extends the debate by playing devil's advocate. She contests some of the students' opinions with statistics and discusses the provenance of the article and its author. She finishes with her own reflections about the value of dialogue.

In these two reflections, we can see how Francesca models dialogue to develop her own critical thinking (Brookfield, 2015) and powerfully reflects on the impact it had on her teaching. Francesca becomes more aware of her own dialogic stance using a structured approach centred around The Source Tool and develops her own and students' metacognition about reasoning within Science.

Thinking together to develop criticality

The next teaching examples are provided by Nina, who is a business educator. Nina reflects on how she creates a dialogic environment to establish the foundations which foster her students' confidence to develop their critical voices in a democratic classroom space (Cui and Teo, 2021). She explains the particular significance of this to her practice, as her cohort of students may not have experienced the opportunities to develop their oracy or critical thinking skills within their secondary educational contexts. Nina is keen not to view this as a 'deficit' in her students and position them as lacking skills (Gravett, 2019). Instead, she uses dialogic techniques to enhance her own teaching practices for the benefit of all her students:

> I don't want to be critical of students. If they didn't have that fear of saying 'I don't know, I don't understand.' There will always be students like that, especially our lot, because they are not very confident. It's how to foster a climate in the classroom where it's good to ask questions. How do you create that atmosphere right at the beginning where you can say to students, 'Great question, I am so glad you asked it because it gives me the opportunity to elaborate to make it clearer,' and do that systematically all the time and maybe even reward students, allowing their questions to be teaching points for the rest of the class?

In this example, Nina illustrates how she has created an open and democratic environment which underpins classroom talk and enables thinking critically to evolve and be encouraged (Cui and Teo, 2021). Nina commits to creating this environment on a regular basis, investing time and effort into developing an established and inclusive classroom culture (Alexander, 2006). This provides the basis for her next teaching example.

Next, Nina explains how she uses dialogue, particularly questions and co-creation with students, to support teaching case studies using The Case Tool (Wason, 2016). The Case Tool supports students in applying theories and concepts to real-world business examples. It contains a worksheet with a series of questions which help develop the criticality needed when approaching a case study: how to recognise assumptions, analyse, interpret, and assess quality of information, use deductive reasoning, and draw conclusions. Nina constructs her sessions around the following questions to scaffold student learning and to encourage engagement:

- What is the key problem, and what are the challenges the case is addressing?
- What is the focus of the case?
- Which concepts or theories do you think are being illustrated or applied?
- Does the case present information/solutions from a number of different viewpoints?
- Can you find flaws in any of the evidence, data, or arguments?

Nina uses The Case Tool to teach students about how IKEA develops their pricing strategy. In the following extract, she illustrates how she provides students with the freedom to carry out some independent research about the company, as well as answering The Case Tool questions. Students then bring their findings and questions to the classroom. Nina uses these to design her session using a set of PowerPoint slides and a quiz. This shows how teacher and student are thinking together to co-create the content of the session:

> I use a lot of case studies to help students transfer their theoretical knowledge to existing businesses. In this particular case, we were looking at the pricing strategy for IKEA for the launch of new products. It was about teaching that. But sometimes I take a bit of freedom and say 'Why don't you go away and take 5 minutes to research this?' I send students to research something to enrich the discussion co-creating it with my students. One week before the session, I ask them, 'Listen, help me prepare for the case for the class. Can you give me some material?' And because they did it, I thought okay, I am not

going to ask them to present, but I used the material to create the quiz. I made sure that the slides were in the name of the students who contributed so that the rest of the class could recognise the contribution of that particular group of students. And then I created the quiz just to reinforce the concept and to add a bit of fun.

I find that asking questions like this and asking students to come with one fun fact or one interesting quirky fact about the company that we are studying on that particular day breaks the ice and gets them engaged in a fun manner. I would say about a third of the class, because I did some analysis afterwards, contributed some fun facts Then we did the quiz and then we got into the case. I try to use a variety of active learning methods.

Nina's next step is to build on this exploratory discussion using the questions from The Case Tool to organise a structured dialogue about the case. Students debate in groups and write down their answers on the Case Worksheet, comparing and contrasting their findings. Through thinking together, they make sense of the case within the session. Here, Nina reflects on the success of the approach:

That was a very nice way to discuss everything in two hours. I like that I used different styles of teaching and learning in the class . . . 5 or 10 minutes to read the work, the Case Worksheet, and the case study. Obviously, they should have already done it, and that's why I gave them 5 or 10 minutes. But on the other hand, I delivered quite a full session . . . the PowerPoint presentation, the quiz, the dialogue and communication with students about the case study, and the fun facts. At the end, the discussion focussed on that specific section, on that specific worksheet. I had everything all together in one place.

In these examples, we see Nina using 'supportive,' 'purposeful,' 'cumulative,' and 'deliberative' dialogic teaching principles (Alexander, 2020) to teach her students case studies in a structured and systematic manner. Encouraging them to think with her and to think together makes the learning more enjoyable but also more genuinely participative. Nina shows how she is narrowing the social distance between her and students, developing their agency and independence in their learning.

Talking and thinking with numbers

Our final educator, Zola, uses a range of dialogic moves supported by questions from The Practitioner Insights Tool to help students interpret, analyse, recognise assumptions, and assess the quality of information and data from business reports and secondary sources of information (Wason, 2016). Zola is particularly interested in helping her students to be critical about quantitative data, to assess the reliability of claims made about statistics, as well as about the robustness of the methodologies for finding this data. She organises her instruction by adapting the following questions from The Practitioner Insights Tool:

- What is the volume and value of the market?
- What is the brand share of this company? Its competitors?
- What are the growth rates of this market

- Which tools could you use from your degree course to help you interpret and present this information?
- Can you identify the theories or concepts that underpin the company's approach?
- Is any new marketing thinking highlighted?
- What is your opinion of this data? Do you agree with the findings? Is there any information missing? Are there any contradictions? How does it compare with any other information collected?

Zola scaffolds her approach by starting off asking questions using examples of data from everyday life. She creates a culture of dialogic education to support students to explore their views about secondary data, not to interpret it at face value but to think deeply and critically about what it could mean. She reflects on the challenges of doing so:

> So, I have tried to start with getting students to be critical right from the get go. But one of the things I find really difficult is using the discourse and getting them to be a bit more theoretical about it. So, they are quite happy talking about answering, 'Can you identify the advantages and disadvantages or can you talk about the benefits or the pros and cons?' They are quite happy with that language. But as soon as you start saying, 'Okay, let's be critical,' they think, 'Gosh, this is a whole new thing. I don't know where to start with this, and don't know what I am doing, and I don't know how to do it.'

To help her students overcome these challenges, Zola uses a range of dialogic moves, beginning with elicitation (Cui and Teo, 2021). This helps get them started with expressing their views about the data from adverts, an everyday source which students are more likely to be familiar with, as she explains:

> There are a lot of very badly presented graphs, and there are a lot of badly claimed statistics. So, we go through this right from the very beginning. We watch a couple of adverts, what are the claims made, what might be the issues with those claims made. So, I try to build them up and to start talking about, 'What are the advantages and disadvantages, what is good about this graph, what is not good about this graph?' And we use a lot of industry data. I did this in the first couple of weeks. They used one of the graphs again in one of the more formal critical thinking exercises I did. What was really nice was that recall of what makes something good, what might be a gap, what might be a lack of explanation of the methodology – that was a lot quicker for them to recall. Em . . . but their confidence . . . I think one of the big boundaries is about confidence with the discourse. And actually, they know most of what they are doing. They have started talking about, for example, if we are looking at a measure of average, we say, 'What is good about the mean, what might make it not such an important measure to use in certain circumstances?' Getting them into that critical mindset, being critical of everything they do.

As this activity helps her students build up their confidence in talking about data, Zola extends the classroom dialogue. She asks students to elaborate more and corroborate their thinking, challenge their own and one another's contributions, and make connections between their points. Using the dialogic moves of extension, challenge, and critique (Cui and Teo, 2021) helps students to apply their critical thinking to more complex activities involving critiquing data:

> What I found very encouraging was that we had a graph, it was an attitudinal graph, and it highlighted the percentage of people who answered 3 or 4 in this survey where 4 was very satisfied, and 1 was not satisfied. We talked about, 'Okay, hold on, where's the gap, what are they not telling us? They have given us this sample size, but what does 3 mean, etc.?' So, it's just getting them to question and not just assuming that what they are getting is accurate, faithful, appropriate, and representative. And I think they seem to be more comfortable with this approach. Being able to scaffold that discourse and that discussion around a couple of the tools from the critical thinking skills toolkit I think really helped too.

In a final reflection, Zola nicely illustrates how her students are feeling comfortable in a dialogic environment where they are building their own metacognition – understanding what it means to be critical about numbers and making their learning more accessible and practical. She sees how thinking through the numbers is developing her students' confidence in critical thinking. This encourages her to embed dialogue more fully and regularly in her teaching and assessment practice and to connect it across different teaching activities and at different levels of the degree:

> I think that it's hugely important to build up students' confidence when using critical thinking in any situation. And that confidence and that feedback loop helps them think, 'Oh okay, I can do this' and then go ahead and be even more critical and develop those skills. Well, I have my students filling in the Source and Practitioners' Insights for one piece of data, which they are then going to use for another assignment. So, I will be marking it, and it will be nice to see whether they have adapted and can apply what we have done in class. I will definitely be using this approach again and seeing what I can do to integrate it more into level 5 and level 6. Now that we have started introducing the discourse, we will be using this much more widely in the rest of the module because now that they are much more confident, they can understand and see how it can be extended throughout – to keep it going, basically.

Insights and implications

This chapter provides a glimpse into the authentic classroom experiences of three HE educators who use dialogue to teach critical thinking. It shows how their students are developing their criticality within their subject discipline. As such, rather than provide best practice models, it offers some practical insights and ideas which HE educators might like to try in their own practice.

Underpinned by resources from a *Critical Thinking Skills Toolkit* (Wason, 2016), designed to develop a common language of Facione's (1990) critical thinking skills, teachers reflect on a range of dialogic moves and techniques to support the development of their students' critical voices. Using the toolkit to set the purpose and goals of the discussion, we can see how Francesca, Nina, and Zola are developing their own dialogic stance and modelling criticality for their students, steering and guiding their thinking processes and reflecting on how this is working for them. Using the questions from the tools as an overall framework, we see how they are using some of the principles of dialogic teaching and dialogic moves to help students rationalise their own thought processes and articulate their own thinking. In doing so, teachers are making critical thinking more meaningful and relevant to the needs of their students, as well making their disciplinary knowledge more accessible.

Based on the teachers' experience in this chapter, there are several recommendations that HE educators might like to consider to develop thinking through talk in their own practice.

- Think about your own practice and the different modules and programmes which you work on. Where do dialogue and critical thinking development currently live in these spaces? How could you explicitly introduce or refine your learning outcomes to include the development of critical thinking skills through dialogue to stimulate students' criticality?
- Ask your own metacognitive questions. Critically reflect on how you use speaking and listening in your own practice to develop students' criticality. You might want to ask yourself the following:
  - How do I encourage students to share their thinking about the concepts I am teaching?
  - Do I currently plan my discussion with a particular learning objective in mind? If not, how might I do so?
  - What types of questions do I ask students? How do I encourage them to answer them and build on their responses?
  - How do I provide feedback on students' ideas?
  - Is there an opportunity for pair and group work? How do students discuss learning tasks together? Do they listen to each other in group work? How do they critique each other's ideas as well as build on each other's contributions?
- Create an inclusive, supportive, and active learning environment, regardless of the size of classroom, which provides students and teachers with a democratic learning and teaching space. This enables the development of agency and self-determination over learning and narrows the social distance between teacher and student.
- Harness the principles of dialogic teaching, specifically argumentation, discussion, and questioning, to support students' cognitive development.
- Develop a taxonomy of questions which relates to your disciplinary content and which encourages students to think critically within the context of your disciplinary knowledge.
- Use the Critical Thinking Skills Toolkit (Wason, 2016)[1] in order to provide context and set a purpose and goal for the discussion. Align these activities to your programme and module learning outcomes and assessment criteria and develop some activities from the toolkit which could be set as pre-session activities for students to complete and bring their findings to class. Use the repertoires of dialogic teaching and dialogic moves to support the discussion around the tools.

Note

1 The toolkit is produced under Creative Commons licence. Please contact the author for a copy if you want to try it in your practice.

References

Abrami, P.C., Bernard, R.M., Borokhovski, E., Waddington, D.I., Wade, A. and Persson, T. (2015) Strategies for teaching students to think critically: A meta-analysis. *Review of Educational Research*, 85(2), pp. 275-314.

Alexander, R. (2006) *Towards Dialogic Teaching. Rethinking Classroom Talk*, 3rd edn. York: Dialogos.

Alexander, R. (2020) *A Dialogic Teaching Companion*. London: Routledge.

Bali, M. (2015) Critical thinking through a multi-cultural lens: Cultural challenges of teaching critical thinking. In Davies, M. and Barnett, R. (eds.) *The Palgrave Handbook of Critical Thinking in Higher Education*. Basingstoke: Palgrave Macmillan, pp. 317-334.

Barnett, R. (1997) *Higher Education: A Critical Business*. Buckingham: SRHE and Open University Press.

Brookfield, S. (2013) *Powerful Techniques for Teaching Adults*. San Francisco: Jossey-Bass.

Brookfield, S. (2015) Speaking truth to power: Teaching critical thinking in the critical theory tradition. In Davies, W.M. and Barnett, R. (eds.) *The Palgrave Handbook of Critical Thinking in Higher Education*. Basingstoke: Palgrave Macmillan, pp. 529-543.

Cui, R. and Teo, P. (2021) Dialogic education for classroom teaching: A critical review. *Language and Education*, 35(3), pp. 187-203.

Cui, R. and Teo, P. (2023) Thinking through talk: Using dialogue to develop students' critical thinking. *Teaching and Teacher Education*, 125, pp. 1-11.

Facione, P. (1990) Critical thinking: A statement of expert consensus for purposes of educational assessment and instruction. *The Delphi Report*. Available at: https://philarchive.org/archive/faccta (Accessed: 1 May 2024).

Freire, P. (1998) Pedagogy of freedom: Ethics. In *Democracy, and Civic Courage*. New York: Rowman and Littlefield, Inc.

Gravett, K. (2019) Making learning happen: Students' development of academic and information literacies. In Lygo-Baker, S., Kinchin, I. and Winstone, N. (eds.) *Engaging Student Voices in Higher Education*. Basingstoke: Palgrave Macmillan, pp. 175-190.

Heron, M. (2018) Dialogic stance in higher education seminars. *Language and Education*, 32(2), pp. 112-126.

Heron, M. (2019) Making the case for oracy skills in higher education: Practices and opportunities. *Journal of University Teaching and Learning Practice*, 16(2), pp. 9-18.

Heron, M., Dippold, D., Hosein, A., Khan Sullivan, A., Aksit, T., Aksit, N., Doubleday, J. and McKeown, K. (2021) Talking about talk: Tutor and student expectations of oracy skills in higher education. *Language and Education*, 35(4), pp. 285-300.

Heron, M. and Wason, H. (2023) Developing dialogic stance through professional development workshops. *Innovations in Education and Teaching International*, pp. 1-13.

Janssen, E., Meulendijks, W., Mainhard, T., Verkoejen, P., Heijltjes, A., van Peppen, L. and Van Gog, T. (2019) Training higher education teachers' critical thinking and attitudes towards teaching it. *Contemporary Educational Psychology*, 58, pp. 310-322.

Mah, A.S.H. (2016) Oracy is as important as literacy: Interview with Christine C. M Goh. *RELC Journal*, 47(3), pp. 399-404.

Teo, P. (2019) Teaching for the 21st century: A case for dialogic pedagogy. *Learning, Culture and Social Interaction*, 21, pp. 170-178.

Wason, H. (2016) Embedding a critical thinking framework for undergraduate business students. In Remenyi, D. (ed.) *Innovation in the Teaching of Research Methodology Excellence Awards: An Anthology of Case Histories*. Reading: Academic Conferences and Publishing International.

Wason, H. (2023) *Learning to Teach Critical Thinking in Higher Education*. EdD thesis. Milton Keynes: The Open University.

15 Talk is the answer

Taking control of teaching and learning

This book started life as an idea born of our experience of teaching – Meghan's as a primary school teacher who saw what was possible when you dispense with a didactic approach to education and give children voice, and Paul's as a teacher educator who has seen increasing levels of state control and regulation of education based on an ideology determining not only what is taught but increasingly *how* it is taught. We toyed with the idea of calling the book *Taking control of teaching and learning* because in many ways, that is what it is about. Good education requires teachers who feel empowered to take control of curriculum and pedagogy and who understand their role as professionals, who can exercise judgement and discretion in their daily interactions with students. The current educational climate makes this extremely difficult. Students, too, need to be empowered to see themselves as valuable members of society who have some control over their learning and, through questioning and discussion, are given the opportunity to develop independence of mind. But in the end, we gave it the title we did because it encapsulates our philosophy of education. Talking together allows us to raise questions and deepen our understanding – understanding of ideas and knowledge and understanding of each other as people.

But while this book is a plea for the proper inclusion of talk in learning, this must not be as a performative tool, a bolt-on to the curriculum, students' outcomes measured against age-related or other expectations. Talk needs to form part of a process which encompasses curriculum and pedagogy. It must be contextualised and embedded within everyday classroom learning experiences. Dewey makes an analogy of knowledge with a map. The student is an explorer, learning how to interpret the map – the accumulated wisdom of the species – and trying to find out the best routes to take (1902, p. 136). The teacher is a guide. They need a good understanding of the knowledge to 'translate' the map into a form that activates the thinking of young people at different stages of development and guides them in their choice of routes. Because the map represents knowledge in a very different form from the terrain that students experience in their day-to-day lives, giving it meaning is not just about transmitting information. It requires a teacher who knows their pupils, their interests, and their motivation and discusses, interacts and engages with them, and encourages them to engage with each other, as we have seen in the examples in this book. The knowledge itself comes in the form of information and skills but also in the form of developing ways of thinking and acting. A good teacher can mediate between students' everyday knowledge

DOI: 10.4324/9781003451044-18

and the key ideas central to different disciplines to enable them to develop their skills and understanding. As Campbell so memorably expressed it in his *Report of the New Education Fellowship Conference* in 1937, 'It is not what we do to the child that educates him (sic), but what we do to enable him to do for himself, and this is equally true for the young infant, the school child and the adolescent' (Darling, 1994, p. 36).

How to go about it

Throughout the book, we have discussed and demonstrated examples of how to bring talk to life. And although much of the focus has been the primary classroom, there are many points of similarity between this sector and the others represented here – further and higher education. The list here encapsulates the main findings from research evidence and classroom practice, suggesting how to go about it:

- **Create a community in your classroom:** for talk to flourish, the classroom needs to be a place of trust. The teacher needs to make themselves open and accessible to the students. They need to encourage the students to listen to each other, too. Building a community like this should be a principle aim of every teacher because, although it might take time to establish, it will soon pay off, and any time 'lost' at the start will be more than made up when students are on their journey of discovery together. One of the first steps in creating a community of learners is doing away with a 'right answer' culture. A supportive environment where it is okay to have a go and to make tentative attempts to articulate your understanding is an important step in developing that understanding. Students and teachers need to build on what others say, learning to validate each other's statements but also to disagree respectfully. Teachers need to show they can be wrong and share a bit of themselves with their classes.
- **Encourage exploratory talk:** doing away with a 'right answer' culture means the teacher is not the only one who asks the questions. In fact, encouraging children to explain their understanding by asking questions should be a natural next step. It should not mean they become dependent or need to ask about everything, but encouraging a 'what happens if?' approach, whether it is a science experiment, writing a story, or painting a picture, is a natural element of human creativity and innovation, the very thing we should be encouraging for children to become confident and successful, not feeling inhibited by not doing things in 'the right way.' This is, incidentally, also true about children as emergent readers and writers, who are often inhibited by teachers who have been told that phonics is the only way children learn how to read and getting spellings correct is more important than the composition and effect of what is written.
- **Teach pupils how to reason:** at the heart of good classroom discussion is reason. We have seen a variety of strategies in use across the different education phases represented in this book. To support pupils to develop their reasoning skills, the lesson could start with a question. This can be generated by the pupils, as is common practice in P4C, or it can be the theme for a discussion or debate, as seen in the chapter on further education. Non-verbal strategies like use of the classroom space, for example, the concept line we saw students use in the Introduction to the book, or the agree/disagree approach taken

in the chapters on further and higher education play their part also. These approaches may be useful at the start or end of a lesson to get discussion going or to summarise. But to develop reasoning itself, students need to be introduced to the discourse norms of discussion and debate, understanding the need to be appreciative and respectful. Taking turns to discuss a question, listening to each other and not interrupting, using eye contact, and non-confrontational body language are all essential ground rules. The phrases 'I agree' or 'I disagree,' with a reason given, 'building on what X has said,' and other words such as 'position' in phrases such as 'I am not sure that I would take that position' are all necessary to allow a full discussion to flow. But lessons with talk will not always be full-on enquiries. So, other strategies for the teacher to use such as 'Recap' and 'Reformulation' (Mercer, 2000) will help talk flow, as well as provide the ability to tease out concepts after careful listening with phrases such as 'are you talking about the concept of . . .?'

- **Provide evidence for what you say:** another crucial aspect which is necessary for good reasoning is being able to provide evidence to support what you have said. We saw a good example of this in Chapter 12 where a Year 5 class were comparing Islam and ISIS. The reason the boy Imran reached the conclusion he did in the discussion was based on his research of what the then leader of ISIS had proclaimed. Likewise, in Chapter 14, higher education lecturer Nina explains how she sends off students to do some research on a topic, which she then incorporates into her teaching the following week. Teachers should encourage students to substantiate what they say in class discussions or tentative talk situations with evidence from research or personal experience or understanding. This not only helps them in their academic enquiry and decision making, but it is an excellent skill for life and work where decision making is required. Skills of reasoning and providing evidence are often not taught until children are in secondary school, and that is often through the medium of meeting the learning objective or because the mark scheme requires it. Students are taught the jingle 'Point, Evidence, Explain' when writing essays in secondary school, but this approach is just as useful in spoken discussion.

- **Introduce concept words:** the power of concept vocabulary, whether you are studying Maths or Science, or encouraging discussion in PSHE, RE, English, or Geography, allows students to think about things in a different way. We have seen many lessons discussed in this book which show how the careful introduction of words such as *freedom, influence, class, power,* and *adversity* has enabled pupils to think about issues in their lives or in the subject they are studying differently, by providing a 'peg' to hang their thoughts on. Primary school teachers, further education tutors, and higher education lecturers have all discussed the power of introducing what Vygotsky called 'scientific' language to pupils to reorganise their experiences and articulate what they think.

- **Don't take everything at face value:** whilst much learning, especially in the early years, requires pupils to take things at face value and trust what the teacher says, the ability to scrutinise and evaluate - to ask questions - becomes increasingly important throughout schooling. But this is not reflected in current curriculum and pedagogy. Even the students in Nina's university class were inclined to take a magazine article at face value in Chapter 14 until she began to develop their critical reasoning skills through talk. Much of this is because of an approach to learning which discourages pupils from asking questions or talking together. But, as we have seen, much younger age groups can learn to ask questions of the books they are reading or projects they are studying, and it can lead to very productive debate and encourage a cast of mind that we would sometimes describe as 'thinking out of the box.' These critical reasoning skills are exemplified by the question, 'Why are things the way they are?' followed by such obvious follow-ups as 'Have they always been this way?' 'Need they be this way?' Can we imagine them differently?' and 'What would be the advantages and disadvantages of this new way – and to whom?'

- **Embrace creativity:** in many lessons in schools and colleges and in assessments at university, the teachers determine the 'outcome.' It might be a piece of writing or artwork. Sometimes students get to plan a science investigation or design a piece of technology, but always pre-specifying the expected outcome limits student creativity and innovation. One of the advantages of P4C, as seen in practice, is that at times a teacher can send children away after an enquiry to respond in whatever way they see fit. In many of Meghan's lessons, children could choose whether to respond by drawing, writing poems, doing 'philosophical play,' or some other response, such as the boy in Chapter 11 who made a Lego aeroplane after a class discussion with the question, 'Does Adversity make you stronger?'

A manifesto for hope?

Education policy and practice has, over recent decades, been tied to what governments think will make their country more economically competitive. In other words, it has been instrumentalised. In England, this has meant the Department for Education, with all its different names over the years and under administrations of different political colours, has given itself many new powers, principally those of surveillance. It has passed several curriculums into law, set targets for children's attainment at different phases of their education, made it a legal requirement to teach reading in a particular way, legislated teaching standards that professionals have to meet, and even written a teacher training curriculum which providers have to follow or they are designated 'non-compliant.' This command-and-control culture, exemplified by Ofsted and school league tables, has made schools, which should be places of hope and positivity, often develop a climate of fear. These feelings, which are a response to the pressure of constant scrutiny and surveillance, make teachers feel they have little authority to exercise professional judgement and make decisions. Yet despite this unhealthy and regrettable climate, many schools and colleges are able to create the conditions for pupils to flourish, as we have seen from just some of the examples in this book. Talk is encouraged, and pupils not only become more knowledgeable and able to reason but more confident in themselves, which will help them in their lives. You may have done similar work in your own schools, or be planning for it, or as a student you may be planning to include opportunities for talk in your classroom. In the wider world, the value of talk is evidenced in so many different ways from the work of activist groups that force discussion onto a national stage, such as Greta Thunberg's Climate Action movement and the school strikes it yielded, to the Good Friday Agreement which after exhaustive talks brought an end to years of violence in Northern Ireland. In South Africa, the Truth and Reconciliation Commission enabled painful discussions to acknowledge some of the immense suffering caused by years of Apartheid. At an individual level, talk therapies are in major use in psychotherapy to treat many different conditions.

We hope that this book has fired your imagination and shown you what is possible. Talk is increasingly being recognised as a major factor in life chances, and a recent resurgence of interest in developing children's spoken language skills has led to primary and secondary schools in the UK integrating talk activities and assessments into their taught programmes. There is also a growing literature on talk and dialogic teaching. Books such as Rupert Knight's *Classroom Talk in Practice: Teachers' Experiences of Oracy in Action* (2022), which covers primary and secondary education, and Amy Gaunt and Alice Stott's *Transform Teaching and Learning Through Talk: The Oracy Imperative* (2019) born out of the work of School 21, which, together with the oracy charity Voice 21, supports the work of hundreds of schools across the country. Have a look at Oracy Cambridge, the Hughes Hall Centre for Effective Spoken Communication, which has a bank of useful resources, or the SAPERE website, where you will find opportunities for staff training in Philosophy for Children as well as teaching resources.

Education is about the future. The future can often seem bleak. We may become concerned about political discourse, the prevalence of hate speech, the perversion of facts by 'fake news,' or the potential of AI to influence and misrepresent. But if we can shift public thinking to see the value of talk to individual wellbeing, life opportunities, and as a bulwark to support the fragile nature of our democracy by engaging with people with differing views and opinions, rather than hiding behind the convenient digital screens of social media, we shall be doing ourselves, our children, and our children's children, a service.

Last thoughts

This book is about empowering children and young people through talk. It is only when we open the classroom or lecture hall space to talk that we are able to hear their voices. How often are we, as teachers and parents, surprised at the ideas, the reasoning, or just the good common sense expressed by young people when this occurs? They are always more able to reason than we give them credit for. As this book is about learning to hear their voices, it seems appropriate to end with some, so here are the voices of two young ten-year-old boys and a nine-year-old girl reflecting on what they feel about classroom discussions and enquiries (Gurton, 2022, pp. 90–91):

> [T]eachers just give like a bit more of, like, our way . . . rather than them always, like telling us what we're supposed to be doing.
>
> – Catherine

> You don't have to, like, hear the teacher every single time, you get to hear other people in your class, and you're kind of, like, intrigued to hear what they think.
>
> – Zephaniah

> It helps us talk to more of our classmates . . . instead of us, the children, talking to the teacher. So, we are engaging with others more, and we can see different points and how other people think. . . . It's given me more understanding about the wider world, and it's got rid of some of my assumptions about certain groups of people, and it's made me share my opinion with other people.
>
> – Liam

References

Darling, J. (1994) *Child-Centred Education and Its Critics*. London: Paul Chapman.

Dewey, J. (1902) *The Child and the Curriculum*, reprinted in Garforth, F.W. (1966) *John Dewey: Selected Writings*. London: Heinemann.

Gurton, P. (2022) *Teacher Talk and Pupil Talk: A Case Study of a Thinking Skills Approach to Learning in an English Primary Academy*. University of Wolverhampton. http://hdl.handle.net/2436/625068.

Mercer, N. (2000) *Words and Minds: How We Use Language to Think Together*. London: Routledge.

Index

Note: page numbers in *italics* indicate figures and page numbers in **bold** indicate tables.

Printed in the United States
by Baker & Taylor Publisher Services